O Brave New Words!

O Brave New Words!

Native American Loanwords in Current English

By Charles L. Cutler

UNIVERSITY OF OKLAHOMA PRESS : NORMAN AND LONDON

Chapter 11 is adapted from "Indianisms in Current English," *English Language Notes* (March 1992), copyright © 1992 by *English Language Notes.*

Library of Congress Cataloging-in-Publication Data

Cutler, Charles L.
    O brave new words! : Native American loanwords in current English / by Charles L. Cutler.
        p.   cm.
    Includes bibliographical references and index.
    ISBN 0-8061-2655-8 (alk. paper)
    1. English language—United States—Foreign words and phrases—Indian.   2. Indian languages—Influence on English.   3. Indians of North America—Languages.   4. Languages in contact—United States.   5. Americanisms.   6. Vocabulary.   I. Title.
PE3102.I55C88   1994
422'.97—dc20   94-15764
                                                              CIP

The paper in this book meets the guidelines for permanence and durability of the Committee on Production Guidelines for Book Longevity of the Council on Library Resources, Inc. ∞

1   2   3   4   5   6   7   8   9   10

TO KATHY
with love and devotion

Miranda. O brave new world
        That has such people in't!
Prospero. 'Tis new to thee.

Shakespeare, *The Tempest*

Contents

List of Illustrations xi
Preface xiii
Using This Book xvii

1. Voyage into a New Awareness 3
2. Adventurers and Settlers 14
3. A Forest of Languages 23
4. "Wild Beasts and WilId Men" 32
5. First Words from the New World 44
6. Reports from the Frontier 53
7. Renaming a Continent 67
8. Opening Up the West 79
9. Of Kayaks and Igloos 92
10. Words along the Fiery War Trail 102
11. Indianisms in Current English 123
12. The Twentieth Century and Beyond 136
Epilogue 152

Glossary 1. English Loanwords from the North American
Indian Languages (North of Mexico) 154
Glossary 2. English Loanwords from the Eskimo and
Aleut Languages 217

Appendix. English Loanwords from the Latin American
Indian Languages 221
Notes 248
Bibliography 257
Index 275

Illustrations

Chart of North American Indian Loanwords in English   2

Map of American Indian Language Groups   25

Preface

ALIEN YET FAMILIAR, NATIVE AMERICAN LOAN-
words are a haunting presence in the English language of
North America. They name much that is unique to the
continent—both in human history and in natural history.
They act as a reminder, conscious and subliminal, of peoples
whose cultural influence has often been slighted. More than
four centuries of communication and miscommunication
may be traced in the chronicle of these words.

It is not surprising that Native American loanwords have
been taken for granted. Some—such as *powwow*, *tomahawk*,
and *wampum*—are obviously Indian. But others—such as
hominy and *woodchuck*—have become so naturalized as to blend
with ordinary American discourse. Further Native American loanwords such as *bayou*, *hickory*, *and Sasquatch*—may
pass without notice by most people who utter them.

Back in 1971, as a contributor to *American History Illustrated,* I thought that the story behind American Indian
loanwords might have considerable historical value. But to
my dismay, I could find no comprehensive account of the
subject. Extended research on Indian loanwords turned up
only stray articles and brief discussions in various histories
of the English language.

After my article "The Battle the Indian Won" appeared
in *American History Illustrated* in January 1972, I undertook
to compile a full list of current Indian loanwords—since I
could not find even that in print. My method was direct: I
read all the way through *Webster's Third New International*

Dictionary. I chose this reference work as a standard because it was authoritative and the most nearly complete gathering of words specific to the American vocabulary. For cultural reasons, the focus of my research was on northern Native American loanwords. After many months, I had assembled a list of more than one thousand Native American (North American Indian north of Mexico, plus Eskimo and Aleut) words and incidentally more than fifteen hundred Latin American Indian loanwords.

Professor David P. McAllester, then Professor of Anthropology at Wesleyan University, encouraged me in what had become a book-length project. But he wisely suggested that I exclude place-names, on which so much work was already being done by others. Accordingly, I have limited my treatment of place-names derived from Native American languages to a single chapter, which discusses borrowing trends in general. This book, in fact, deals mainly with common nouns rather than proper nouns (eschewing, for example, the names of Indian tribes).

During my twenty years of research and writing, I have done my best to cope with some knotty problems. The field of Native American languages is so vast, the historical research so demanding, and the determination of vocabulary origins so complex that I more than once gave up in despair. But the fascination of the topic and the need for a full-length account of it always drew me back. The following is an explanation of the principles that have finally formed this book.

Etymologies. This is not a work of linguistics but a *history* of Native American loanwords and loan terms in English and the various ways they have entered the language. Words have been included by virtue of their etymology even when they may not derive directly from Native American culture. I have given the etymological background wherever feasible, relying on the best authorities. My main sources have been *The Random House Dictionary of the English Language: Second*

Edition—Unabridged and *The American Heritage Dictionary of the English Language.* Special acknowledgment is due Ives Goddard, Department of Anthropology, Smithsonian Institution, whose expertise on these two reference works has been extraordinarily valuable. The eminent linguist William O. Bright has also been helpful in this respect while offering encouragement at several points during this project.

Currency. I have written primarily about Native American loanwords in current use. The standard for currency is again *Webster's Third New International Dictionary* and its supplements. Yet some of the words included might better be classified as historical. I have preferred to risk erring, if at all, on the side of inclusiveness.

Dating. Since the organization of this book is mainly historical, it focuses on loans with a datable first use in English. *The Oxford English Dictionary*, second edition; *A Dictionary of Americanisms* by M. M. Mathews, and the *Dictionary of Canadianisms* were most helpful in this respect. My own research has yielded new first dates for several dozen loans. Deciding the first use of a word can be difficult. I differ from some authorities in not counting an appearance in a foreign language context (usually French). And, unlike some others, I accept as appropriate only a use of the word in the *sense* being documented. But decisions about first use are sometimes judgment calls and always subject to revision with the discovery of a new document. I will gratefully receive improved dates and thank the senders.

Cultural Links. An important thesis of this book is that the number and the kind of North American Indian (north of Mexico) loan terms borrowed have generally reflected the shifting cultural relations between Native Americans and others. As a result, some sweeping examinations of certain periods of American history appear in these pages. I have tried in such passages to achieve simplification without oversimplification.

Thanks are due to the following people, who have given me invaluable help on various aspects of this book: George H. J. Abrams, Lyle Campbell, Rudolph H. Cutler, Robert Devereux, Brian W. Dippie, Victor Golla, William T. Hagan, Edwin A. Hoey, William L. Leap, Vincent Marteka, Laura Martin, Rev. Stanislaus Maudlin, Frank Menchaca, Janina Montero, Donald J. Orth, Stephen J. Perrault, Rev. Francis Paul Prucha, Susan C. Rennie, Harriet Rockwell, Dr. Wil Rose, Robert M. Utley, Willard B. Walker, Jack Weatherford; the staff of Olin Library at Wesleyan University, including Joan Jurale, Alexa Jaffurs, Erhard Konerding, Margery May, Shirley Rosseau, Ed Rubacha, and Elizabeth Swaim; and the staff of Levi E. Coe Memorial Library in Middlefield, Connecticut, including Karen Smith, Jeanne Taylor, and Patricia White. Virginia Rex did a praiseworthy job of deciphering and typing the manuscript for the two Glossaries. Special thanks go to Teddy Diggs, who skillfully edited the manuscript.

CHARLES L. CUTLER

Rockfall, Connecticut

Using This Book

THIS BOOK IS ORGANIZED ON HISTORICAL LINES, with background chapters interspersed among narrative chapters. The earlier narrative chapters discuss all the words of each era examined. Later narrative chapters conclude with lists of the numerous words for which there was no room in the chapters themselves.

The two Glossaries and the Appendix serve as supplement and reference. You will find a glance through the Glossaries rewarding. They offer an overview of *all* the North American Indian and Eskimo and Aleut words current in English—many pronunciations, dates of first recorded use where known, etymologies based on sound scholarship, and brief definitions. The Glossaries throw additional light on the words you will encounter in the text as well as illuminate words not otherwise discussed. The Appendix, a list of Latin American loanwords, consists simply of words and some definitions, yet it reveals the far-reaching influence of ancient American civilizations.

O Brave New Words!

North American Indian Loanwords in English

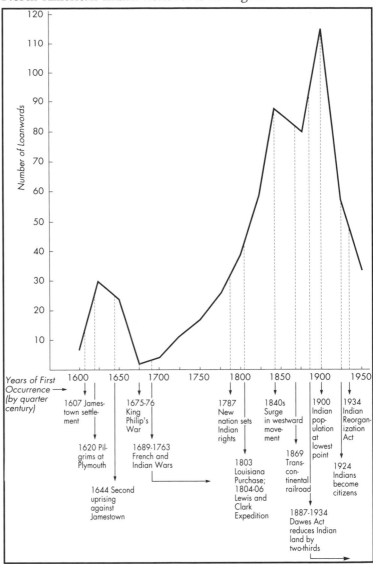

The peaks and troughs of loanword borrowing in English from North American Indian languages (north of Mexico) generally correspond to historical fluctuations in white-Indian relationships. Borrowing is greatest during the period 1875–1900, but Indian population and cultural influence are then already starting to decline.

CHAPTER ONE

Voyage into a New Awareness

RAIN RATTLED ACROSS THE VAULTED CHURCHES and rickety tenements of London in 1583. It raked the masts of ships moored in the Thames, ships returning from trips up the coast or from distant, hazardous voyages. It beat a tattoo on the leaded roof over Thomas Harriot's chamber high in Durham House, the palace Queen Elizabeth had enabled her beloved Walter Raleigh to lease in part.

Twenty-three-year-old Thomas Harriot had the air of an Oxford undergraduate. Only three years out of the university, he still wore the black required of undergraduates there. Now he was watching a cup placed under the downspout outside his latticed window. Carefully he counted his pulse to time the rise of water in the brass cup, jotting down the results with sharpened quill. On a whim, he was calculating how much rainwater would fall into his room in one day if a roof did not cover it.[1]

Raleigh had installed Harriot in the 21½-by-12½-foot room on the top floor of Durham House, next to his own apartment. Just as Raleigh enjoyed a panoramic view of the Thames from his turret-study overlooking the river, Harriot could survey the ever-changing prospect of a London reaching to the limits of the known world and beyond—toward lands recorded only in fable or in fragmentary accounts of travelers who had barely escaped to tell their tales.

Harriot rarely had leisure to gauge rainfall or muse on the

view. Hearing of his brilliance and far-ranging interests, Raleigh had recruited him for a special mission. An attempt by Raleigh's stepbrother, Sir Humphrey Gilbert, to prepare a colony in Newfoundland had failed. Raleigh expected Harriot to lay the theoretical and practical groundwork for establishing England's first colony in the New World.

The initial problem Harriot had to grapple with was how to navigate the largely uncharted Atlantic Ocean. English sailors were accustomed to coastal journeys, in which a captain relied on time-tested charts and, typically, years of experience. To prepare Raleigh's sailors for the open sea, Harriot studied not only the existing navigation texts written in English but similar works in Spanish and Portuguese as well. And Harriot bristled with an energy that prevented him from resting content with written descriptions. He went among the docks stretching below Durham House to question old salts who had proven themselves on voyages throughout the growing network of English exploration and trade.

Around the end of 1583, Harriot was able to set up a class in navigation for Raleigh's mariners. He wrote a textbook, *Arcticon,* that embodied the best-known techniques of ocean navigation, organized and expanded by the author. One can imagine the young scholar patiently expounding his subject to burly sailors, most older than he and possibly sitting in a classroom for the first time in their lives. Harriot introduced his students not only to theory but also to his own improved versions of navigational instruments such as the cross-staff— a tool for taking the altitude of celestial bodies, especially the sun.

Pleased at Harriot's analysis of the navigational challenges of an Atlantic crossing, Raleigh had the young man help design and ready the two ships planned for the voyage. Harriot participated in assembling the crews. He even kept Raleigh's accounts, working with his employer to secure financial backing for the costly trip.

In 1584, Raleigh finally launched his two ships on an expedition to reconnoiter the coast of the New World between Florida and the northeastern region of North America. After a two-month voyage, the ships reached the Carolina area. The sailors found the Indians admirably open and courteous. A welcome on Roanoke Island especially impressed the sailors, who were treated to a banquet in a large cedar dwelling. Captain Arthur Barlowe extolled the lush beauty of the islands and the hospitality of the natives in a report ostensibly addressed to Raleigh but mainly designed to attract support in Parliament for Raleigh's planned settlement.

As evidence for his sanguine account, Barlowe brought back two of the Indians who had welcomed him—Manteo and Wanchese. Did Harriot personally help bring the Indians back? There is no direct evidence of his participation in the expedition he had prepared. But he soon established a close relationship with the two Indians—especially Manteo—a remarkably close relationship if he did indeed first meet them in England. Within a few months of the Indians' arrival, Harriot was able to converse freely with them in their dialect of the Algonquian family of languages. Harriot furthermore developed an ingenious phonetic alphabet to transcribe the language. This alphabet—a pioneering venture into linguistics—has disappeared, along with many of Harriot's other papers.

While improving his Algonquian in long conversations with Manteo (dressed English-style in brown taffeta), Harriot also acquired a detailed knowledge of the peoples and natural history of the coastal area Raleigh had decided was the ideal place for his settlement. This information was essential both to equip a new expedition properly and to gain backers for the risky and expensive undertaking.

On April 9, 1585, Raleigh dispatched his second expedition to the New World, this time with Harriot definitely aboard. Seven ships made up the squadron, with a total of about six hundred men. Harriot sailed on the *Tiger*, the main ship of the expedition, undoubtedly refining the course he had charted for the ships. When the ships reached the West Indies, Harriot switched to his role as naturalist and gathered samples of native products to carry back to Raleigh as possible objects of trade.

Two and a half months after setting out, the expedition finally reached the island of Wococon in the Carolina outer-banks. Soon the expedition leader accepted an Indian offer to move his headquarters to Roanoke. From there, the settlers explored the nearby islands and coastline over a range of about one hundred miles.

Harriot's subsequent report is not clear about which of these sorties he accompanied. But his unique value as an interpreter with the Indians and the number of observations he made of the area indicate that he sailed along the coast-line and up mainland rivers, visiting Indians who inhabited the numerous thriving villages. At the same time, he was one of the few members of the expedition to live in his own house outside the fort that had been built. He probably needed a place of his own to store and study the specimens of plants and animals he was cataloging for Raleigh.

In addition, Harriot shared a laboratory inside the fort with Joachim Gans, a metallurgist. The two tested metal-lic substances they had obtained from the Indians or had found. In 1992, archaeologists described the discovery of four-hundred-year-old crucibles, ointment pots, and distill-ing apparatus at the fort's site. "This is the beginning of science on this continent, trying to extract natural resources to build a country's wealth," William Kelso, archaeologist for the Thomas Jefferson Memorial Foundation, declared.[2]

Throughout his investigations, Harriot also worked closely with John White, the expedition artist and surveyor. The two were companions on many surveying trips into the re-gions surrounding Roanoke. When Indian villagers welcomed them, they stayed in bark-covered houses. In the wilderness, they slept under the stars. White's drawings are as circumstantial and lively as Harriot's descriptions. Together, the two developed a portrait of the Carolina Indians rivaling any previous studies of native peoples.

White, assisted by Harriot, also carefully mapped the area they traversed. The main purpose was to assist Raleigh's plans for colonizing Virginia, but the renderings have much value in themselves. White's map of the region between Cape Fear and Chesapeake Bay has been praised as the most carefully detailed map of any part of North America in the sixteenth century.[3]

Meanwhile Manteo helped the surveyors while smoothing relations with the Roanoke Indians, on whom the settlers depended for food. But clashes broke out nonetheless. A series of disagreements and misunderstandings led to the slaying of Wingina, the Roanoke chief, by his white guests. Harriot almost surely disapproved of this act, chiding in his report some members of the expedition for being "too fierce, in slaying some of the [Indians]."[4] The position of the settlers became less tenable. During a visit of Sir Francis Drake's fleet in June 1586, the men jumped at the chance to sail back to England when Sir Francis invited them to do so.

Just as the settlers were hastily gathering their belongings to escape Roanoke, a severe storm of several days' duration lashed the island and Drake's ships. Sailors threw overboard most of the baggage that the fleeing people were trying to save. Into the frothing waves went maps, manuscripts, specimens, and other memorabilia from the year Raleigh's expedition had spent in the New World. Among the losses were many of White's drawings and some of Harriot's notes.

Harriot wrote up his surviving observations on returning to England. These appeared in 1588 as a forty-eight-page pamphlet printed on inexpensive paper and sold for pennies.

The lengthy title of the publication begins straightforwardly—
A briefe and true report of the new found land of Virginia. But
the continuation reveals the pamphlet's main purpose, *of the
commodities there found and to be raysed, as well marchantable, as
others for victuall, building and other necessarie uses for those that
are and shalbe the planters there; and of the nature and manners of
the naturall inhabitants. . . .* Raleigh ordered its publication,
which might well never have occurred otherwise, as a way of
promoting his plan to colonize the New World.

A *Briefe and True Report* includes much of absorbing interest on the natural history of the Carolina coast and the local
Indians before the influence of white settlement. But here
we will deal with only one of Harriot's far-ranging achievements—the introduction into English of Indian loanwords.

Harriot's pamphlet includes thirty-seven different American Indian words, not counting proper names. That these
words are only a fraction of those he originally recorded we
know from comments in the pamphlet. He said, "Of al sorts
of fowle I haue the names in the countrie language of foure-
score and sixe." He also mentioned having the names of
"eight & twenty seuerall sortes of beasts." Further, he noted,
"There are many other strange trees whose names I know
not but in the Virginian language."[5]

Four of Harriot's recorded Indian words are of West Indian origin—*canoe, cassava, guaiacum* (lignum vitae), and
maize—previously accepted into English. For more on these
and other loanwords from Latin American Indian languages,
see chapter 5.

A still-current plant name that Harriot introduced into
English apparently from an Indian source is *cushaw* (*cocúshaw*
in Harriot), a winter squash with a typically crook-necked
fruit. This name may come from an Algonquian language in
Virginia or North Carolina. (The locations of Indian loanwords in Harriot's pamphlet are given at the end of the
notes to chapter 1.) The cushaw, along with pumpkins and

other squashes, is a native of North America. *Squash* itself in this sense is a North American Indian word discussed in chapter 4. A name in Harriot for a related plant is *macock* (*macócqwer* in Harriot), a kind of melon or pumpkin. This name comes from an Algonquian language in Virginia or North Carolina.

One of the key Indian words that Harriot first published is *werowance,* still used in historical writings for an Indian chief or tribal official. Ralph Lane, governor of Virginia when Harriot was there, earlier employed the word in 1585 in a report to Raleigh.[6] But his report was not published until 1589. *Werowance* is a Carolina Algonquian word apparently from *wilaw-* (rich, valuable, precious) + *antesi* (have such a manner of life).[7]

On his visits to Indian villages, Harriot engaged the inhabitants in discussions of their religion. He has been described, in fact, as the first Englishman known to have done missionary work in North America.[8] But Harriot was as interested in learning the Indian point of view as he was in converting Indians to the Anglican faith.

In describing the Indian religion, Harriot introduced into English what appears to be an early version of the Algonquian word for deities or forces of nature, *manitou* (*montóac,* Carolina Algonquian).[9] "They beleeue that there are many Gods, which they call *Montóac,* but of different sortes and degrees; one onely chiefe and great God, which hath bene from all eternitie. Who as they affirme when he purposed to make the worlde, made first other goddes of a principall order to bee as meanes and instruments to be vsed in the creation and gouernment to follow; and after the Sunne, Moone, and Starres as pettie gods, and the instruments of the other order more principall." Harriot's further comments indicate a struggle to grasp the Indian religious outlook, one not easily capsulized.

Harriot was not alone in borrowing words. He refers to

"*Tsinaw* a kinde of roote much like vnto yt which in England is called the China root brought from the East Indies." This Carolina Algonquian word is believed to be derived from the word *China*—specifically from the Smilax *China*, a plant thought to have healing properties. Scholars suggest that Manteo or Wanchese, Harriot's Indian friends, may have adopted the word from the English and reintroduced it to Harriot.

At almost the same time that Harriot was preparing his *Report,* a stray Indian loanword entered English through a would-be colonizer of the New World from France. A French Huguenot named René Goulaine de Laudonnière wrote a history of two abortive attempts to settle Florida's eastern coast during the 1560s. His book, translated by the geographer Richard Hakluyt in 1587, furnishes a first use in English of *cassina* (or *cassena*) for the *ilex vomitoria,* a holly whose leaves are used as a tonic or an emetic. *Cassina* comes from the Timucua (an Indian language of Florida) word *kasine.* "Afterward he [an Indian chief] commandeth Cassine to be brewed," Laudonnière said of a sacred ceremony he witnessed. "They make so great account of this drink that no man may taste thereof in this assembly unless he hath made proof of his valure in the warre."[10] This widely used herb later also came to be called in English by the Catawba word *yaupon,* which will be discussed in chapter 6.

Harriot's New World experience was the opening chapter in an extraordinary career that brought him renown among the scholars of Europe. During a long life by Elizabethan standards, he conducted many scientific experiments in fields such as ballistics and light. A pioneer in algebra, he introduced the "more than" and "less than" signs in mathematics. He was the first Englishman to build a telescope and use it to make astronomical observations. Among his correspondents were some of the great minds of Europe, including the astronomer Johannes Kepler. In fact, Harriot suggested an amazingly contemporary thought experiment to Kepler for research on the rainbow. "I have now conducted you to the doors of nature's house, where its mysteries lie hidden," he wrote in 1606. "If you cannot enter, because the doors are too narrow, then abstract and contract yourself mathematically into an atom and you will easily enter, and when you have come out again, tell me what miraculous things you saw."[11]

During most of this time, Harriot was in the employ of Raleigh—a circumstance that in itself placed him at the political and social center of Elizabethan England. It was to Harriot that Raleigh turned for help in preparing his defense at his trial for treason in 1603. And Harriot is known at least to have been present when Raleigh was finally beheaded in 1618 as delayed punishment. Among Raleigh's generous bequests to Harriot were "such blacke suites of apparell as I haue [in Durham House]."[12]

By that time, however, Harriot was also enjoying the patronage of Henry Percy, ninth earl of Northumberland. This enlightened nobleman treated Harriot as a member of his household and an intellectual companion, with plenty of free time for scientific research. From Northumberland, Harriot received an estate and an independent income—a major improvement in his social status.

But Harriot paid a penalty for his association with Raleigh and Northumberland. As they came under political and religious suspicion, so did he. In 1603, Lord Chief Justice John Popham viciously accused Harriot of heresy during Raleigh's trial. After exposure of the Gunpowder plot to blow up the Houses of Parliament in 1605, Northumberland was arrested for his association (almost surely innocent) with the conspirators. Harriot spent some time in jail as a result of his connection with Northumberland. Despite considerable discomfort, Harriot survived these embarrassments.

He was not so fortunate in his cultivation of a smoking

habit. One of the words he borrowed from the Indians is *uppówoc,* a Carolina Algonquian word, now archaic in English, for tobacco. In *A Briefe and True Report,* he claimed that through *uppówoc* smoking, Indians were "notably preserued in health." He added, "[They] know not many greeuous diseases wherewithal wee in England are oftentimes afflicted." He, Raleigh, and Northumberland were all heavy smokers and helped popularize the Indian custom among the English nobility.

Apparently Harriot was the first person to be recorded by his physician as a smoker.[13] In his mid-fifties he developed nasal cancer. Was this affliction connected with smoking? Recent medical findings would point to the possibility. Harriot's death on July 2, 1621, at the age of about sixty, almost surely as the result of smoking, makes him a forerunner in this as in so many other respects.

A memorial plaque in the chancel of St. Christopher's Church in London characterized Harriot in Latin as one

> Who cultivated all the sciences
> And excelled in all—
> In Mathematics, Natural Philosophy, Theology,
> A most studious searcher after truth.[14]

Yet Harriot's reputation, so high among the foremost thinkers of his time, quickly fell into decline. The main reason was his curious failure to publish any of his thousands of pages of scientific research and other discoveries—except for *A Briefe and True Report.* To make matters worse, Harriot's executor also did not publish any of the voluminous records left in his care. Not until this century have Harriot's achievements been adequately recognized and studied.

Why did Harriot fail to publish? Some have suggested that he was too much the perfectionist to offer the world anything in which he might later find a flaw. However that may be, Harriot took pride in his one publication, despite its lack of completeness. In 1603, he noted with apparent satisfaction that that work had already appeared in four languages.

Almost twenty years passed after the publication of *A Briefe and True Report* before another Englishman displayed the same acute interest in American Indian culture as Harriot. But Harriot's pamphlet opened the door for other early ethnologists of the New World. His introduction of Indian words into English led the way for the later adoption of more than one thousand still-current North American Indian (north of Mexico) loanwords. Although numerically small in comparison with the total English vocabulary of about half a million words, this linguistic legacy forms a colorful and indispensable part of the modern English language—in fact, one of its major vocabulary sources outside the Indo-European language family. Harriot's contribution in this respect, though it represents only one aspect of his genius, is a monument worthy of the man.

CHAPTER TWO

Adventurers and Settlers

ON THE AFTERNOON OF JULY 18, 1605, THE MATH-
ematician and mariner George Waymouth eased his ship, the
Archangel, into Dartmouth harbor. He had spent several months
leading an expedition to what is now Maine. *A True Relation
of the most prosperous voyage made this present yeere 1605 by Cap-
taine George Waymouth,* by James Rosier, who sailed with
Waymouth, was published a few months later. The book
attracted wide attention in outward-looking England.

But five Indians Waymouth had kidnapped made a more
vivid impression. Rosier related that it took five or six sailors
to get two of the captives aboard ship, "for they were strong
and so naked as our best hold was by their long haire on
their heads."[1] Along with the Indians, Waymouth brought
back two of their canoes and their bows and arrows. The
display of the Indians and their gear to some of England's
most influential figures gave substance to the rhetoric that
the New World so often inspired in European visitors.

The English drive to colonize North America had faltered
after 1590. Walter Raleigh had sent a party of 117 people in
1587 to try a third time to establish a colony. The colonists
set themselves up once again on Roanoke Island. By the
time the colony's absentee leader, John White (the artist
who had previously accompanied Thomas Harriot to Roanoke Island), returned three years later, the settlement lay in
ruins. All the colonists had vanished, never to be found
again. English plans for North American settlement lan-
guished for more than ten years.

Waymouth's Indians reached an England more receptive to them than it had been to Harriot's Indian friends (and possibly a few other, less heralded, Indian captives). Sir Ferdinando Gorges, governor of Plymouth's Fort, commandeered the five, whom Rosier quaintly described as "a Sagamo or Commander," three "Gentlemen," and "a servant."[2] Gorges took several into his own home and questioned them about the teeming shores and forests of their native land. Communication was possible because, according to Rosier, members of Waymouth's expedition had taught the Indians some English.

After examining his guests, Gorges wrote that Waymouth "brought five of the Natives . . . ; they were all of one nation, but of several parts and several families; this accident must be acknowledged the means under God of putting on foot and giving life to all our Plantations."[3] Several of the Indians would in fact serve as guides for later expeditions.

Backing the witness of the Indians, of course, was Rosier's book. Rosier said in his foreword that he was reserving a list of four hundred or five hundred Indian words for "those that shal goe in the next Voyage."[4] But his text introduced two key Indian words to English readers:

> *powwow,* medicine man or a meeting—from Narragansett *powwaw,* Indian priest; *Baugh, Waugh* in the text: "One among them (the eldest of the Company, as he [one of Waymouth's party] judged) riseth right up, the other sitting still, and looking about, suddenly cried with a loud voice, Baugh Waugh: then the women fall downe, and lie upon the ground, and the men all together answering the same, fall a stamping round about the fire with both feet, as hard as they can, making the ground shake, with sundry outcries, and change of voice and sound." (For the exact source of this and other Indian loanwords in this chapter, see the end of the notes to chapter 2.)
>
> *sagamore,* chief or leader—Eastern Abenaki *sàkama;* in the text, describing the taking of a whale: "When they have

killed him and dragged him to shore, they call all their chiefe lords together, and sing a song of joy: and those chiefe lords, whom they call Sagamos, divide the spoile, and give to every man a share."

At the end of his book, Rosier offered a short glossary of Indian words. The following evidently appeared for the first time in print:

> *caribou,* the animal—Micmac *khalibu,* perhaps originally "shoveler of snow"; *Coribo* in Rosier, defined as "Fallow Deere."
> *moose,* the animal—Eastern Abenaki *mos; Moosurr* in Rosier, defined as "Red Deere."
> *pone,* corn bread—compare Virginia Algonquian *poan, appoans;* this word appears in the later and redundant *corn pone; Paune* in Rosier, defined as "Bread."
> *tomahawk,* a light ax—compare Virginia Algonquian *tamahaac,* hatchet; *Tomaheegon* in Rosier, defined as "An Axe or Hatchet."

The words that Waymouth's Indians themselves uttered found an enthusiastic audience. Two of the Indians went to Lord Chief Justice John Popham. Just two years earlier, it will be recalled, he had branded Harriot a heretic at Raleigh's trial. But Popham and his influential friends harbored an interest similar to Harriot's (though hardly so sophisticated) in developing the New World.

Their excitement over the Indians sparked the formation of a major joint-stock company—one in which stock was held jointly by company owners—for the development of Virginia. At that time, "Virginia" included the entire Atlantic Coast north of Florida. Company operations were to be divided into a northern and a southern branch, each to have its own resident council.

One person drawn to this enterprise was twenty-seven-year-old John Smith, an intrepid soldier and adventurer.

Smith was a short but powerful man with a long moustache and full beard. He asserted that he had fought in Hungary and elsewhere and that he had been captured and for a time enslaved by the Turks. Historians long dismissed his more extravagant claims as bombast, but recent research at least partly confirms many of his once-doubted assertions.

Smith's record as an adventurer undoubtedly recommended him to the Virginia Company for a seat on the seven-member local council designated to rule a colony in the southern branch of Virginia. After months of delays because of bad weather, an expedition of three ships—with Smith aboard—set sail early in 1607 and reached the Chesapeake Bay area in April. The peninsula chosen on the James River for Jamestown, the first settlement, turned out to be unfortunate. Although well located for defense against European threats by sea or Indian threats by land, it was swampy, with brackish water that undermined the health of those who drank it. Furthermore, the 105 Jamestown settlers included a high percentage of gentlemen ill-equipped and unmotivated for the hard work needed to build an outpost in the wilderness.

Smith played a key role in establishing Jamestown. His war experiences in Europe were surely valuable in building the town's fortifications. His readiness to parley with Indians helped the settlers develop trade with them and gain vital information about Indian customs, intentions, and fighting strength.

One of Smith's expeditions resulted in the adventure for which he is perhaps best known. In December 1607, Smith led a party up the Chickahominy River north of Jamestown. Indians surprised the group, capturing Smith and killing his men. Only Smith's coolness and potential value as a hostage saved his life. Conveyed from village to village, Smith was at last delivered to the great chief Powhatan.

Smith gave an account of this meeting in a letter of about forty pages published in 1608 without his permission, *A*

True Relation of such occurrences and accidents of note, as hath hapned in Virginia. In this work, Smith introduced English readers to a version of the word *raccoon*—Virginia Algonquian *aroughcun.* In describing Powhatan, he used a variation of this word: "Arriving at Werawocomoco, their Emperour proudly lying uppon a Bedstead a foote high upon tenne or twelve Mattes, richly hung with manie Chaynes of great Pearles about his necke, and covered with a great Covering of *Rahaughcums.*" Smith had a hard time with this jawbreaker, spelling it four different ways in his writings.

Powhatan closely questioned Smith before ordering his execution. According to Smith, only the intervention of Pocahontas, Powhatan's thirteen- or fourteen-year-old daughter, saved his life. Many historians have challenged this story, but the warm friendship between Smith and Pocahontas before and after her marriage to the Englishman John Rolfe points to a special relationship between the two.

On Smith's return to Jamestown, authorities there threatened him with execution for negligently causing the death of two of his men. But later in the year, in a characteristic reversal of fortune, he was elected president of England's only colony in North America. Under Smith's leadership, the situation at Jamestown began looking up. The settlers repaired their church, constructed a blockhouse, and built twenty new houses. They cleared thirty or forty acres of farmland and stepped up their output of tar, glass, and soap ash. Nor did Smith neglect maintaining the delicate relationship between the colony and the surrounding Indians.

But a series of misfortunes overtook President Smith. Rats were discovered to have infested the casks of corn stored for the winter. Orders came from England that the colony was to be recognized as part of a larger colony under an "absolute governor," a plan that immediately began to undermine Smith's authority. Friction developed between Indians and some unruly settlers. Finally an accidental explosion of a powder keg badly injured the beleaguered Smith. Overwhelmed, he retreated to England in October 1609.

Smith had already earned undying credit for his role in establishing the first permanent English colony in North America. Yet he was still under age thirty. Once recovered from his injuries, he began a restless search for activities that could again engage his talents and energy. In 1612, he published his *Map of Virginia, with a Description of the Countrey, the Commodities, People, Government and Religion.* This thirty-nine-page volume, with map, gave an overall description of Jamestown and its environs.

Smith had become familiar with some Virginia Algonquian tongue and is referred to as a translator by at least one companion. It is in *A Map* that he best shows this knowledge by introducing his greatest number of Indian words: *assapan* (the American flying squirrel), *chinquapin, cockarouse* (a person of importance among American colonists), *hickory, hominy, maracock* (a passionflower), *matchcoat* (an Indian mantle), *muskrat* or *musquash,** *netop* ("friend," used by colonists in greeting Indians), *persimmon, puccoon* (plant yielding a red or orange dye), and *tuckahoe* (arrow arum root).

Smith went on a final expedition in 1614, this time to New England—which he named. Most of his remaining life, until he died in 1631, was spent writing in London. The main fruit of these later years was *The Generall Historie of Virginia, New-England, and the Summer Isles,* published in 1624. Here he introduced another Indian word into English: *roanoke,* wampum—*rawranoke,* Virginia Algonquian, perhaps meaning smoothed shells. (For *Roanoke* as probably the earliest surviving North American Indian place-name in English, see chapter 7.)

But John Smith was not alone in his detailed interest in

---

*George Percy earlier recorded this word as *Muskats* in his 1607 account of Virginia, but publication of his report did not occur until 1625 (*Purchas* 18:415).

Indian language. About the time Smith's *Map* appeared, William Strachey, a Cambridge-educated writer well known in London literary circles, compiled a lengthy glossary of Indian words. Strachey was on friendly terms with the playwright Ben Jonson. The poet John Donne referred to him in a letter as "allways my good friend," and the poet Thomas Campion called him in Latin "my old companion."[5]

Strachey is now best known for supplying Shakespeare with the main source for *The Tempest*. In 1606, Strachey had lost his job as secretary to the English ambassador in Constantinople because of a quarrel with his employer. Three years later, while on his way to a similar position as secretary and recorder for the governor of Virginia, he was shipwrecked in the Bermudas. There he and his companions spent the winter before sailing to Jamestown in two small ships they had constructed. The manuscript of a narrative letter he wrote describing that adventure found its way into Shakespeare's hands well before publication in 1625, after Strachey's death.

Students of Indian culture too are indebted to Strachey. While in Virginia, he drew up his list of eight to nine hundred Indian words (the inclusion of phrases makes an exact count difficult). This glossary was appended to the unfinished *The Historie of Travell into Virginia Britania*, written by him about 1609–12.[6] Not published until 1849, this work contains many of the same words that Smith introduced—*assapan, chinquapin, hickory, maracock, matchcoat, muskrat, netop, persimmon, puccoon, raccoon,* and *tuckahoe.* Strachey was influenced by Smith's report, but he records several other Indian words that entered the English vocabulary as well:

> *cantico,* a dancing party—modification of Delaware *kəntka,* to dance; "Kantokan—to daunce," in Strachey.
> *pecan* (?), the nut—Virginia Algonquian *paccan:* "a walnut— . . . Paukans."

supawn, hasty pudding (corn mush)—akin to Massachuset *saupaun,* mush (literally softened by water); "Asapan" in Strachey's glossary; some trace *spoon bread,* the name of a custardlike bread traditionally made in the South with corn-meal, to this source.[7]

wicopy, leatherwood—Eastern Abenaki *wikᵊpi,* inner bark suitable for cordage; "Hemp—Weihkippeis" in Strachey's glossary.

Strachey died in 1621, poor and obscure, dogged by bad luck to the end. He had lost a considerable amount of inherited property years before, and the major projects on which he had labored remained unfulfilled. Centuries would pass before his talent won him the recognition that had eluded him while alive.

Meanwhile, French explorations yielded other Indian words that passed into English. A classic early work on the French in Canada is Marc Lescarbot's book translated under the title *Nova Francia, a description of Acadia.* When a friend invited him to Canada, Lescarbot was a prominent lawyer in Paris and a man of extensive learning. Disillusioned with law, he accepted the invitation because of a "desire to flee a corrupt world and to examine this land with [his] own eyes."[8] The book he published after his return to France is a sympathetic and urbane account of the New World from the perspective of world history as then known. A translation appearing in London in 1609 presented two Indian words novel to English readers:

moccasin, footwear—compare Natick *mohkussin;* Lescarbot wrote: "Besides these long stockings, our savages do use shoes, which they call *mekezin,* which they fashion very properly, but they cannot dure long, specially when they go into watery places, because they be not curried nor hardened, but only made after the manner of buff, which is the hide of an elan [moose]."

totem, an animal or other object serving as emblem of a clan or family—Ojibwa *nindoodem,* "my family mark" (Lescarbot's version is *aoutem*).

Two other Indian words introduced into English early in the seventeenth century are animal names:

opossum, the animal—Virginia Algonquian *aposoum:* "There are Arocouns and Apossouns, in shape like to pigges" (*A true declaration of the estate of the colonie in Virginia,* 1610); the shorter form, *possum,* is given as *possowns* in *Good Newes from Virginia* by Alexander Whitaker, 1613.

terrapin, the animal—Virginia Algonquian *torope;* in Whitaker, *Good Newes:* "I have caught with mine angle . . . the Torope or little Turtle."

Most of the first English loanwords borrowed directly from the North American Indians denote plants and animals specific to America. But further loanwords reflect the culture of the Indians—a culture that Europeans tried to understand out of curiosity as well as for utilitarian reasons. It is fortunate that the first explorers included sophisticated people like Harriot, Lescarbot, and Strachey, capable of imaginative insight into the New World.

Smith lacked the formal education of these three. "I be no scholer," he wrote the Virginia Company.[9] Yet his travels among the Indians and his close ties with them gave him a familiarity with their language and culture that produced the greatest number of Indian loanwords in the early seventeenth century.

CHAPTER THREE

A Forest of Languages

WHAT EVEN THE MOST TALENTED OF THE EARLY English explorers could not realize was the richness of New World languages. The Indians encountered by Thomas Harriot and John Smith were speakers of coastal Algonquian tongues. Beyond them dwelt—amid the vast forests and mountains of North America—Indians speaking a multitude of other languages rivaling in their variety those of any continent in the world. It is estimated that at the time of Columbus, the Indians in the New World had more than 1,000 and possibly 2,000 different languages.[1] Compare this profusion of tongues with the approximately 6,000 languages spoken in the entire world today!

The Smithsonian Institution Department of Anthropology has placed the number of languages spoken in North America (north of Mexico) at the time of Columbus at 350. Other authorities place the total at more than 500. Some 200 of these languages are still spoken.[2] The rest disappeared as their speakers died out, leaving descendants who could not speak the languages or sometimes leaving no descendants at all.

The lack of writing among the northern American Indians made their languages dependent on a living tradition. Some Indian groups oppose, on principle, the writing down of their languages. Harold Dean Salway, president of the Oglala Sioux, feels this way about Lakota, his tribal language. He noted, "Writing it is bad, I think, because you have a tendency to lose some of the spirituality when it's down in black and white."[3] Even now, there are no dictionaries for many North American Indian languages. Published grammars for these languages are unusual.[4] As a result, the languages are a fertile field for the researches of linguists. Major uncertainties remain—for example, exactly how many language families the Indian tongues of North America represent.

In his *Language in the Americas* (1987), Joseph H. Greenberg divided all Native American languages into only three broad groups: Eskimo and Aleut, Na-Dene, and Amerind. *Eskimo and Aleut* is a traditional category, with Eskimo divided into Yuit and Inuit. *Na-Dene* includes languages of the Pacific Northwest and Athabaskan (Apache, Navajo, etc.). All the rest, according to Greenberg, fall into the massive group he calls *Amerind,* which includes hundreds of Indian languages from the Algonquian* family in North America to Yaghan in southernmost South America.

But other leading linguists hotly dispute Greenberg's classification. For the purposes of this book, we will use a commonly accepted list of seven language phyla (superstocks): Eskimo-Aleut, Na-Dene, Macro-Algonquian, Macro-Siouan, Hokan, Penutian, and Aztec-Tanoan. These phyla are further subdivided into fifty-seven families. See the map for the location of many of the languages.

The variety of North American Indian languages north of Mexico made communication a problem for Indians of different groups. The inability to converse easily among themselves hindered cooperation among Indians. It had much to do with the failure of Indian tribes and nations to unite against white encroachment, even when survival was at stake.

Yet some intertribal languages did permit communication across many cultures. Often such languages took the

---

Sometimes spelled *Algonkian* or *Algonkin,* as in several sources quoted in this chapter.

American Indian Language Groups

ARCTIC OCEAN

ESKIMO

ATHABASKAN

ALEUT

ESKIMO

ESKIMO

TLINGIT

HAIDA

TSIMSHIAN

WAKASHAN · SALISH

ATHABASKAN

ALGONQUIAN

BEOTHUK

SALISH

CHIMAKUAN

ALGONQUIAN

SALISH
SAHAPTIN-NEZ PERCE

SIOUAN

CADDOAN

SIOUAN

IROQUOIAN

ALGONQUIAN

PACIFIC
OCEAN

UTO-AZTECAN

HOPI

SIOUAN

ALGONQUIAN

CHEROKEE

ESSELEN
YOKUTS
SALINAN
CHUMASHAN

UTO-AZTECAN

ZUNI

KERES

CADDOAN

SIOUAN

YUCHI

CATAWBA

ATLANTIC
OCEAN

ALGONQUIAN

KIOWA
ATHABASKAN

CADDOAN

TUNICA

TANOAN

TONKAWA

MUSKOGEAN

YUMAN

ATHABASKAN

COMANCHE

SERI

ATAKAPA

NATCHEZ

TIMUCUA

UTO-AZTECAN
COAHUILTECAN

CHITIMACHA
KARANKAWA
COMECRUDAN

UTO-
AZTECAN

UTO-AZTECAN

Gulf of Mexico

CHINOOKAN

SALISH

YAKONAN

SAHAPTIN-NEZ PERCE
KALAPUYA
MOLALE
KALAPUYA
COOS
TAKELMA
KLAMATH-
MODOC
SHASTAN

CAYUSE

ATHABASKAN
KAROK
YUROK
WIYOT
CHIMARIKO
ATHABASKAN
YUKI
POMO
WAPPO

UTO-
AZTECAN

PALAIHNIHAN

YANAN

MAIDU

UTO-
AZTECAN

MAIDU

MIWOK

WASHO

COSTANOAN

0   100 MI
0 150 KM

0   200 400 600 MI
0   300 600 900 KM

UTO-AZTECAN

▓ Eskimo-Aleut	▦ Hokan	☐ Uninhabited areas
▨ Na-Dene	⸭ Penutian	■ Nonsubject area
▒ Macro-Algonquian	▧ Aztec-Tanoan	⬚ Language isolates and families with undetermined affiliations
▩ Macro-Siouan		

The map indicates the phyla, or broad groups, into which many linguists divide North American Indian languages. Within each phylum are languages related to one another. From C. F. and F. M. Voegelin, *Map of North American Indian Languages,* copyright 1966 by University of Washington Press.

form of a lingua franca, such as the Chinook Jargon. This trade language, based on the Chinook tongue with words borrowed from other languages, flourished around the Columbia River and along the Pacific coast as far as Alaska. The Comanche language by itself served as a trade language among tribes in the southwestern Great Plains.

One of the most ingenious approaches to intertribal communication was the sign language employed by Plains Indians. These Indians refined their nonverbal language to a high degree. "By a system of several hundred signs, representing all parts of speech, the Indians of the Plains conversed together—near at hand or sometimes at such distances that the signs could only be silhouetted against the sky, with a flow of motion which equaled the articulatory dignity of spoken speech,"[5] wrote John P. Harrington of the Smithsonian Institution. Often an Indian making the signs would simultaneously speak in his own language. From the Rio Grande into southern Canada, Plains Indians speaking more than a score of different languages bartered and bantered among themselves using gestures of the sign language.

Although archaeologists have discovered evidence of a sign system among eastern tribes, this apparently never achieved the range and effectiveness of that of the Plains.[6] Early Europeans and the Indians they dealt with had to learn words to communicate at any length. Nearly all the languages the Europeans first encountered belonged to the Algonquian family. Partly because of this primary—and often most vivid—contact, about half the North American Indian (north of Mexico) loanwords in English come from Algonquian languages.

Between forty and fifty Algonquian languages are known to have been spoken, from far north along the Atlantic seacoast down to North Carolina and across much of northern North America to the Great Plains. Linguist Frank T. Siebert, Jr., places the homeland for Algonquian speakers at

Table 3.1 Algonquian Languages

Those languages with an "O" after them are no longer spoken. Some of the others are on the verge of extinction.

Abenaki (Eastern)	Loup O
Abenaki (Western)	Mahican O
Arapaho-Atsina-	Malecite-Passamaquoddy
Nawathinehena	Massachusett O
Blackfoot	Menomini
Carolina Algonquian O	Micmac
Cheyenne	Mohegan-Pequot-Montauk O
Connecticut-Unquachog-	Montagnais-Naskapi
Shinnecock O	Nanticoke-Conoy O
Cree	Narragansett O
Delaware	Ojibwa-Algonquin-Ottawa
Fox-Sauk	Potawatomi
Illinois-Peoria-Miami O	Powhatan O
Kickapoo	Shawnee

Adapted from Karl V. Teeter in Thomas A. Sebeok, *Native Languages of the Americas* (New York, 1976), 1:507.

the eastern Great Lakes region. His research indicates that the period of latest unity of these speakers was from 1200 B.C. to 900 B.C.[7] Scholars are now reconstructing the Proto-Algonquian language these people are believed to have spoken. See table 3.1 for a list of twenty-six of the Algonquian languages.

Algonquian is characterized, like several other Indian language families, by *polysynthesis*—the expression of many sentence elements within a single word. The elements of such a word act as nouns, verbs, adverbs, and other parts of speech. "The structure of the language often forces an assemblage of concepts that impresses as a stylistic discovery," wrote Edward Sapir. "Single Algonkin words are like tiny imagist poems."[8] This linguist cites as an example of polysynthesis the following from the Algonquian language Fox: *eh-kiwi-n-a-m-oht-wa-ch(i),* which means "then they together kept (him) in flight from them." The root element is *kiwi,* signifying "indefinite movement round about, here and there."[9] The prefix and suffixes convey the rest of the meaning.

The more sympathetic early whites noted the expressiveness of Algonquian and other Indian languages. These languages often vividly render a complex object or idea through a joining together of terms for simpler things. The Algonquian language Cheyenne, still spoken by thousands in Montana and elsewhere in the West, furnishes many examples of this process.

The Cheyenne word for nightingale is *voenåhtóohehe,* literally "all night-hollering." In the same language, nut is *ooˀxôseoˀo,** "crack-with teeth." Interpreter is *éestomótåxeváhe,* "speak for someone-person." The continuing vitality of Cheyenne appears in modern coinages such as automobile, *amahoˀhestôtse,* "burns while it goes-thing," and UFO, *tse-sáa-nanóhehane ameˀhahtôtse,* "the-not-recognized flying-thing."**[10]

Another charming, if not so prevalent, feature of Indian languages is onomatopoeia. Walt Whitman wrote in *Leaves of Grass* of

The red aborigines,
Leaving natural breaths, sounds of rain and winds, calls as
of birds and animals in the woods, syllabled
to us for names.[11]

---

*ˀSignifies a glottal stop, the closure and explosive release of the glottis that occurs between the two elements of "oh-oh!"

**In the South Pacific during World War II, the famed Navajo Code Talkers—speaking their language over the radio to keep messages secret from the Japanese—developed similar equivalents in Navajo. A colonel became "silver eagle" in Navajo, a dive bomber "chicken hawk," and an aircraft carrier "bird carrier" (Ringle, "Indecipherable Heroism").

An early apparent example of onomatopoeia in an Algonquian language can be found in *A Key into the Language of America* (1643) by Roger Williams. He gives the Narragansett word for horse, which the eastern Indians had known for only a few decades, as the neighing *naynayoûmewot*.[12] The following apparently onomatopoetic words come from several other Algonquian languages: chicken—*kokôhéaxa* (Cheyenne);[13] owl—*gokookhoo* (Ojibwa); great horned owl—*oohoomsii* (Ojibwa); chickadee—*jigjigaaneshiinh* (Ojibwa);[14] whippoorwill—*wikwĕlĕĕch* (Micmac); to caw—*kakoojooweese* (Micmac); and frog—*chechowĕch* (Micmac).[15]

Despite their strong oral tradition, Indians often impressed whites as sparing in their use of language. In 1635, William Wood said in his *New England's Prospect:* "Garrulity is much condemned of them, for they utter not many words, speak seldom, and then with such gravity as is pleasing to the ear. Such as understand them not desire yet to hear their emphatical expressions and lively action."[16] Witness after witness described the quiet watchfulness of Indians.

But Indian silence was meaningful. Members of tribes such as the Apache and Navajo frequently said nothing when they were unsure about a stranger or even uncertain about the attitude of a member of their family.[17] Conversation would begin only when doubts were resolved.

Silence among Indians often preceded a discussion of sacred matters. Chased-By-Bears, a Santee-Yanktonai Sioux, noted: "Before talking of holy things, we prepare ourselves by offerings . . . one will fill his pipe and hand it to the other who will light it and offer it to the sky and earth . . . they will smoke together. . . . Then will they be ready to talk." Or silence itself was considered sacred. Ohiyesa (Dr. Charles A. Eastman, a Sioux) wrote: "If you ask [the Indian]: 'What is silence?' he will answer: 'It is the Great Mystery!' 'The holy silence is His voice!' If you ask: 'What are the fruits of silence?' he will say: 'They are self-control, true courage or endurance, patience, dignity, and reverence. Silence is the cornerstone of character.'"[18]

This quietness was balanced by an oratory that ranged from fiery defiance to a tragic expression of doom. Indians sometimes offered lengthy ritual prayers that had to be recited exactly, down to the last syllable. Tribal matters, on the other hand, were debated extemporaneously for hours or days until a consensus was reached. Here the Indian developed a rhetoric rivaling that of any other language.

Some of the most quoted Indian speeches are those delivered as the Indian accepted defeat with unconquerable dignity. Thus Chief Joseph vowed in 1877, "From here where the sun now stands I will fight no more forever."[19] In about 1848 Colonel Cobb, a Choctaw chief, lamented to a government agent: "My people are scattered and gone; when I shout, I hear my voice in the depths of the forest, but no answering voice comes back to me—all is silent around me!"[20]

The still-widening silence of Indian languages deeply concerns linguists and Indians alike. Federal government policy—starting in the 1860s and lasting into the middle of this century—was to promote the use of English among Indians as a way to further their economic development and to move them into the mainstream of American society.

But more recently, the cultural loss caused by the disuse of native tongues has been widely recognized. Distinctive customs and traditions often disappear with the languages in which they were conveyed. "Perhaps some very gross features of a tribal people's world view and perceptions can be transferred to English, but by and large the disappearance of a language means a major alteration in such a world view," wrote Robert Thomas, an anthropologist at the University of Arizona and a Cherokee. "More, it means . . . that such a people have surrendered their intellectual autonomy and independence to another society."[21]

To counteract the loss of Indian languages, language-renewal programs have arisen among Indian groups across the nation. William L. Leap, professor of anthropology at American University, is a leader in this movement. He has actively supported Indian-language renewal projects as well as programs to strengthen the English skills of Indians in Arizona, New Mexico, Oklahoma, Wisconsin, and other states. He notes the rise in Indian-language projects funded under the U.S. Bilingual Education Act, the attendance of hundreds of educators and others at Indian-language conferences during the 1980s, and the movement among a number of tribes to foster their native languages. In 1990, the federal government passed a law officially supporting the renewal of Indian languages. Sponsored by Senator Daniel K. Inouye of Hawaii, the bill established "as the policy of the United States the preservation, protection, and promotion of the rights of Native Americans to use, practice, and develop Native American languages."[22]

What is the future of the relatively few Indian languages remaining out of those that once abounded in North America north of Mexico? Professor Leap estimated in 1991 that a third of the Indian languages still spoken in the United States were threatened with extinction.[23] Words and names from many vanished Indian languages survive, ironically, only in the English terms derived from them.

CHAPTER FOUR

"Wild Beasts and Willd Men"

GOOD FRIDAY OF 1622 MARKED A VIOLENT END to apparently friendly relations between the settlers and the Indians of Virginia. Indians infiltrated scores of white settlements and homesteads. Once among the trusting settlers, they suddenly attacked. So complete was the surprise that Indians picked up muskets and tools that belonged to the settlers and turned them on their owners. Farms, houses, and public buildings went up in flames as Indians torched the hated symbols of white encroachment. Some 347 settlers died out of an estimated total of 1,300.

The settlers crushed the uprising, then took steps to discourage another outbreak. Once the advocate of friendship with the Indians, John Smith joined in an outcry for their destruction. It is no accident that the borrowing of words in Virginia—the source of most of the first North American words in English north of Mexico—came to an almost complete halt.

Yet even as that tragedy unfolded, a new settlement was getting under way in the north. Pilgrims had arrived in Massachusetts late in 1620. Half died that first winter, and the survival of the rest hung in the balance for months. The Pilgrims endured, however, and set about organizing a community quite different from the one in Virginia.

No William Strachey among the Pilgrims learnedly examined the New World and its inhabitants. William Brewster, the Pilgrim elder, was the only one in the little congregation to have attended a university (Cambridge). The rest had been farming folk and followers of trades.

Nor did curiosity with an eye to profit play as great a role in Plymouth, or the slightly later Massachusetts Bay Colony, as in Virginia. William Bradford, Plymouth Colony's second governor, explained in his classic *Of Plimoth Plantation* that the Pilgrims fled an exile's home in Holland to preserve their culture from being overwhelmed by Dutch influence. But he concluded his list of reasons for their migration by declaring, "Lastly, (and which was not the least,) a great hope and inward zeall they had of laying some good foundation, or at least to make some way therunto, for ye propagating and advancing ye gospell of ye kingdom of Christ in those remote parts of ye world."[1]

The Pilgrims had less contact with Indians initially than did the early settlers of Virginia. As fate would have it (providence, the Pilgrims felt), the *Mayflower* landed at a place denuded of Indian inhabitants four years earlier by a plague that previous European visitors had introduced. Instead of a village, the Pilgrims discovered graves and empty wigwams.

The Pilgrims, furthermore, were under less pressure than the Virginians to learn the Algonquian languages of nearby Indians. Two English-speaking Indians soon appeared; one was Squanto, a tall man belonging to the Patuxet tribe (who had inhabited the site the Pilgrims settled). His history was a strange one. He had been kidnapped from Cape Cod in 1614 by Englishmen and sold as a slave in Spain. Redeemed, he went to England, then sailed on an English ship to Newfoundland and back. Finally he jumped ship on a new trip to America and returned to Cape Cod in 1619. There Squanto found that the plague had wiped out his tribe. He became friends with Samoset, an Abenaki who had apparently learned the rudiments of English from fishermen along the coast of Maine.

Squanto served as an intermediary between the Pilgrims and Massasoit, chief of the plague-weakened Wampanoags. This chief apparently welcomed the newcomers as potential allies against the powerful Narragansett tribe. Squanto assisted the Pilgrims in many ways, acting as interpreter and teaching them about farming and food gathering. Historians now debate the extent to which Squanto was making a bid for personal power against Massasoit. But without his help, the Pilgrims might never have survived in a land Bradford had called "a hidious and desolate wilderness, full of wild beasts and willd [*sic*] men."[2]

Until Squanto's death of a mysterious ailment in 1622, the Pilgrims were dependent on him, even overly dependent. Writing the year after Squanto's death, the Pilgrim leader Edward Winslow said: "As for the [Indian] language, it is very copious, large, and difficult. As yet, we cannot attain to any great measure thereof: but can understand them, and explain ourselves to their understanding; by the help of those that daily converse with us."[3]

Mourt's Relation, published in 1622 by George Morton, who may have been the author, is the only contemporary description of the *Mayflower* voyage and the early months of Plymouth Colony. Reflecting the strongly ethnocentric outlook of the Pilgrims, this work used few Indian loanwords and introduced only two:

sachem, an Indian leader—of southeastern New England Algonquian origin; *sâchim* in Narragansett; Morton wrote, "The next day . . ., many of their Sachims, or petty Governours came to see us, and many of their men also." (For the exact source of this and other Indian loanwords in this chapter, see the end of the notes to chapter 4.)

squaw, Indian woman—from Massachusett *squà,* younger woman; in Morton: "Also the *Squa Sachim,* or Massachusets Queene was an enemy to him [another sachem]." (*Squaw* as a noun apparently first occurred in William Wood's *New England's Prospect* (1634), to be discussed.)

In *Plimoth Plantation,* Bradford was similarly sparing in his use of Indian loanwords, employing fewer than ten different words from Algonquian languages. This paucity of Indian loanwords is all the more striking in a work the length of Bradford's—528 pages in the 1898 edition.

Bradford, however, did introduce *wampumpeag,* wampum, in his book in 1627—from *wampumpeage,* southeastern New England Algonquian, literally "white strings." In connection with the trade for beaver and other animal skins, Bradford noted a Pilgrim "stock of furrs, fells, beads, corne, wampampeak, hatchets, knives, &c."[4] Shorter forms of *wampumpeag* later appear as *peag* (also spelled *peage* or *peak*) in 1634[5] and as the more familiar *wampum* in 1636.[6]

Wampum held profound significance for the Indians. They put it to ceremonial use—as a ratification of treaties, as a badge of chieftainship or a token of honor, as a call to confess religious transgressions, and as an offering to the Creator. Bands of wampum could be six feet or longer, with intricate designs in white and purple shell beads. Tribes handed down the most significant wampum bands from generation to generation.

Since the Indians obviously prized wampum and sometimes used it in barter, whites came to treat it as currency. The Dutch led the way for the commercial use of wampum in the early seventeenth-century Northeast. The Dutch-transmitted term for unstrung wampum is *sewan* (or *seawan* or *seawant*), from *sé-wan,* Munsee Delaware language, literally "that which is in a scattered state." One observer noted in 1627, "As an employment in winter they [the New York Indians] make seawan, which is an oblong bead that they make from cockle shells."[7]

While the Pilgrims were still securing a foothold at Plymouth, other Englishmen had been exploring what is now Maine with an eye to settling there. One of the explorers was William Levett, a native of York, England. Levett had been promised six thousand acres of his choice within a vast area assigned to Sir Ferdinando Gorges in northern New England. After beginning his search in 1623, Levett chose an island in the mouth of Portland harbor and stationed ten men to hold it while he returned to England for supplies and more men.

To raise money and to arouse interest in his plans for a settlement, Levett wrote an account of his adventures. For some reason, *York and Portland* was not published until 1628. Offering an early description of the northern New World and its inhabitants, the book also introduced two Indian words:

> *wigwam*, house—Eastern Abenaki *wikɔwam* house; "We built us our Wigwam, or house, in one houres space, it had no frame, but was without forme or fashion, only a few poles set up together, and couered with our boates sailes which kept forth but a little winde, and less raigne and snow," Levett wrote in run-on style about his makeshift shelter.
>
> *sannup*, a married male Indian—Massachusett *sanomp* man; Levett claimed, "The Sagamores will scarce speake to an ordinary man, but will point to their men, and say *Sanops* must speake to *Sanops,* and *Sagamors* to *Sagamors.*"

As English settlements in the New World increased in the early seventeenth century, so did the English public's appetite for news about America. The Massachusetts Bay Colony in 1630 and Maryland in 1634 became outposts of England along with Virginia and Plymouth. Back home, people wanted to know more about the reputed wonders of these newly settled areas as well as their economic potential.

Meanwhile, despite the troubles in Virginia, a few loanwords from the southern Indians were trickling into English. *Atamasco lily,* the "fairy lily," comes from the Virginia Algonquian *attamusco.* "The Virginia Daffodil. . . . The Indians do call it Attamusco," occurs in 1629 in the publication *Narcissus Virgineus.*[8] The Algonquian *pocosin,* a mainly regional word meaning a swamp in an upland area, was recorded in Virginia in 1634. From Maryland in the same year came *poke* in the sense of tobacco. "After this was brought . . . a great Bagg, filled with a large Tobacco-pipe and Poake, which is the word they use for our Tobacco."[9] The word derives from a variation of Virginia Algonquian *puccoon,* pokeweed.

One of the best books written to meet the demand for information about New England was William Wood's *New England's Prospect,* avowedly published for "the mind-travelling Reader" and "the future Voyager."[10] Little is known about Wood other than that he had spent four years in Massachusetts, returning to England in 1633. His book was published in London the following year and sold at the Three Golden Lions shop. The success of this detailed and mostly accurate account of early New England can be gauged by new editions of the book issued in 1635 and 1639.

Wood's care to present local color led him to add a glossary of Indian words to his book. In his text and list, he introduced four novel Indian loanwords:

> *nocake,* cornmeal dried and pounded into a powder— Algonquian, akin to Narragansett *nokehick,* parched cornmeal; Wood wrote, "The best of their victuals for their journey is *Nocake* (as they call it), which is nothing but Indian corne parched in the hot ashes."
>
> *papoose,* young Indian child—Narragansett *papoòs,* baby; in Wood: "This little Pappouse travels about with his bare footed mother to paddle in the Icie Clammbankes."
>
> *skunk,* the animal—Massachusett *squnck;* in Wood: "The beasts of offence be squunckes, ferrets, foxes."
>
> *squanter-squash,* summer squash—*isquotersquash* from Narra-

gansett *askútasquash;* in Wood: "In summer, when their corne is spent, Isquoter squashes is their best bread, a fruite like a young Pumpion."

The early settlers of Massachusetts had felt ambivalent toward their Indian neighbors from the first. On the one hand, many whites valued the friendship of Indians and appreciated their help. On the other hand, settlers had heard tales of Indian ferocity even before arriving in the New World and shuddered at subsequent reports of troubles in Virginia. Early Massachusetts laws kept Indians at a distance, long forbidding the trading of guns to them while controlling their movements in towns. False alarms of Indian uprisings kept whites in the scattered and vulnerable settlements on edge. In 1632, for example, fear of a rumored Indian plot led the people of Massachusetts to double the number of their guards. At that time, all men except magistrates and ministers were furnished with weapons, which they were trained to use.

Frictions between the two dissimilar peoples led to real clashes. The killing of a trader from Massachusetts near Block Island in 1636 sparked a move by New England whites against the Pequot tribe of Connecticut, which was deemed responsible for the murder and other outrages. The Pequots had been regarded for some time as a threat not only to whites living in Connecticut but also to traders from other parts of New England. Massachusetts leaders further feared that the Pequots might ally themselves with other powerful tribes such as the Narragansetts. In 1637, a New England army of several hundred men, accompanied by Indian forces, attacked a Pequot stronghold in Mystic (despite its appearance, *Mystic* is a Pequot-Mohegan name meaning "the great tidal river"). Taking the fort by surprise, the attackers massacred some six hundred of the Pequots in a victory as decisive as it was horrible. Over the following months, surviving

Pequots were hunted down with a thoroughness that prevented the tribe from recovering for centuries.

The Pequot War was a powerful blow for white dominance in New England. Yet whites remained apprehensive. Tribes such as the Narragansetts of Rhode Island and the Mohegans of Connecticut still had to be acknowledged and placated. Rumors of Indian uprisings continued to sweep New England from time to time.

A first-recorded use of the loanword *powwow* as a verb in 1642 nevertheless reflects the attempt of many New England Indians to come to terms with English culture. "They will have their times of *powaheing,* which they will, of late, have called Prayers, according to the *English* word," appears in the book *Plain Dealing.*[11]

One New Englander who became closely attuned to the Indians, despite repeated alarms, was Roger Williams—an exception in this respect as in so many others. Forced out of the Massachusetts Bay Colony in 1636 because of his liberal religious views, Williams was next urged to leave even the more tolerant Plymouth Colony. The individualistic minister finally established his own settlement, Providence, with a democratic government and a policy of religious toleration.

In his new home, Williams developed warm relations with the neighboring Narragansett Indians. He regarded them as a people with a natural virtue superior to that of the whites, though lacking the revelation of Christianity. Williams traveled among the Narragansetts, traded with them, and learned their language. As a trusted friend, he became an intermediary and peacemaker between them and the English.

Williams described the Narragansett language in *A Key into the Language of America,* published in 1643. More than just a work on language, *A Key* presents a portrait of the Narragansett people and their customs. Introduced in it are native words for various foods, several of which became a permanent part of the American diet:

> *nasaump*, coarse hominy (hulled and dried kernels of corn)—Narragansett *nasàump*, cornmeal mush; in Williams: "Nasàump. *A kind of meale pottage, unpartch'd.*"
>
> *samp*, coarse hominy (etymology above); in Williams: "*Samp*, which is the *Indian* corne, beaten and boild, and eaten hot or cold with milke or butter, which are mercies beyond the *Natives* plaine water, and which is a dish exceeding wholesome for the *English* bodies."
>
> *squash*, plants including summer squash, winter squash, and pumpkin—akin to *isquotersquash* from Narragansett *askútasquash*; in Williams: "*Asqútasquash*, their Vine aples, which the *English* from them call *Squashes* about the bignesse of Apples of severall colours, a sweet, light wholesome refreshing."
>
> *succotash*, corn and usually lima beans cooked together—Narragansett *msíckquatash*, boiled whole-kernel corn; in Williams: "*Msíckquatash.* Boild corne whole."

The location of the Narragansetts on the New England coast is reflected in five marine fish and shellfish loanwords from their language: *menhaden*, mossbunker—*munnawhatteaûg*; *mummichog*, a silver-and-black killifish—*moamitteaûg*; *quahog*, the edible clam—*poquaûhock*; *scuppaug* (later *scup*), food fish like the porgies—*mishcuppaûg*; and *tautog*, the edible blackfish—*tautaûog*, plural of *taut.**

In his book, Williams demonstrates that the adoption of words from Indians was not one-sided. He gives several instances in which the Narragansetts took over English words denoting objects they had not been familiar with: *Monéash*

---

*The account of George Waymouth's voyage in 1605 defines *Tattaucke* as *cunner fish* in its glossary. Blackfish and cunner fish both belong to the family of wrasses and look much alike, making their Algonquian names almost surely cognate. But Williams established the modern loanword meaning of *tautog*.

for "money"; and *Côwsnuck, Gôatesnuck,* and *Hógsnuck* or *Pígsnuck* for the farm animals the whites introduced.[12]

Williams's *A Key* proved not to be the beginning of a more enlightened relationship between settlers and Indians but an isolated instance of true communication that, if it had continued, would have benefited both peoples. But in both New England and Virginia, Indian resentment was building up explosively. By the time settlers realized the degree of hostility they inspired, the time for a reconciliation had passed.

In 1644, an Indian uprising again shattered Virginia. The Powhatans rose up once more under Opechancanough, who had led them in 1622. This time, however, settlers were well prepared and greatly outnumbered the Indian attackers. Though at the cost of several hundred killed, the settlers put down the uprising and ended the power of the Powhatan Confederacy. So complete was the victory that at the war's conclusion, the Virginia General Assembly declared the Indians "no longer a nation."

News of the bloody conflict alarmed Indians and whites along the eastern seaboard. In distant England, the philosopher Thomas Hobbes was influenced by the settlers' views of Opechancanough's uprising when he claimed in 1651 that American Indians possessed virtually no real government. He had the Indians in mind when he made his famous declaration that the life of people in the state of nature is "solitary, poore, nasty, brutish, and short."[13]

Slower to erupt but just as drastic was the Indian uprising in New England in 1675–76. Indians there, like those of Virginia, found themselves crowded by the ever-increasing number of English settlers. Haughty treatment by magistrates and one-sided trading practices inflamed even those Indians trying to reach an accommodation with colonial society. King Philip (Metacom), son of Massasoit and chief of the Wampanoags, grew restive at the steady decline of

Indian lands and self-sufficiency under relentless white pressure. At last, he conceived the plan of organizing a league of Indian tribes throughout New England and in New York up to the Hudson River to oust the oppressors.

Philip's alliance, though powerful, failed to attract sufficient support for his purpose. But his warriors dealt the region its worst disaster in history: twelve settlements totally destroyed; twelve hundred homes burnt down; eight thousand cattle slaughtered; and hundreds of fighting men and noncombatants killed. He lost nonetheless; he was killed, and his wife and son (Massasoit's grandson) were sold into slavery by the merciless victors. New England would never be the same. Indian political power in the region was permanently broken. The impetus for cultural exchange between Indians and settlers dwindled. In New England as well as in Virginia, the borrowing of Indian loanwords—which had been declining since mid-century—almost ceased. Note the trough on the chart, "North American Indian Loanwords in English," page 2.

Only the following loanwords can be gleaned from North America in the second half of the eighteenth century:

> *seapoose* (also *sea puss* or *sea purse*), shallow inlet or tidal stream in Long Island, or swirling of undertow—Unquachog *seépus* river; "[They] are to have for their paines 3s per day at the seapoose" (in Southampton, New York, town records for 1650).[14]
>
> *sagamité*, hulled corn or a porridge made of hulled corn—Algonquian; "Then my father made a speech shewing many demonstrations of vallor, broak a kettle full of Cagamite with a hattchett" (in a travel book published in 1665).[15]
>
> *woodchuck,* groundhog—an anglicization of a word presumed from a southern New England Algonquian language; compare Narragansett *ockqutchaun,* woodchuck; "The natural inhabitants of the woods, hills, and swamps, are . . . rabbits, hares, and woodchucks" (in a 1674 source).[16]

In addition, previously adopted loanwords were used in compounds to create the picturesque *Canada goose* (1676), *moccasin flower* (lady's slipper) (1680), and *pokeroot* (1687). *Tomahawk* as a verb came into use around 1650. *Huskanaw,* which names the harrowing initiation rite for youths at puberty practiced by Indians in Virginia, was recorded by 1692.

CHAPTER FIVE

First Words from the New World

THOMAS HARRIOT'S REPORT ON VIRGINIA IN 1588, filled though it was with the rapture of discovery, used words from the New World already well established in English. Christopher Columbus had led the way for the adoption of American Indian words into European languages. *Canoe* and *cassava* (plant source of tapioca), in Harriot, had earlier been noted by Columbus during his first voyage to America in 1492. Columbus also introduced other West Indian words into Spanish—*cacique* (Indian chief), *cannibal,* and *hammock.*[1] Translations into English of early Spanish and Portuguese travel accounts included these and other new words that matched the wonders that had opened up to explorers.

Exotic words for tropical plants and the mysteries of Indian civilizations poured into English. Latin American Indian tongues have supplied English with more than fifteen hundred words—about half again as many as those coming from North American Indian tongues north of Mexico. Before examining the reasons for this disproportion, let's take a look at the arrival of the loanwords themselves.

The first American Indian word to enter English may have been the West Indian (Arawakan) *guaiacum*—lignum vitae, a source of timber and resin. "Yet hath this woode Guaiacum alwayes been there used," appears in T. Paynell's translation of a medical book in 1533.[2] The oil guaiacol served as an expectorant and a reputed cure for syphilis.

Guaiacum still finds use in the screening test for fecal occult blood and in other medical applications.

Representing another, now-debated, side of West Indian life is *cannibal*. While exploring the West Indies in 1492, Columbus began receiving reports of a fierce people living on some of the islands. Arawakan-speaking neighbors of the people called them *caribe* or *caniba,* meaning "brave" or "daring." Caribs (the modern form of the name) specialized in conquering other West Indian peoples by storming their villages at dawn. Victorious Caribs allegedly ate enemy corpses on the battlefield. They then carried off the women to be slaves and the surviving men to participate in a five-day ceremony during which the male captives were tortured, shot with arrows, clubbed to death, and cooked before being eaten—according to contemporary accounts.

The name of the Caribs survives in the *Caribbean Sea;* but Columbus used its alternative form in introducing *cannibal* into Spanish. *Cannibal* entered English through Richard Eden's 1553 translation of a Latin book (using some terms from the Spanish), *A treatyse of the newe India, with other new founde landes and Ilandes. . . .* In this book, Columbus is described as visiting a Carib village from which the inhabitants had fled. "And when oure men came into theyr houses, they found in theym certayne young men bound to postes, and kept to be made fatte, and lykewyse many olde womenne whiche these *Canibales* kepte to be their drudges."[3] Another cognate English word through Spanish is *caribe,* meaning piranha. The name *Caliban,* belonging to the ogreish character in Shakespeare's *Tempest,* may be an altered form of *cannibal*. In recent years, a number of scholars have argued that such usages malign the Caribs.

In 1555, the same Richard Eden published his translation from the Latin of another pioneering work on the New World—*The Decades of the newe worlde, or west India, etc.,* by Peter Martyr. This book, full of curious lore, introduced several Latin American loanwords into English. Two of Martyr's descriptions illustrate why his book gripped the popular imagination and fixed so many loanwords in standard English. He introduced *hurricane* in a complaint about the familiarity some of the Indians allegedly had with the devil. "Lykewyse when the deuyll greatly intendeth to feare theym, he threteneth to sende them great tempestes which they caule *Furacanas* or *Haurachanas,* and are so vehement that they ouerthrowe many howses and great trees." In introducing *maize* (a word Columbus brought back to Europe from his third voyage to the New World), Martyr wrote: "The graynes wherof are sette in a maruelous order, and are in fourme somwhat lyke a pease. While they be soure and unripe, they are white: but when they are ripe they be very blacke. When they are broken, they be whyter than snowe. This kind of grayne, they call *Maizium.*"4

ARAWAKAN

Hurricane and *maize* come from the Arawakan family of languages, the source of most of the earliest Latin American Indian loanwords in English. Out of some seventeen Latin American words introduced by Eden (several originally from Columbus), sixteen are Arawakan—*cacique, cannibal, canoe* (ultimately of Cariban origin), *cassava, guaican* (remora, or sucking fish), *guava, hammock, henequen* (a fiber used for making twine), *hurricane, iguana, maguey* (plant used for making a beverage), *maize, potato, savannah, tuna* (prickly pear), *yuca* (cassava).5

Speakers of the languages in this family were the first Indians Columbus encountered—his introduction to New World peoples. Columbus repeatedly noted their friendliness and charm and called them "very well-built people, with handsome bodies and very fine faces."6 They lived in a lush tropical environment on various islands and the coasts of Central and South America. Their related languages included Arawak, Taino, Lucayo, and the Arawakan-based Island Carib.

Unfortunately, the more than one million speakers of Arawakan languages proved no match for European diseases and Spanish rule. Within a century, they had almost disappeared. The Spanish had to import slaves from Africa to keep their sugar plantations going.

But, along with crafts of exquisite workmanship, the Arawakan-speakers left behind a significant legacy of words. Besides those in Eden, listed above, the following come from the Arawakan family: probably *barbecue, carey* (a turtle), *mangrove,* and possibly *tobacco* (some authorities suggest an Arabic source for this). For about three hundred additional Arawakan loanwords, see the Appendix, "English Loanwords from Latin American Indian Languages."

CARIBAN

As noted, the Caribs often clashed with more peaceful peoples in the region. They originally migrated from northeastern South America and spread through the Lesser Antilles. There they encountered Arawakan-speaking residents, whom they often drove away to other islands. Yet some Caribs mingled sufficiently with the original inhabitants to develop an Arawakan-based pidgin sprinkled with many Cariban words—known as Island Carib.

Under Spanish occupation, the Caribs fared little better than the Arawakan-speakers. But, though savaged by their Spanish conquerors, the Caribs transmitted a number of their words through Spanish to English: *caiman* or *cayman* (a crocodilian animal), *canoe, curare,* probably *manatee, peccary* (a piglike animal), *pirogue* (dugout), and *yaws.* More are listed in the Appendix.

NAHUATL

Once established in the West Indies, the Spanish turned to the American mainland. In 1517, they discovered Mexico. Hernán Cortés began his invasion of the Aztec empire two years later. The conquest of Mexico resulted in a cultural blending that became modern Mexico, with a large infusion of Indian words into Spanish and subsequently English. The main language the Spanish encountered among the Aztecs was Nahuatl, part of the Uto-Aztecan language family spoken widely in Central America and North America. Related languages in North America are Ute, Pima, and Shoshone.

Cacao, from Eden's 1555 translation of Martyr, may be the first Nahuatl word in English. "They [the Mexicans] have not the use of golde and syluer money; but use in the steade therof the halfe shelles of almonds, whiche kynde of Barbarous money they caule Cacao or Cacanguate."[7] Ten cacao beans would buy a rabbit, and the price of a slave was one hundred.

Cortés witnessed in the Aztec emperor Moctezuma II the reason for the value of the beans. All day long, Moctezuma sipped golden goblets full of chocolate or *chocolatl*—the Nahuatl *xocoatl,* from *xococ* (bitter) + *atl* (water). The Aztecs ground *cacao* beans to form a powder, which they mixed with water, maize, and spice. A dash of chili (Nahuatl *chilli*) gave zest to the cold and unsweetened beverage. Aztecs not only liked the taste of this spicy drink but regarded the concoction as an aphrodisiac.[8]

Besides the words cited above, the English vocabulary numbers some three hundred words from Nahuatl. Food names are common among them: *avocado, cocoa, enchilada, guacamole, tamale,* and *tomato* are a few. Animal names include *coyote* and *ocelot.* An important ingredient in the gum base used for chewing gum is *chicle,* obtained from the evergreen tree *sapodilla.* The hallucinatory drug *peyote* is derived from *mescal,* a cactus.

TUPIAN

While the Spanish were subduing Mexico, the Portuguese started to colonize Brazil. Among the Indian groups living in that vast area were Carib and Arawak peoples. But warlike and cannibalistic Tupian-speaking peoples dominated much of Brazil. They migrated along the Brazilian coast and up the Amazon River. One object of their travels was to find the Land of the Grandfather, a paradise believed to offer eternal youth.

Jesuit priests mastered Tupi and promoted the language as a lingua franca for much of Brazil. In some cities, clergy regularly preached in Tupi. During the seventeenth and eighteenth centuries, three times as many Brazilians spoke Tupi as Portuguese.[9] But the Portuguese language prevailed at last, and the Tupian languages declined along with the Tupian people. (The related Guarani, however, retains its vitality as a major language of Paraguay, spoken by 95 percent of the people there.)

The number of Tupi-speakers is now down from the original several million to fewer than one hundred thousand. But the Tupian languages have enriched the Brazilian Portuguese vocabulary. And around three hundred Tupian words, listed in the Appendix, have percolated through Portuguese and Spanish into English. This wealth of words reflects Brazil's abundance of natural life, the most varied in the world. Consider the fierce *cougar, jaguar,* and *piranha;* the showy *macaw, tanager,* and *toucan;* the delicious *cashew* and *manioc,* basis of *tapioca;* and the medicinal *ipecac. Buccaneer* comes from the Tupi *buccan,* a wooden frame such a person used to preserve meat by drying or smoking it.

QUECHUA

On the other side of Brazil, Francisco Pizarro's invasion of Peru in 1532 reverberated throughout South America. Over the next thirty years, the Spanish finally broke the Inca resistance. Much of the most highly developed civilization in the Western Hemisphere crumbled under an onslaught that left the surviving Incas virtual slaves. For another century, rebellions threatened colonial rule. But the Spanish kept control and made Peru the center of their power on the continent.

Walls of cunningly fitted stone, palaces, and stretches of some of the best roads in the world remained as testimony of the Inca achievements. Some Inca customs and beliefs endured, especially in remote areas. But the most notable cultural legacy from the Incas is the ancient Quechuan family of languages. About thirteen million people in South America, including half of modern Peruvians, speak Quechua—a greater number than at the time of the Incas. In 1975, the government of Peru declared Quechua an official language of the country, equal to Spanish.

Probably because of Peru's distance from the United States, English has obtained only about half as many loanwords from Quechua as from Nahuatl. Yet the approximately 150 Quechuan words listed in the Appendix compose a valuable and colorful addition to the English vocabulary. Animal names are prominent among these words: *condor, llama, puma,* and *vicuña* are a few. Two potent drugs bear names of Quechuan origin: *cocaine,* from the *coca* plant, and *quinine.* Additional Quechuan words are *caoutchouc* (natural rubber), *guano* (the bird and bat droppings used as fertilizer), and *jerky* or *charqui* (beef cut in strips and dried).

The North American Indian (north of Mexico) contribution of loanwords to English, rich though it is, does not approach the abundance of loanwords in English from Latin American Indian languages. This might seem improbable, given the nearness of North American Indians to English-speaking whites and the innumerable cultural and social links between the two peoples over four centuries. Why the contrast? The explanation seems to be threefold: the nature of the environment; the level of civilization; and differences in receptivity to Indian culture.

Environment. Latin America is unrivaled in the world for the variety and number of its plants and animals. According to Alan B. Durning of the Worldwatch Institute, "The Amazon basin holds the largest concentration of living things on earth." A few acres of Amazon rain forest, he says, may contain a greater diversity of flora and fauna than found in the entire United States. Terry L. Erwin, curator of insects for the Smithsonian Institution, estimates that thirty million insect *species* live in the Amazon jungle canopy.[10]

Additional rain forests in Central America, tropical islands in the Caribbean, the soaring Andes Mountains, the rolling pampas of Patagonia, and other varied regions of Latin America contribute to the region's bounty of wildlife. It was natural for Europeans to adapt many Native American names for the thousands of plant and animal species unique to Latin America.

Civilization. The cultural level of the North American Indians needs no defense. Their arts and crafts, their subtle relationship to the environment, their leagues and complex associations, all reflect an impressive level of accomplishment. But in the sixteenth century, the Aztec and Inca peoples of Latin America maintained civilizations of a complexity rivaling any in the world. These empires provided governmental and economic systems for millions of people. The Incas, for example, set up a network of paved roads and stone way stations that stretched thousands of miles.

Justifiably awed, the Spanish conquerors adopted many accomplishments of the Latin American civilizations—and frequently kept the original vocabulary for them.

Cultural receptivity. Spanish and Portuguese newcomers to the New World mingled more readily with Native Americans than did the Anglo-Saxons. One reason was that the early Spanish and Portuguese explorers less often had wives with them than did the English colonists. Close social relationships with Indians, furthermore, may have seemed more natural to the Spanish and Portuguese, who had lived for centuries alongside Moors. The social hierarchies of the Latin American civilizations meshed readily with those of the European invaders, fostering intermarriage along class lines.

Spanish conquerors, as the historian Edward F. Tuttle has pointed out, deliberately used native languages in their drive to colonize Latin America. "[The Spanish] encountered two indigenous imperial languages of great prestige, the Aztecs' Nahuatl and the Incas' Quechua. In their respective spheres both became the parallel main sources of loans to Spanish. Each was seized upon by local Spanish administrators and missionaries as a lingua franca for their complementary ends."[11] As noted, the Portuguese used the same strategy in Brazil.

Finally, the native peoples of fifteenth-century Latin America spoke perhaps 1,500 languages, compared with some 350 in North America. This sheer profusion of languages placed an immense new vocabulary at the disposal of the Spanish and Portuguese conquerors.

CHAPTER SIX

Reports from the Frontier

DURING THE YEARS 1711–12, JONATHAN SWIFT was afraid to go out in nighttime Dublin. "Did I tell you of a race of rakes called the Mohocks, that play the devil about this town every night, slit people's noses, and beat them, etc.?" he wrote in his journal to the protégée he called Stella. "It is not safe being in the streets at night."[1] To emphasize the gratuitousness of their crimes, the widely feared Mohocks did not stoop to rob their victims.

Mohock, apparently first recorded in this sense by Swift, is a variant spelling of *Mohawk.* As applied to well-born ruffians in the eighteenth century, the name reflects the bad press American Indians often received. Mohawk Indians had become notorious as the most ferocious members of the Iroquois Confederacy. They did, in fact, have a long history of tyrannizing other Indian tribes, and they behaved just as pugnaciously toward whites they considered enemies. The name *Mohawk* itself originated in the dread this tribe inspired among other Indians. It comes from the Narragansett *mohowaúg,* meaning maneaters. Now *Mohawk* conveys more faintly threatening overtones in the term *Mohawk* or *Mohawk haircut,* in which a person's head is conspicuously shaved to leave a ridge of hair down the middle of the scalp, or as a name for a current U.S. Army aircraft used to monitor enemy movements.

But the British of Swift's day felt an ambivalence toward American Indians, an ambivalence that was especially acute in the case of the Mohawks. In 1710, four Mohawk sachems visited London, where they were hailed as the "Four Kings of the New World." Queen Anne received them and accepted their gift of several belts of wampum. She reciprocated with a set of communion plates and a commission to have their portraits painted. The sachems took the London tour reserved for foreign dignitaries, dined with prominent Londoners including William Penn, reviewed four troops of Life Guards, visited churches and palaces, and viewed numerous other attractions in the city and its environs. Ordinary Londoners greeted the visitors with enthusiasm. When the sachems attended a performance of *Macbeth,* playgoers would not allow the play to go on until the manager seated the Indians onstage.

Yet the "Four Kings" left behind an unexpected legacy. It was directly from the honored visitors that the rakes who terrorized the people of Dublin and London derived their name. Daniel Defoe, writing in the *Spectator* in 1712, explained the name's origin. "The *Mohock,* or *Mohawks,* are, or rather were, *for they are Extinct now, or very near it,* a Small Nation of *Savages* in the Woods, on the back of our two Colonies of *New-England* and *New York.*" Defoe's additional comments illustrate how far public opinion about the noble visitors had fallen, for he goes on to assert that the Mohawks "were always esteem'd as the most Desperate, and most Cruel of the Natives of *North-America.*"[2]

But even in the time of Swift and Defoe, people were challenging the negative stereotyping of American Indians. In a widely reprinted book translated in 1703 as *New Voyages to North America,* the French philosopher and baron Louis-Armand de Lahontan described the Hurons of Canada as noble savages. This book incidentally introduced *carcajou,* wolverine, into English from the Montagnais *kuàkuàtsheu.* "Carccaious, an animal not unlike a Badger," the English translation reads.[3]

Several books by Englishmen living in the New World lent support to Lahontan's admiration of Indians for remaining close to nature and thus leading lives of greater purity than Europeans, with a presumably more artificial and corrupt civilization. Robert Beverley offers a firsthand appreciation of the Indians in *The History and Present State of Virginia,* published in London in 1705. A member of the Virginia gentry and a keen observer, Beverley was the first to offer a comprehensive account of the established colony and Virginia's original inhabitants. "I am an *Indian,* and don't pretend to be exact in my Language," he wrote in his preface. "But I hope the Plainness of my Dress, will give [the reader] the kinder Impressions of my Honesty."4

Beverley lived a comfortable life, revising his history, speculating in frontier land, and tending his magnificent estate. A bleaker fate awaited John Lawson, another early historian of the colonial southern frontier. Lawson was at loose ends in London in 1700 when a stranger informed him "that *Carolina* was the best Country [he] could go to."5 Impulsively, Lawson boarded a ship in the Thames about to sail for America. Within months of his arrival in Charleston, South Carolina, he plunged into the Carolina wilderness with a party of six Englishmen and four Indians, who were soon dismissed. The Englishmen then explored Indian trails and settlements on their own, completing a journey of about one thousand miles.

Lawson settled in eastern Carolina for several years. He participated in the incorporation of Bath, North Carolina, in 1705. A surveyor by occupation, he also wrote his classic *A New Voyage to Carolina, Containing the Exact Description and Natural History of that Country . . . ,* published in London in 1709. "We look upon [Indians] with Scorn and Disdain, and think them little better than Beasts in Humane Shape, though if well examined, we shall find that, for all our Religion and Education, we possess more Moral Deformities, and Evils than these Savages do, or are acquainted withal," he asserted in *New Voyage.*6

But benign though the Indians of the Southeast had been to Lawson and his companions, they could be extraordinarily cruel if provoked. They subjected prisoners of war, Lawson noted, to tortures as extreme as the "Devils themselves could invent, or hammer out of Hell." In perhaps the worst example, they stuck pitch-pine splinters all over a victim's body until he looked like a porcupine. They then ignited the splinters, which burned "like so many torches." Lawson said that the torturers made the victim "dance round a great Fire, every one buffeting and deriding him, till he expire[d]."7

In 1711, Lawson and Baron Christopher de Graffenried, a developer, embarked on an expedition up the Neuse River to see how far it could be navigated. They were seized upstream by Indians, who brought the two men before King Hancock of the Tuscaroras. At first, the Indians leaned toward releasing both captives. But Lawson and a visiting chief quarreled. After several council meetings, the Indians spared de Graffenried. As for Lawson, he was tortured to death—reportedly turned into the human torch he had so graphically described.

Yet Lawson's book lives with Beverley's as a compassionate and informative account of the Southeast Indians. In his work, Lawson introduced three still-current Indian words into English, including the following two:

> *mananosay,* soft-shell clam—probably Algonquian; Lawson noted, "Man of Noses . . . are valued for increasing Vigour in Men, and making barren Women fruitful."
> *yaupon,* a holly used for making medicinal tea—Catawba *yopún,* a diminutive of *yop* tree; in Lawson: "drinking vast Quantitities of their *Yaupon* or Tea, and vomiting it up again, as clear as they drink it."8

Lawson's martyrdom reflected the dilemma of Indians and whites on the eighteenth-century frontier. A significant number of whites felt genuinely friendly to the Indians. The

English government tried to foster amicable relations with what it perceived as Indian governments in America. It had welcomed the "Four Kings." In 1730, seven Cherokee chiefs went to London and agreed to an alliance with King George II. Meanwhile, the English scientist Robert Boyle furnished funds for an Indian school, established in Williamsburg, Virginia, in 1723.

But whites often valued Indian friendship mainly as an aid to developing the highly profitable trade in furs. The English sent caravans of up to one hundred horses into the interior, laden with goods such as guns, blankets, and kettles. The Indians traded deerskins in return. At best, this trade promoted friendly relations between whites and Indians— including marriages of traders with Indian women. At worst, whites cheated the Indians with inferior goods or plied them with the rum that demoralized entire tribes. Often, as in earlier contacts, the white man's diseases wrought greater havoc among the Indians than military battle.

Still, naturalists and others continued the southern exploring tradition of Beverley and Lawson. In 1722, the Englishman Mark Catesby embarked on a three-year study of the wildlife in South Carolina, Georgia, and Florida. The first volume of his renowned *The Natural History of Carolina, Florida, and the Bahama Islands,* illustrated with over two hundred plates etched by himself, was completed in 1731. He introduced two Indian words to English readers:

> *catalpa,* any of several North American trees having whitish flowers—Creek *katalpa,* "head with wings," from *ka-* (head) + *taɬpa* (wing), from the shape of its flowers (/ɬ/ is a sound rather like *lth* in the English word *wealth*); "The Catalpa Tree . . . was unknown to the inhabited parts of Carolina till I brought the seeds from the remoter parts of the country. . . . It is become an ornament to many of their gardens."

tupelo, any of several flowering trees—Creek *'topilwa,* "swamp tree," from *íto* (tree) + *opílwa* (swamp); "The Tupelo Tree . . . the Grain of the wood is curled and very tough, and therefore very proper for Naves of Cart-Wheels, and other Country-Uses."[9]

Soon, from the opposite end of North America, came the loanword *tepee,* recorded as *ti pee* in 1743 by James Isham, who ran an English trading post on Hudson Bay. This word for the Plains Indian cone-shaped tent comes from the Siouan *tipi,* from *ti* (dwell) + *pi* (noun suffix). Appearing in an Assiniboine word list that Isham compiled, the word seems to have occurred so far north because of close relations between the northern Crees and the more southern Assiniboines.

Isham borrowed another key word from his Indian clients. Trappers and others who ventured on trips into the wilderness learned from Indians to carry compact and nourishing trail food of a type still eaten by campers and explorers, though with varying ingredients. "Pimmegan as the Natives styles itt, is some of the Ruhiggan [meat dried and pounded fine] fatt and Cranberries mixd. up togeather, and Reckon'd by some Very good food by the English as well as Natives," Isham noted in 1743.[10] The word comes from Cree *pimihkaam,* meaning "he makes pemmican" or "he makes grease." *Pemmican* originally was prepared by pouring hot fat into a leather pouch containing meat and berries.

The West too was beginning to beckon many Americans. As pioneers began flocking in that direction, many rode in the *Conestoga wagon.* The name of this broad-wheeled covered wagon, typically loaded with families and furniture, comes from the Pennsylvania town where it was first made—Conestoga, named after an Iroquoian tribe that became extinct in 1763. The term apparently first appeared in 1717 and by mid-century had been adopted as the name of a Philadelphia tavern, "Conestoga Waggon." Later *stogie,* meaning "cheap cigar," would gain its name from the cigar-smoking drivers of Conestoga wagons.

Politics added to the hazards of explorers and pioneers. The frontier, running deep into the Southeast and up through New York, was in turmoil. It had become a battleground for European powers as well as for individual groups of settlers and the Indians they pressed upon. A series of wars between the English and the French, conflict mainly over the fur trade, ranged across inland America from 1689 to 1763. Indians fought on both sides and suffered when allies were defeated. Some Indian tribes held out against white encroachment, but the response to their resistance could be devastating.

Caught in this frontier fighting was a twenty-three-year-old Virginia officer named George Washington. Early in 1755, he had narrowly escaped death in the rout of General Edward Braddock's expeditionary force by the French and Indians. Washington was commissioned a colonel a few months later to take charge of Virginia's colonial troops defending the western frontier. He had his hands full trying to organize the few hundred ragtag militia under his command. In September 1755 another officer, writing to Washington about one of the frequent clashes with Indian raiders, introduced a word still well known to hunters and others who trek through snowy terrain. "The Indians discover our Parties by the Track of their Shoes. It would be a good thing to have Shoepacks or Moccosons for the Scouts."[11] The word now spelled *shoepac* or shortened to *pac* refers to a waterproof, laced boot of leather, canvas, or now rubber—from Delaware *sippack* or *seppock* shoe. (Note how the borrowers of the word assimilated the first part to the familiar *shoe.*)

With Britain's triumph over its European opponents in 1763, a kind of peace descended along much of the frontier. A treaty formally eliminated France from the North American continent. Spain gave up Florida to Britain, receiving the French lands west of the Mississippi River. Potentially most important for many Indians, a proclamation by King George III offered them apparent safeguards against white incursions. This decree prohibited American colonists from settling west of the Appalachian Mountains and ordered settlers on western lands to move. The settlers, however, could not be controlled from London; they kept pushing into Indian lands despite royal disapproval.

France's enduring influence on North America, regardless of treaties, can be seen from the way the French language continued serving as a medium for the transmission of Indian loanwords into English. In Louisiana and throughout much of the northern part of the continent, the French traded, prayed, and lived with Indians. The result was an intimate cultural exchange that the more reserved English rarely achieved. *Bayou* came from Louisiana French by 1763. This word for a creek or marshy body of water derives originally from Choctaw *bayuk,* with similar meaning. *Pecan* came through the French from Illinois *pakani* by 1712 (though see chapter 2 for a possible earlier source).

Meanwhile, *caucus* had entered English as a by-product of the conspiratorial activities in Boston that helped ignite the American Revolution. "This day learned that the Caucas Clubb meets at certain Times in the Garret of Tom Daws, the Adjutant of the Boston Regiment," John Adams wrote in his diary in 1763.[12] The clique was one of several such associations formed to place favored persons into positions of power. This kind of influence was soon being used by Samuel Adams and others to mobilize protests against royal authority. Of much debated origin, *caucus* has often been regarded as probably Algonquian (see *cockarouse,* "person of importance," in chapter 2). But expert opinion currently holds it more likely to have come from Latin *caucus,* drinking vessel. (Adams testily surmised that Caucas Clubb members drank "Phlip," a mixed alcoholic drink, while they made their plans.)

The borrowing of Indian loanwords did not flourish during the American Revolution, at least partly because of cultural disruptions during the war. And at war's end, various problems arose between the Indians and citizens of the new nation. Major Indian tribes, including four in the powerful Iroquois League, had sided with the British. These Indians found themselves in a weak bargaining position, although the U.S. government made a conscientious effort to provide Indians with legal protection. "The utmost good faith shall always be observed toward the Indians. Their land and property shall never be taken from them without their consent," promised the Northwest Ordinance of 1787. Nevertheless, the policy set by the government failed to sway settlers on the distant frontier. Indians, furthermore, did not respond well to the government's expansionist policy of "civilizing" them as a way of reducing their need for huge tribal landholdings.

Most of the slightly more than two dozen datable words from the eighteenth century after the revolutionary war originated with travelers and naturalists. Like the earlier loans of the century, these new words tended to reflect the wilderness and, to a lesser extent, technology learned from the Indians.

•In 1789, a British soldier's published account of Lake Champlain noted, "It abounds with great quantities and varieties of fish; sturgeon, black bass, masquenongez pike of an incredible size, and many others."[13] His version of *muskellunge*, referring to the large game fish, illustrates the passage of this word through French from Ojibwa *maashkinoozhe*.

•*The History of New Hampshire*, 1792, stated: "On some mountains we find a shrubbery and spruce, whose branches are knit together so as to be impenetrable. . . . These are called by the Indians, Hakmantaks."[14] The *hackmatack* is a kind of larch or tamarack (itself an Indian word), probably from Western Abenaki *hakmantak*.

•In keeping with the practical character of most new Indian loanwords in this era, a naturalist introduced *pipsissewa* in a 1789 issue of the *American Philosophical Society Transactions*. This evergreen plant was regarded as medicinal by Indians and settlers alike because of its diuretic and astringent properties. Its name perhaps comes from Eastern Abenaki *kpi-pskwáhsawe*, literally "flower of the woods."

•For carrying a pack in the wilderness, an Indian aid that whites found helpful was the *tump* or *tumpline*, a strap around the chest or forehead. "I was a novice at making canoes . . . and tumplines, which was the only occupation of the squaws," recounted the author of the *Captivity of Mrs. Johnson* in 1796.[15] The word comes from southern New England *mattump*.

•Indians and whites smoked *kinnikinnick*, a tobaccolike substance composed of various barks, sumac leaves, and other dried vegetable matter. An observer wrote in 1796 of "a pouch, which . . . contained tobacco, killegenico, or dry sumach leaves which they mix with their tobacco."[16] The word comes from Unami Delaware *kǝlǝkkǝniíkkan*. (*Kinnikinnik*, a variant spelling, is reputedly the longest palindromic word in English.)

Two-thirds of the datable Indian (north of Mexico) loanwords from the eighteenth century, listed at the end of the chapter, are from the Algonquian family of languages—the languages that prevailed among Indians along the eastern seaboard and across much of Canada. But it is significant that the remaining third of the loanwords come from a variety of non-Algonquian Indian languages—a striking contrast to the overwhelming Algonquian borrowings of the seventeenth century.

The deeper white penetration of the Southeast appears in loanwords from that region. Ten of these words come from the Muskogean family of the Southeast—*bayou, busk, catalpa, Chickasaw plum, choupique, coontie, mico, sofkee, tupelo,* and

water tupelo. Chunkey and *yaupon* additionally come from Catawba, a southeastern member of the Siouan language family.
Cassioberry derives from the Timucuan language of Florida.

Tepee and *pemmican* represent an increasingly northern and
western reach of white explorers, traders, and settlers. But
other words too testify to the spread of white activities in
those directions. *Seneca oil, Seneca root, senega,* and *Seneka snakeroot* point to the Senecas, who lived and still live in western New York. *Canada jay, Canada moonseed, Canada porcupine, Canada thistle,* and *Canadian holly* are early members
of a large group of terms—mostly from natural history—
that bear the name of that nation. *Eskimo dog* and *tyee* (boss),
the latter from the Chinook Jargon of the Pacific Northwest, also reveal the greater range of white traders and
others.

The eighteenth century saw a huge increase in the white
population of North America and in the portion of the continent that it controlled. Yet the number of datable Indian
(north of Mexico) loanwords entering English rose from about
fifty-seven in the seventeenth century to only about ninety
in the eighteenth century. Why was the rise in loanword
borrowing not comparable to the rise in the white presence
on the continent and the greater extent of white contact
with Indians?

The answer may lie in the raw antagonism that marked so
many of the relationships between whites and Indians. Frictions often marred trading exchanges and offset the cultural openings that trade offered. "By its very nature the
Indian trade constantly bred avarice, corruption, degrada-
tion, and violence," wrote the frontier historian Douglas
Edward Leach.[17] The near-perpetual state of war along the
frontier further chilled the sympathetic interest more whites
might have had in Indian culture and the creative response
that Indians might have made to peaceful contact. It is,

perhaps, not surprising that the borrowing of Indian words increased only gradually throughout the eighteenth century.*

LOANWORDS AND LOAN TERMS FROM THE EIGHTEENTH CENTURY

1700–1709

carcajou 1703
pignut hickory 1705
poke (pokeweed) 1708

chunkey 1709
mananosay 1709
yaupon 1709

1710–1719

Mohock 1712
pecan 1712

windigo 1714
Conestoga wagon 1717

1720–1729

tawkee 1725

Seneka snakeroot 1728

1730–1739

catalpa 1731
tupelo 1731
water tupelo 1731
wampum snake 1736

mico 1737
senega 1738
skunkweed 1738

---

*A further possible reason was the decline in overall English vocabulary growth during the eighteenth century. A graph from Geoffrey Hughes, *Words in Time* (p. 102), for the period from 1500 to 1800 shows a peak in vocabulary growth in 1600 followed by a steep drop bottoming out from 1700 to 1750 and a slow rise to 1800. Is this near parallel to the rate of borrowing from North American Indian languages significant?

1740–1749

coon (n.) 1742
namaycush 1743
pemmican 1743
shaganappi 1743

tepee 1743
wavey 1743
wejack 1743
whisky jack 1743

1750–1759

white hickory 1750
pokeweed 1751
shagbark hickory 1751
skunk cabbage 1751
Oswego tea 1752

cassioberry 1753
wawaskeesh 1754
shoepac 1755
Oswego bass 1758
busk (festival) 1759

1760–1769

Chickasaw plum 1760
pekan 1760
pembina 1760
watap 1761
bayou 1763

?caucus 1763
choupique 1763
baggataway 1767
musquashweed 1767
punkie or punky 1769

1770–1779

wahoo (not Dakota) 1770
Canada jay 1772
Eskimo dog 1774
pokeberry 1774
muskeg 1775
Seneca root 1775
winter squash 1775

hog and hominy 1776
wakan 1776
Narragansett pacer 1777
moosewood 1778
scoke 1778
mocock 1779

1780–1789

Shawnee (or Shawanese)
   salad 1780

Illinois nut (pecan) 1781–82
totemism 1768–82

1780–1789 (continued)

Indian poke 1784
moosebush 1784
balsam hickory 1785
Canada moonseed 1785
Canadian holly 1785
chinquapin oak 1785
Kentucky coffee tree 1785
black hickory 1787
Canada porcupine 1787

cawquaw 1787
mathemeg 1787
pogamoggan 1787
cohosh 1789
mooseberry 1789
muskellunge 1789
pipsissewa 1789
tullibee 1789
vulpine opossum 1789

1790–1799

coontie 1791
hackmatack 1792
tyee (boss) 1792
Seneca oil 1795
kinkajou 1796

kinnikinnick 1796
murine opossum 1796
sofkee 1796
tump or tumpline 1796
Canada thistle 1799

CHAPTER SEVEN

Renaming a Continent

IN 1584, MEMBERS OF WALTER RALEIGH'S FIRST
expedition to the New World had received a welcome beyond their fondest hopes. Sailing along what is now the
North Carolina coast, they had visited several thickly wooded
islands. The one that impressed them most was Roanoke—
about twelve miles long, with a cluster of nine cedar houses
at one end surrounded by a palisade (see chapter 1).

Indians there greeted the sailors, ushered them into a
room, and washed them and their clothes. Refreshed, the
sailors were treated to a banquet of venison and a variety of
vegetables and fruits. "We found the people most gentle,
loving, and faithful, voide of all guile and treason, and such
as live after the maner of the golden age," wrote Captain
Arthur Barlowe in his enthusiastic report to Raleigh.[1]

The name *Roanoke* comes from Virginia Algonquian *raw-
ranoke,* which probably means smoothed shells, or wampum
(see chapter 2). The word would go down in history as more
than the site of Raleigh's attempts at colonizing. According
to George R. Stewart, the authority on U.S. place-names,
Roanoke is the first Indian name "to be taken over by the
English, and to survive."[2] The island, the river near it on the
mainland, a county, and several cities still bear the name.

The custom spread across the entire continent, dotting
the map with reminders of Native Americans who had been
pushed back or wiped out. Thousands of Indian names endure as the most widespread memorial of North America's
original inhabitants. And the acquisition of Indian place-

names, far outstripping other kinds of Indian words, illumi-
nates the borrowing of Indian words in general.

Many Indian place-names lose in the translation. Their
meanings seem to be matter-of-fact and utilitarian—describing the physical appearance of a place, distinctive plants, the
direction of a place, or an associated event. The origin of the
names and thus the names themselves could be transient.
"Flaking stone," "pleasant ground," "long river," "at the
dwelling of the owl," and "salmon fishing place" are typical
translations. Whites gave permanence to many of the names
that might never have lasted otherwise among the Indians.

In their original forms, the names could be deeply evoca-
tive. Walt Whitman was not alone in hearing in them "calls
as of birds and animals in the woods"—and writers of songs
and works of literature have used the names tellingly. Indians themselves were highly sensitive to the music of their
nomenclature. "I was born in an age that loved the things of
nature and gave them beautiful names like 'Tessoualouit'
instead of dried up names like 'Stanley Park,'" Dan George,
chief of the Capilano Indian tribe in British Columbia, recalled in 1975. "I was born when people loved nature and
spoke to it as though it has a soul: I can remember going up
Indian river with my father when I was very young. I can
remember him watching the sunlight fires on Mount Pé-
Né-Né. I can remember him singing his thanks to it as he
often did, singing the Indian word 'thanks' very very softly."[3]

The scope of surviving Indian names can be seen in those
for the major natural features of the United States. Consider
the following names of Indian origin:

  • thirteen of the nineteen largest U.S. rivers (by volume
  of flow)—Mississippi, Ohio, Yukon, Missouri, Tennessee,
  Mobile, Atchafalaya, Stikine, Susitna, Arkansas, Tanana,
  Susquehanna, and Willamette;
  • ten of the major U.S. lakes—Michigan, Erie, Ontario,

Okeechobee, Winnebago, Tahoe, Upper Klamath, Utah, Tustumena, and Winnibigoshish;

• numerous of the nation's other natural wonders—including the Niagara and Yosemite waterfalls; the Adirondack, Allegheny, and Appalachian mountains; and the Denali, Sequoia, and Shenandoah national parks.

The percentage of Indian names for political divisions in the United States lags behind that of such names for natural features. The pattern for this discrepancy dates almost from the beginning of the Anglo-Saxon settlement of the New World.

In 1614, John Smith—recovered from his ordeal in Virginia—embarked on a major exploration of a more northern part of America. His *Description of New England,* published in 1616, already displayed the ambivalence of the English between adopting Native American place-names or applying their own. On the one hand, Smith applied *New England* to the coastal area from Massachusetts into Maine. On the other hand, Smith adopted *Massachusetts* (Algonquian, "Great Blue Hill" or "Big-hills-at") for the Boston area, including the Charles River and the Blue Hills. Prince Charles, invited to examine Smith's work, exercised one of his royal prerogatives by making English substitutions for several of Smith's recorded Indian place-names. For example, the prince renamed Smith's Massachuset River after himself, making it the Charles River.

The early settlers of New England readily accepted Indian names for natural features, and such names are widespread down to this day. Out of some twenty rivers in eastern Massachusetts, more than a third still have Indian names. These, like thousands of Indian names of hills, ponds, and brooks throughout New England, often survive in truncated or anglicized form.

But in the naming of towns, the settlers showed a single-minded determination to plant their own distinctive communities in an alien wilderness. In the Massachusetts Bay Colony, none of the towns named before 1690 had an Indian name. In Plymouth Colony during the same period, only two out of twenty towns had Indian names—*Scituate* and *Monomoy* (which later became Chatham). The settlers of Connecticut followed suit. Only one of the towns established there before 1844 retains an Indian name, and this is the anglicized *Norwalk* (from the Algonquian *Norwauke*). That this custom was deliberate can be seen from a resolution of the Connecticut Court on March 11, 1658. "Whereas, it hath been a commendable practice of the inhabitants of all the Colonies of these parts, that as this Country hath its denomination from our dear native Country of England, and thence is called New England, so the planters, in their first settling of most new plantations have given names to those plantations of some Cities and Towns in England, thereby intending to keep up and leave to posterity the memorial of several places of note there."[4]

According to Stewart, "there was a definite feeling" against Indian names for political divisions among Virginians as well. In 1619, for example, he notes that the people of Kiccowtan asked the House of Burgesses to change that "savage name"; the town became Elizabeth City.[5]

Indian names struck many settlers both as uncomfortably alien and uncouth in sound. Yet as time passed, the names became not only acceptable but increasingly admired by some. William Penn, writing from Pennsylvania in 1683 to a London society of traders, said about the Algonquian tongue he understood, "I know not a language spoken in Europe, that hath words of more sweetness or greatness, in accent or emphasis, than theirs: for instance, Octocockon, Rancocas, Oricton, Shak, Marian, Pequesien; all of which are names of places, and have grandeur in them."[6]

The naming of states reflected the growing acceptance among whites of Indian place-names. At first, such state names were the exception. Only *Massachusetts* and *Connecticut* along the first-settled Eastern seaboard bear names of Indian origin. Both originate from prominent geographical features: Massachusetts Bay and the Connecticut River.

The turbulent relations between whites and Indians in the eighteenth century did not favor the adoption of additional Indian names for states. But whites, with the upper hand in the East toward the end of the century, became more tolerant of Indian culture. Two-thirds of the last thirty-six states entering the Union, since the late eighteenth century, bear Indian names.

This trend emerged for the most part naturally, in response to local usage. Indian names clung with special tenacity to rivers and other watercourses. The names were taken up by whites for regions; and it was to regional names that Congress began to turn. *Kentucky,* originally a county of Virginia, led the way in 1792. Both the region and a major river running through it had been called by that name.

Tennessee became established as a state name next, though only after several alternatives had been tried. In 1784, three counties of what was to be the state organized themselves as the State of Franklin—in honor of Benjamin Franklin and perhaps in hopes of his help. Five years later, North Carolina gave the Tennessee region to the United States. The federal government bureaucratically called it the Territory of the United States South of the River Ohio. Legend has it that young Andrew Jackson successfully proposed the more popular name *Tennessee* for the state in 1796, after the mighty tributary of the Ohio River that flows through much of the state.

The zest for conferring Indian names on new western states spilled over into the choice of names for other places and objects. "The names of the newest states and territories have been chosen with excellent taste," asserted the nineteenth-century builder Edward Clark. He urged New York City to follow suit—with Montana Place for 8th Avenue,

Wyoming Place for 9th Avenue, Arizona Place for 10th Avenue, and Idaho Place for 11th Avenue. The city did not adopt these suggestions, but Clark indulged himself in 1884 by giving the name *Dakota* to his famed apartment house completed in 1884 (at West 72nd Street next to Central Park).[7]

So the number of Indian names of new states increased into and through the nineteenth century, the great era of state-making. The list of these states, with dates of admission to the Union, reveals the long shadow of Indians being harried ever westward: *Ohio* 1803; (Indiana 1816); *Mississippi* 1817; *Illinois* 1818; *Alabama* 1819; *Missouri* 1821; *Arkansas* 1836; *Michigan* 1837; *Texas* 1845; *Iowa* 1846; *Wisconsin* 1848; *Minnesota* 1858; *Oregon* 1859; *Kansas* 1861; *Nebraska* 1867; North *Dakota* 1889; South *Dakota* 1889; *Idaho* 1890; *Wyoming* 1890; *Utah* 1896.

The naming of the two latter states demonstrates the extent to which Indian names had become the norm. The Wyoming Valley in Pennsylvania was the scene during the revolutionary war of a massacre in which more than two hundred whites died at the hands of Indian warriors and white Tory rangers. A popular poem dramatized the disaster; the poem, together with the name's musical sound, persuaded authorities to apply *Wyoming* arbitrarily to a place far removed from its original location.

Meanwhile, the Mormons had organized their territory in the Rocky Mountains as *Deseret,* a name from the Book of Mormon. But the federal government was suspicious both of the religion practiced by the Mormons and of their alleged wish to set up an independent government. Overriding religious sentiment, Congress called the state *Utah* after the local Ute Indians.

The nineteenth century was a no less fruitful period for the spread of Native American names—both Indian and Eskimo (Inuit)—for political divisions in Canada. Having apparently at least as high a percentage of such names as the

United States, Canada started acquiring them in French at an even earlier date.

The name *Canada* itself was recorded by the great explorer Jacques Cartier in the report of his second voyage to the New World in 1535. His Indian guides used the Huron-Iroquoian term *kanata,* meaning "village" or "community," to indicate a section of territory occupied by Indian cabins. Official status for the name came with the Canada Act of 1791, and countrywide status arrived with the British North American Act of 1867, which created the Dominion of Canada.

The latter act also established Canada's oldest province, Quebec—whose Algonquian name means "where the river narrows." In addition, the act changed Upper Canada to the province of Ontario—its name said to be from the Iroquoian phrase *kanadario,* "sparkling or beautiful water." Manitoba became a province in 1870. Its name is believed to come from a Cree or Ojibwa word that means "strait of the manitou, or spirit." According to one tradition, the name arose from the roar of storm-driven pebbles against the rocky shore of an island in the strait.

In 1898, the Yukon Territory was established adjacent to Alaska, with an Indian name meaning "the river" or "big river." The Indian theme in naming Canadian provinces continued with the inauguration of Saskatchewan as a province in 1905—making this the fourth Canadian province with an Indian name (out of what would become a total of ten provinces after the admission of Newfoundland in 1949). The name *Saskatchewan* comes from Cree *kishiska* ("rapid") + *djiwan* ("current"), the name of the river flowing through the lower part of the province.

Enthusiasm for Indian names in the nineteenth century was not confined to states and provinces. Numerous features of the landscape received Indian names as the last Indian threat to the whites was being crushed. These names were often more picturesque than appropriate, frequently borrowed from other localities or even concocted. Still, many of North America's most apt and cherished Indian place-names entered the atlas during the nineteenth century.

The memoirs of Lafayette Houghton Bunnell, M.D., noted by Stewart, describe the naming of one of the world's most spectacular natural wonders. In 1851, a battalion of California mounted militia rode into the Sierra Nevada pursuing Indians. Bunnell, familiarly known as "Doc," accompanied them as interpreter. He had a breadth of learning considerably in excess of his companions and a love of poetry that undoubtedly seemed out of place in the group.

At the end of one day, the men suddenly found themselves at the edge of a chasm whose immensity dazzled them and brought tears to Bunnell's eyes. Following an Indian trail, they made their way to the bottom of the valley below, where a river meandered. While the company relaxed and puffed on their pipes, Bunnell suggested that they provide a name for the stupendous valley they had discovered.

Addressing a man who had been drenched looking for a ford across the river, Bunnell urged, "You are the first white man that ever received any form of baptism in this valley, and you should be considered the proper person to give a baptismal name to the valley itself." The man replied: "If whiskey can be provided for such a ceremony, I shall be happy to participate; but if it is to be another cold water affair, I have no desire to take a hand. I have done enough in that line for tonight."

But gradually the men warmed to the idea. Soon they were shouting suggestions—romantic, exotic, biblical. "As I did not take a fancy to any of the names proposed," recalled Bunnell, "I remarked that 'an American name would be the most appropriate'; that 'I could not see any necessity for going to a foreign country for a name for American scenery—the grandest that had ever yet been looked upon. That it would be better to give it an Indian name than to import a strange and inexpressive one; that the name of the tribe who had occupied it, would be more appropriate than any I had heard suggested.'

"I then proposed 'that we give the valley the name of Yo-sem-i-ty, as it was suggestive, euphonious, and certainly *American;* that by so doing, the name of the tribe of Indians which we met leaving their homes in this valley, perhaps never to return, would be perpetuated.'"

This proposal was generally welcomed. But, Bunnell noted: "I was here interrupted by Mr. Tunnehill, who impatiently exclaimed: 'Devil take the Indians and their names! Why should we honor these vagabond murderers by perpetuating their name?' Another said: 'I agree with Tunnehill; ———— the Indians and their names. . . . Let's call this Paradise Valley.'" Finally a Texan spoke up: "Hear ye! Hear ye! Hear ye! A vote will now be taken to decide what name shall be given to this valley."

Bunnell concluded, "The question of giving it the name of Yo-sem-i-ty was then explained; and upon a *viva voce* vote being taken, it was almost unanimously adopted." It was later learned that the name means "Grizzly Bear" in the language of the Miwok Indians, after a local clan totem. The spelling ultimately became the familiar *Yosemite,* possibly because someone thought the name was Spanish.[8]

Three out of the five states admitted to the Union in the twentieth century continued the tradition of Indian names: *Oklahoma* 1907; New *Mexico* 1912; *Arizona* 1912. The other two bear native names from non-Indian languages: *Alaska* 1959, from the Aleut; *Hawaii* 1959, from Hawaiian. And the process of adopting or restoring Indian names goes on. The tallest mountain in North America, Alaska's Mount McKinley, received its name in 1896 when the white dis-coverer called it after the presidential nominee, and subse-quent president, William McKinley. In recent years, Alas-kans have struggled to restore the Athabaskan Indian name

Denali ("Great One") to the majestic, snow-mantled peak. Alaska's members of Congress have repeatedly proposed the restoration, only to be foiled by the congressional delegation from McKinley's home state of Ohio. But the Alaskan Geographic Board has made *Denali* the official name within the state. Furthermore, the immense preserve over which the mountain towers is the Denali National Park.

A growing number of Indians feel that officially disused native names of their localities should be restored to reflect their heritage and culture. The White Mountain Apaches live on a 1.5-million-acre Arizona reservation marked by names such as Baldy Peak, Big Bonito Creek, and Christmas Tree Lake. In the 1980s, Ronnie Lupe, former chairman of the tribe, supervised a project to restore ancient names to the reservation with the assistance of anthropologist Keith H. Basso.

Within a thirty-five-square-mile area in the western corner of the reservation, where he had worked intensively, Professor Basso identified more than six hundred Apache names. Most described the landscape, but many held more than geographic significance. "When you ask Apache people about how places got their names, they tell you the ancestors made these names, and they made them well," he said. "The names are a mnemonic peg on which to hang a social history."9

A site with religious significance to the Apaches was concealed on the map under the name Salt River. This river is of crucial importance to Apache beliefs and worship. Its original name is *Dil Hil I*, "the Black Water." Baldy Peak—the Apache sacred mountain, home of the wind and mountain spirits—is called *Dzil Ligai*, "White Mountain," by the Apaches.

Lupe was at a loss about whether to make sacred places public. He wanted the sites taught to Apache youth as part of their spiritual education. But he did not want to expose the sites to possible desecration by outsiders. Of one thing he was certain. "Every piece of ground here has its Apache name for a reason that is significant to the Apache people," he asserted.[10]

A sweeping effort to restore native names was going on in Canada at the same time. The Executive Council of the Northwest Territory, with an Indian and Eskimo majority, ruled that as of January 1, 1987, local preference would determine place-names of the Northwest. It assigned Randolph Freeman to review the place-names of the region—reaching from Yukon Territory to Greenland and up to the North Pole, an area half the size of the United States.

Freeman ranged across the forbidding terrain by airplane, snowmobile, and tracked vehicle. Although only about fifty thousand people (divided roughly equally among Eskimos, Indians, and whites) lived in the territory, he estimated that it had at least one hundred thousand established place-names. A total of 4.5 million places, he estimated, were nameable.

Some of the existing names honored white explorers. Now local inhabitants wanted the original names restored. For example, the town of Frobisher Bay in the eastern Arctic had been named for Sir Martin Frobisher, the sixteenth-century English explorer. In 1987, the town was renamed *Iqaluit,* an Eskimo name meaning "Place of the Fish."

The Déné Nation, composed of six Indian tribes, simultaneously pressed for a more controversial change. The twenty-six-hundred-mile Mackenzie River, the longest in North America after the Mississippi, had been named in honor of Sir Alexander Mackenzie, who explored it in 1789. The Déné people wanted their own name for it—*Deh Cho,* "Big River" in the Slavey Indian language—to be the official name.

Freeman proposed a compromise between place-names of historical importance to whites and those of cultural or religious significance to native peoples. He urged the adoption of dual names for such places—the existing English or French name with the original Indian or Eskimo name.[11] The same solution has been proposed for some non-Indian names on U.S. reservations and for Indian landmarks elsewhere in this country.

In 1991, much of Canada received an Eskimo (Inuit) name. The Canadian government agreed in principle to turn over a gigantic piece—larger than Alaska and California combined—of the Northwest Territories to the Eskimos (Inuits). Many economic questions had to be settled before the agreement was consummated. But Eskimos (Inuits) named their new land *Nunavut,* which means "Our Land/Country" in Inuktitut, the language of the eastern Arctic.

A 1989 draft of field procedures for the investigation of Native American place-names by the U.S. Board on Geographic Names shows an active concern to preserve native names in the United States. According to the document: "The geographic names of the Native Americans are an important and integral part of the cultural heritage of the United States. The Board on Geographic Names has traditionally supported and promoted the official use of names derived from the Indian and Inuit (Eskimo) languages." The board sensitively alerts investigators to aspects of naming that could easily be overlooked. "In general, the more distinctive a place, the more likely it is to be named. Often, however, minor features will be named; but major features, such as mountain ranges, will be unnamed or vague. Visually indistinct places may have names that have religious or other associations."[12]

The naming and renaming of North America is far from over. Abundant though Native American place-names are in the United States and Canada, many Indians and non-Indians alike feel the need for additional names linked to the ancient past of the two countries. Among continuing influences on the atlas of North America, the Native American heritage is sure to be prominent.

CHAPTER EIGHT

Opening Up the West

"CERTAINLY SO GREAT GROWING A POPULATION, spread over such an extent of country, with such variety of climates, of productions, of arts," wrote Thomas Jefferson in 1813, "must enlarge their language to make it answer its purpose of expressing all ideas, the new as well as the old. The new circumstances under which we are placed, call for new words, new phrases, and for the transfer of old words to new objects."[1] Language was one of Jefferson's many intellectual passions, and he became a pioneer in the study of American Indian languages.

Jefferson had earlier thanked a correspondent for some "little vocabularies" of three Indian languages and commented that he had it "much at heart to make as extensive a collection as possible of the Indian tongues." He added, "I have at present about 30, tolerably full, among which the number radically different, is truly wonderful."[2] He hoped to use these word lists for a comparative study of Indian languages and an investigation into their origins. Thus it was natural that when President Jefferson dispatched an expedition under Meriwether Lewis and William Clark to find the best route to the Pacific for the expanding United States, he also instructed the explorers to learn as much as possible about Indian languages.[3]

The Lewis and Clark Expedition gathered many curious artifacts and facts in its epic journey during 1804–6 from St. Louis to the Oregon-Washington coast and back. On the coast, expedition members wintered in a stockade they called Fort Clatsop after a local tribe. Journals kept by several members are a priceless source of knowledge on the plants, animals, and terrain of the vast region they crossed. Jefferson had furnished Lewis with printed vocabularies of various Indian languages, with blanks left for corresponding words from western tribes. Jefferson later told a friend that Lewis conscientiously took down words from every tribe he encountered.4 These lists unfortunately disappeared when a thief later looted the trunk where they lay and scattered the papers he found there.

But the Lewis and Clark journals yielded some half dozen new Indian loans—among the earliest examples of far western Indian words that were starting to enrich the English vocabulary. Names for regional food plants are prominent among the still-current Indian words noted by Lewis and Clark Expedition members. One member commented in 1805 on the "large quantity of this root bread which they call commass." *Camas,* or *camass*—from Chinook Jargon *kamass*—is a plant of the lily family that served as a staple for Indians of the West Coast. Clark remarked in the same year on "a kind of Surup made of Dried berries" that an old woman presented to him—berries gathered from a small shrub, the *salal,* in Chinook Jargon *sallal.* In 1805 Clark wrote that the *wapatoo,* an arrowroot plant with a Chinook Jargon–derived name, had "an agreeable taste and answers very well in place of bread."5

Yet not all of the Lewis and Clark loans come from the Chinook Jargon, which will be discussed in a few pages. In 1805, Clark introduced *tamarack,* a probably Algonquian word for a kind of larch, in a comment that reflected the hardships of the expedition: "The Mountains which we passed to day much worst than yesterday the last excessively bad & thickly Strowed with falling timber & Pine Spruce fur Hackmatak & Tamerack."6

Meanwhile, Indian words were beginning to pour into English from other sources. The scientist B. S. Barton, writing in the *Scientific Monthly* in 1806, chose *wapiti*—which literally means "white rump" in Shawnee—as a name for the American elk to distinguish it from its European relative. "As the Elk has not to my knowledge been described by any systematic writer on Zoology, I have assumed the liberty of giving it a specific name," he wrote. "I have called it Wapiti, which is the name by which it is known among the Shawnees or Shawnese Indians."7 The *Scuppernong* grape received its southern Algonquian name after the North Carolina river and lake by 1811. (*Scuppernong* wine, a white aromatic wine made from the grape, was so called by 1825.)

Jefferson hoped that the Indians being displaced by whites could be peaceably settled in the regions west of the Mississippi River, but this goal proved illusory. Major Indian groups resisted the white advance, and American generals defeated them in campaigns that in several cases led to political careers. In 1811, at the mouth of Tippecanoe Creek in the Indiana Territory, the future president William Henry Harrison smashed Tecumseh's midwestern Indian alliance and won the political nickname "Tippecanoe." He again hammered Indians combined with British forces in southern Ontario, Canada, in 1813 during the War of 1812. General Andrew Jackson built a national reputation in the same war with the defeat of the Creek Indians in the Mississippi Territory. In 1817, Jackson was again on the march against Indians. This time, he actually led an invasion into Spanish-held Florida to harry the Seminoles. Still later, as president, he sanctioned the forced removal of the Cherokees from Georgia during the 1830s, over Supreme Court opposition, along the "Trail of Tears."

Words from a variety of western Indians entered English, verbal evidence of the nation's westward thrust. Names of inland peoples became loan terms, reflecting the trend. The *Osage orange,* an ornamental tree with an inedible orangelike fruit, was referred to by that name in 1817. The *Cherokee rose,* a fragrant climbing flower, was actually of Chinese origin but received its American name by 1823. The *Navaho blanket,* woven in geometric designs with symbolic meaning, was recorded by name in 1834. The Choctaw language sounded so odd to the ears of whites that by 1839, *choctaw* meant any strange or incomprehensible language. The *cayuse,* a native range horse, received its name by 1841 after the people living in what is now Oregon and Washington.

Some of the loan terms incorporated names that were or would become those of Western states. In 1811, a naturalist reported the *Tennessee warbler,* a small olive-green bird that nests in Canada and winters in South America. *Kentucky* occurs as part of a compound in *Kentucky rifle* (1832), the long-barreled and extremely accurate rifle used in the conquest of the West, and in *Kentucky bluegrass* (1849), which would become a staple of lawns in North America and Europe. The whimsically named *Arkansas toothpick,* a narrow-bladed knife, appeared with an illustration in the *Crockett Almanac* of 1836.

Canada is another place-name, of Huron-Iroquoian origin, especially popular in compounds denoting plants and animals. Thus we find *Canada balsam* (1806), *Canada violet* (1821), *Canada root* (1828), *Canada snakeroot* (1832), *Canada lynx* (1836), *Canada warbler* (1844), and *Canada plum* (1848). And consider *Canadian goose* (1806) and *Canadian goldenrod* (1836).

Some cold-weather words of this period owe their origin to northern Indians. *Toboggan* (1820) originated in Canada. The word comes through Canadian French from Micmac *tophagan,* a hand-drawn sleigh for carrying baggage.

From the United States near the Canadian border came *mackinaw* (1822), referring to a heavy woolen blanket that the U.S. government distributed to the Indians. The name derives from the Fort Mackinac trading post in Michigan that became Mackinaw City—from Ojibwa *michilmachinak,* "island of the large turtle," referring to nearby Mackinac Island. (Sixty-eight spellings of this Indian name have been counted.) In the biting winters of the Great Lakes region, where this settlement was located, a heavy blanket could make the difference between death and survival. In fact, both Indians and whites regularly wore their blankets in winter as well as slept under them. This custom gave rise to the *mackinaw coat,* a short double-breasted coat of woolen cloth, recorded by 1902 but with a tradition going back at least to 1761. Related words are *mackinaw trout* (1840), a large dark lake trout, and *mackinaw boat* (1812), a flat-bottomed boat with pointed prow and square stern once used on the upper Great Lakes.

Chipmunk (1832), another Ojibwa word, is an example of the way many Indian words were adapted to the English-speaker's ear. This word comes from *chitmunk*—which may be a version of the expressive Ojibwa *ačitamo'n'*(the symbol stands for a glottal stop), "headfirst," from the manner in which the animal descends trees.

The American public became increasingly interested not only in the western or other Indians remote from the East but also in the prostrate eastern tribes. In 1814, young Washington Irving described the theme of a school of writing beginning to enjoy vast success among American readers. "The eastern tribes have long since disappeared; the forests that sheltered them have been laid low, and scarce any traces remain of them in the thickly settled states of New England, excepting here and there the Indian name of a village or stream," he lamented in a magazine article. "And such must sooner or later be the fate of those other tribes which skirt the frontiers." He went on to speculate that if any memorial of the Indian survived in the future, "it may be in the romantic dreams of the poet."[8]

Poets and writers were finding promising material in the fading presence of the eastern Indians. Indians were the subject of a number of plays, many about Pocahontas, appearing in theaters during the first half of the nineteenth century. James Fenimore Cooper published eleven novels featuring Indians, such as his classic *The Last of the Mohicans* in 1826. Critics carped that these works contained exaggerations or falsehoods. But Cooper had at least studied the accounts of travelers and historians—using their reports to portray Indians as real people with often estimable character and customs.

The historian David Simpson has suggested that for Cooper and his contemporaries, the dwindling presence of the American Indian east of the Mississippi added to "the poetic appeal of [the Indian's] vocabulary."[9] Easterners no longer felt threatened by an Indian presence. They could view, and in many ways admire, Indians through a golden haze of memory.

In her study of American-history textbooks, Frances Fitzgerald noted that these books further encouraged a sympathetic interest in Indians. She wrote that in the 1830s and 1840s they presented Indians as "interesting, important people—in spite of the fact that they are not Christians." The textbooks, she observed, "give a remarkable amount of attention to the customs, the tools, and the probable origins of the 'native Americans.'" (This textbook concern for the Indians declined, however, as the century wore on.)[10]

Yet Indians could be the object of indulgent ridicule, as some prominent loanwords of the time indicate. In the Massachusett language, *mugguomp* or *mummugguomp* means "war leader." The word was first published in John Eliot's 1663 Indian Bible as a translation of "centurion" in the Acts. By 1832, *mugwump* had come to mean a somewhat ridiculous person who takes an independent position in politics. The term gained historical significance in 1884 when James Blaine won the Republican nomination for president. Many Republicans preferred Grover Cleveland, the Democratic nominee; the *New York Sun* called them "Little Mugwumps."

Some have claimed that the word describes "a sort of bird that sits on a fence with his mug on one side and wump on the other."[11]

Another Natick word that journalism gave currency to at about the same time is *Podunk*. This came to enjoy very modest fame in English as the name of two meadows—one near Worcester, Massachusetts, and the other near Hartford, Connecticut. Its meaning in Natick is "where there is a sinking," or "a boggy place." During the 1830s and 1840s, American humorists not infrequently used place-names— many of them Indian—satirically. An item in the *New Orleans Picayune* (which counted some New Englanders on its staff) used *Podunk* in 1841 as an apparent generic name for a town of little importance. Five years later, the *Buffalo Daily National Pilot* carried a series of humorous articles about an imaginary remote village called Podunk, which reinforced the connotations of the name. Today *Podunk* continues to serve as "an accepted symbol for bucolic coma," in H. L. Mencken's phrase.[12]

But an even greater number of words were entering English from the Far West in the end of the first half of the nineteenth century. Chinookan-speaking Indians on the lower Columbia River (between the subsequent states of Oregon and Washington), Indians described by Lewis and Clark, were a source of new words throughout the century. The Chinook Indians looked unprepossessing by European standards, with sloping foreheads caused by the intentional deforming of babies' heads. Furthermore, the Chinooks struck expedition members as crafty and sometimes menacing. Yet they boasted of a culture admirably suited to the fertile, rainy environment of the Pacific Northwest. They and associated peoples built large cedar-plank houses and were adept at wood carving, both for useful and for dramatically ornamental objects. Their dugout canoes, hewn from giant redwood and cedar trees, enabled them to travel in the sea.

The location of Chinooks along the Pacific coast and the Columbia River made them natural middlemen between European traders of coastal areas and Indians of the interior. The *Chinook Jargon* (1840) developed because of the need of traders converging on the area to communicate with one another. This trade language combined the Chinookan language with Nootka and other Indian, English, and French words. By the middle of the century, the Chinooks had been devastated by western-borne epidemics. But the Chinook Jargon continued to furnish English with colorful words.

One of these loanwords refers to the spectacular custom of Indians along the Pacific Northwest coast: *potlatch* (1847)— Chinook Jargon *pátlač* from Nootka *p'achitl,* to make a potlatch gift. "Potlatch is one of the top 10 terms in anthropology," noted Ann Fienup-Riordan, a cultural anthropologist at the University of Alaska. It is a way of creating honor by dancing, feasting, and bestowing gifts on the occasion of a major social event such as a wedding. Preparations for a potlatch formerly took as long as seventeen years. Currently a year is typical. At the traditional celebration itself, a chief or other eminent sponsor would lavish carved chests, blankets and robes, precious furs, and other luxurious items upon guests to validate his status. Such extravagance might strip the host of material goods. But it left him with "a mountain of wealth in what people think of him and his family," according to the art historian Dr. Aldona Jonaitis. A paternalistic Canada, worried about the apparent squandering of goods, outlawed the custom from 1884 to 1952. The potlatch persisted nonetheless and is still regarded by its participants as central to their cultural identity.[13]

Impressed by the natural wonders of the United States, foreigners played a part in the adoption of Indian words. Fanny Kemble, the nineteenth-century actress and author, traveled widely in the United States and lived for some time as the wife of a southern planter. Probably her American background prompted her to introduce *Niagara* in the figurative sense of "overwhelming flood." The English historian Thomas Babington Macaulay was famous for his erudite monologues, said sometimes to have lasted from morning till evening. "Such a Niagara of information did surely never pour from the lips of man!" Kemble wrote to a friend in 1841 after hearing him speak.[14]

The great Cherokee leader Sequoyah (1760?–1843) won national and some international fame in the nineteenth century. He had been fascinated by English "talking leaves," as some Indians called books and newspapers. After twelve years of effort, he developed a syllabary—list of syllables—for transcribing the Cherokee language. The Cherokees became literate in their own language within months—going on to devise a constitution and government based on those of the United States. In 1847, the Austrian botanist Stephan Ladislaus Endlicher paid fitting homage to Sequoyah by applying a variant of his name to the Redwood *(Sequoia sempervirens)*—the tallest living thing. The name also became attached to the Giant sequoia *(Sequoiadendron giganteum)*—the most massive living thing. Sequoia National Park was established in 1890 to protect the Giant sequoia.

The first two centuries of white settlement in North America north of Mexico were often dark with mistrust directed at the Indian. But by the middle of the nineteenth century, sympathy for Indians had become increasingly evident among some whites, developing into a serious attempt to understand the first Americans and to ameliorate their suffering under the relentless pressure of the westward movement. Simultaneous with interest in the Indian came concern about the forests and wildlife on the North American continent. Jefferson's Lewis and Clark Expedition turned out to be the forerunner of many more explorations by the government, private parties, and adventurous individuals to learn more about the continent's natural history.

The results are evident in the Indian loanwords and loan terms borrowed during the first half of the nineteenth century. Two-thirds of the ascertainable new Indian loans during this period come from the writings of naturalists and travelers. This spate of borrowing constitutes an amount much greater than that of the earlier peak in the early seventeenth century. In both periods, Anglo-Americans needed to expand their vocabulary to include terms for plants, animals, and other natural phenomena nameless in English. But the different and more dynamic element in the nineteenth century was the vaster, seemingly inexhaustible frontier. Most nineteenth-century Indian loans in the United States have a western character that bears out the dawning continental outlook of the American people. Throughout the rest of the century, the expanding United States would acquire vocabulary from ever-more far-flung tribes.

LOANWORDS AND LOAN TERMS FROM THE FIRST HALF OF THE NINETEENTH CENTURY

1800–1809

hickory shad 1800
saskatoon 1800
hickory nut 1802
wampee 1802
squeteague 1803
apishamore 1804
wabeno ca. 1804
camas or camass 1805
Monongahela (kind of
   whiskey) 1805
piskun 1805
salal 1805

tamarack 1805
wapatoo 1805
babiche 1806
Canada balsam 1806
Canadian goose 1806
cous (or cowish) 1806
eulachon 1806
sewellel 1806
shallon 1806
wapiti 1806
musquash root 1807
ouananiche 1808

1810–1819

mockernut hickory 1810
moose elm 1810
Ohio buckeye 1810
water hickory 1810
Kentucky warbler 1811
Mississippi kite 1811
Scuppernong (grape) 1811
Tennessee warbler 1811
Connecticut warbler 1812
mackinaw boat 1812
squantum 1812
broom hickory 1813
catawba rhododendron 1813

Eskimo curlew 1813
bogue 1814
Seneca grass 1814
papooseroot 1815
squawroot 1815
summer squash 1815
hickory horned devil 1816
dockmackie 1817–18
how (greeting) 1817
Osage orange 1817
skunk currant 1817
coonskin 1818
pokelogan or pokeloken 1818

1820–1829

toboggan (n.) 1820
blue cohosh 1821
Canada violet 1821
lye hominy 1821
water moccasin 1821
mackinaw (blanket) 1822
possum (v.) 1822
chebacco boat 1823
Cherokee rose 1823
pung 1825

Scuppernong (wine) 1825
tweeg 1825
titi 1827
black cohosh 1828
Canada root 1828
cocash 1828
squaw-weed 1828
barren ground caribou 1829
Canadianize 1829
quinnat salmon 1829

1830–1839

Canada snakeroot 1832
catawba tree 1832
chipmunk 1832

Kentucky rifle 1832
moosebird 1832
mugwump (n.) 1832

1830–1839 (continued)

nutmeg hickory 1832
opossum mouse 1832
squawbush 1832
wankapin 1832
coon dog 1833
coon (v.) 1834
moose fly 1834
Navaho blanket 1834
raccoon grape 1834
raccoon oyster 1834
Kentucky jean 1835
massasauga 1835
Arkansas toothpick 1836

Canada lynx 1836
Canadian goldenrod 1836
hickory shirt 1836
water chinquapin 1836
klootchman 1837
siscowet 1837
muckamuck (v.) 1838
old-squaw 1838
skookum (n.) 1838
choctaw (strange language)
    1839
moose maple 1839

1840–1849

Chinook Jargon 1840
mackinaw trout 1840
cayuse 1841
dowitcher 1841
Niagara (overwhelming
    flood) 1841
Podunk 1841
chogset 1842
Croton bug ca. 1842
chittamwood 1843
coon's age 1843
skunk (v.) 1843
Canada warbler 1844
cibolero 1844
coon song 1844
Indian moccasin 1844
opossum shrimp 1844

Oregon pine 1845
yamp 1845
Catawba (wine) 1846
sego lily (or sego) 1846
senega root ca. 1846
squash bug 1846
Texas Ranger 1846
toboggan (v.) 1846
totemic 1846
water opossum 1846
muckamuck (n.) 1847
pogy ca. 1847
potlatch (v.) 1847
sequoia 1847
Siwash (an Indian) 1847
skookum (adj.) 1847
stogie or stogy (shoe) 1847

1840–1849 (continued)

tillicum 1847
Canada plum 1848
cisco 1848
pukeweed 1848
scup 1848
wanigan (or wangan, etc.)
  1848

camas rat 1849
cultus 1849
Kentucky bluegrass
  1849
taconic 1849
tobogganing 1849

CHAPTER NINE

Of Kayaks and Igloos

ESKIMOS AND THEIR KAYAKS LOOKED ALMOST AS strange to the English in the sixteenth century as Martians in flying saucers would to us now. The English first encountered the Eskimos while searching for the Northwest Passage to Asia. Both peoples were startled by the experience—though some of the Eskimos may have seen whites before.

In 1576, the Elizabethan sea dog Martin Frobisher sailed around Greenland to Baffin Island off the northern Canadian mainland. At an inlet later known as Frobisher Bay, Eskimos who had apparently been friendly captured five of Frobisher's crew. Retaliating, Frobisher lured an Eskimo in a kayak close to his ship by dangling a bell toward him. Frobisher then managed to haul the man—and his kayak—bodily onto the ship's deck. The captive was so disconcerted that he bit his tongue in two.

Unable to exchange the Eskimo for the captured sailors, Frobisher sailed away with his prize. More skilled as a navigator than as an explorer, Frobisher believed that he had finally discovered the Northwest Passage. At least he found a hero's welcome on returning home. The backer of his voyage described the return of captain and crew to London, "bringing with them their strange man and his bote, which was such a wonder onto the whole city and to the rest of the realm that heard of it as seemed never to have happened the like great matter to any man's knowledge."[1]

Frobisher's Eskimo and his kayak excited the English much

as George Waymouth's Indians and their canoes would a few years later (see chapter 2). But it took a chunk of ore that Frobisher brought back from Baffin Island to raise money for two further expeditions. The explorer carried the stone to several assayers until he found one who would agree that it contained a significant amount of gold. This dubious evidence was enough to get backing for Frobisher's other expeditions, including one thousand pounds and the loan of a ship from Queen Elizabeth.

Ever optimistic, Frobisher intended to plant a settlement on the Arctic island to work the gold deposits he chose to believe were there. But his expeditions produced only several hundred tons of fool's gold and other extraneous minerals. The ventures financially ruined Michael Lok, Frobisher's backer, and ended sixteenth-century England's plans for a colony in the far north. An Arctic waste lacking gold held much less appeal for settlement than did southern lands with forests and grasslands reminiscent of the English countryside.

For centuries, the remoteness of the Eskimos and the harshness of the climate they endure protected their obscurity. Eskimo villages and tiny settlements still sparsely dot a forbidding landscape that lies thousands of miles around and within the Arctic Circle. Eskimos are scattered from easternmost Siberia across Alaska and northern Canada to coastal Greenland. Aleuts, speaking a language akin to that of the Eskimos, live on the eleven-hundred-mile-long Aleutian Island chain that stretches west from the Alaskan mainland.

These peoples, the most far-flung native group in the world, are linked by a common culture and similar artifacts. Only in this century has the traditional Eskimo way of life changed markedly, under the impact of Western technology. But the Eskimos and Aleuts still participate in a language family called Eskaleut. The following table displays the broad outlines of this family.

Table 9.1 Eskaleut

ESKIMO
 Yupik—traditionally spoken in Siberia and southwestern
  Alaska
 Inuit—traditionally spoken from Bering Strait to Greenland
ALEUT—spoken on Aleutian Islands; started diverging from
  Eskimo possibly three thousand years ago

The vocabulary of the Eskimos reflects the numbing climate in which they live. Few words in English describe ice
and icy conditions; scores in at least one Eskimo dialect do.*
In his *Hunters of the Northern Ice,* Richard K. Nelson lists
twenty-two words that Eskimos on the northern coast of
Alaska apply to the age or thickness of ice—words that
translate as grease ice, slush ice, file ice, pancake ice, black
young ice, gray young ice, heavy young ice, winter ice, old
ice, mother ice, rotten ice, and so on. Nelson also lists sixteen Eskimo words for conditions and states of ice movement as well as fifty for sea-ice topography.[2]

Who is right in the controversy over whether to call the
northernmost peoples of the world "Eskimo" or "Inuit"?
Eskimo as a name did not originate with the Eskimos. The
English and other early European explorers picked up this
name from Montagnais, an Algonquian language of northern Quebec and Labrador. "What shoulde I speake of the
customes . . . that may be uttered in the more northerly
partes of the lande amonge the Esquimawes of the Grand
Bay," wrote Richard Hakluyt in 1584.[3] In his question,
which includes the first printed occurrence of *Eskimo* in En-

---

*Widespread, unsubstantiated claims that Eskimos have numerous words for
snow have been challenged by Laura Martin of Cleveland State University
(*American Anthropologist,* June 1986) and linguist Geoffrey K. Pullum (*The Great
Eskimo Vocabulary Hoax,* 1991).

glish, he was speculating on taxes an English government might levy on that people.

The name *Eskimo,* mistranslated as "eater of raw meat," is rejected by some Eskimos as both alien and offensive. But linguists now suggest that the name originally came from Montagnais *ayashkimew,* meaning Micmac.[4] Although Eskimos in Canada are officially called *Inuit,* "people" in their language, numerous others prefer the more familiar *Eskimo.*[5] Following common usage, the latter name will be used here.

Up to the nineteenth century, Eskimo terms were of little concern to English-speaking peoples. "With exploration as their primary goal, the English numbered Eskimos among the curiosities of distant lands rather than as subjects for study," says Eskimologist Wendell H. Oswalt.[6] The fewer than ten Eskaleut loanwords surviving in current English from before the nineteenth century, out of a total of more than forty, reflect the superficiality of early relations between the two peoples. Most of the earliest loanwords were derived from translations of Scandinavian and Russian books.

Despite the wonder Frobisher's captive and his kayak evoked, for example, almost a century passed before the first English record of the loanword *kayak.* A scholar, Adam Olearius, had played host to three Eskimo captives in Denmark. His book, under the translated title *Enlarged Muscovite and Persian Travel Description,* refers in 1662 to "Kajakka, a little Boat."[7] The Eskimo original is *qajaq.*

From the same book comes the English loanword for that other archetypical Eskimo invention, the igloo. As Olearius observes, *iglu* in Eskimo simply means "house."[8] Such a dwelling is by no means necessarily a dome built of snow blocks, as it is so often portrayed. In polar regions, it was most often made of stone. Igloos could also be partly subterranean houses covered with sod. But Eskimos in the central Arctic traditionally did construct igloos from hard-packed snow carved into blocks with bone or ivory knives. The builders stacked these blocks upward in a spiral to form a dome. A hole in the top allowed smoke to escape, and often a pane of ice or animal gut served as a window.

Igloos, heated only by seal-oil lamps and the warmth of human bodies, provided snug protection against howling blizzards. The Arctic archaeologist John E. Lobdell has noted that the igloo "was a remarkable innovation, one that fostered a population explosion about a thousand years ago."[9]

Nearly a century after *kayak* and *igloo*, more Eskaleut words entered English. A Hudson's Bay Company report in 1743 contains the apparent first reference in English to the other principal kind of Eskimo boat—the *umiak* (Eskimo *umiaq*, "women's boat"). This vessel is a large open boat made of skins stretched on a wooden frame, sturdy enough to be used in the hunting of whales. "Several Oomiaks or women's boats filled with women and children were also alongside," noted the report.[10] A translation of a book by the Scandinavian missionary Hans P. Egede, *A Description of Greenland* (1745), introduced the still-current Eskimo loanword *angakok*, "shaman," into English. The angakok learned through arduous training to direct supernatural forces that enabled him to cure the ill, determine the cause of death, and guide people in making personal decisions.

The remaining eighteenth-century source of Eskaleut loanwords in English is a book by the Russian Stepan Glotov. Translated and summarized by William Coxe as *Account of the Russian Discoveries between Asia and America,* it was published in London in 1787 but has a translator's preface dated 1780. In the book are words for two kinds of Eskimo-Aleut clothing—one of them destined to become standard cold-weather garb throughout much of the world.

Glotov states that Eskimos "wear coats (parki) made of bird skins." To this, Coxe appends a footnote: "Partki in Russian signifies a shirt, the coats of these islanders being made like shirts."[11] *Parka,* now meaning a hip-length hooded coat, is an Aleut or Yupik Eskimo word from Russian *párka* and ultimately from a Uralic language of northeastern European Russia. For *kamleika* in Glotov, a waterproof pullover shirt, see glossary 2.

Only a few more Eskaleut words trickled into English before the U.S. acquisition of Alaska. These loanwords, given in glossary 2, are almost completely limited in use to the native peoples from whom they came: *komatic*—a sledge with wooden runners (1824); *muktuk*—whale skin used for food (1835); *tupik*—an Eskimo summer dwelling (1836); and *ulu*—an Eskimo women's knife (1824).

Several apparently Eskimo words dating from this period are, like *Eskimo* itself, ultimately of non-Eskimo origin. One is *husky,* the working dog of the Arctic. The husky is a draft animal of remarkable hardiness. It now is classified into several types; see *Alaskan malamute* below. Recorded in 1852, *husky* is derived from the name *Eskimo. Mush!*—used as a command to a team of huskies and recorded in 1862—comes from American-French *moucher,* "to walk, go."

The U.S. purchase of "Russian America" in 1867, under Secretary of State William Seward, inspired critics to scoff at "Seward's folly," "Seward's icebox," and "Polaria." The Departments of the Army, Treasury, and Navy successively ran Alaska under a policy of benign neglect. In 1884, the growing development of the salmon industry and the early discovery of gold led to the Organic Act, which made Alaska a judicial district and established a school system in the region. Not until 1912 did the U.S. possession become the Territory of Alaska, with its own elected legislature.

But however casual the government was in its early treatment of Alaska, the American people took an interest in it. Naturalists, clergymen, and journalists began flocking north shortly after the purchase, braving cold weather and rugged terrain to see it for themselves. Their reports, often displaying awe at the picturesque landscape and amazement at the exotic peoples there, led to a spurt of loanwords from Eskimo and Aleut.

The name *Alaska* itself is an Aleut word—spelled variously *Alaeksu, Alachschak, Alaschka,* and *Alaxa*—meaning "mainland."[12] U.S. Senator Charles Sumner proposed the name under the misapprehension that it meant "great land." Choosing a native word for the name of a region was in keeping with the nineteenth-century trend toward giving Native American names to most new U.S. states (see chapter 7). A number of new loan terms incorporating *Alaska* soon entered English.

(For linguistic reasons, this chapter is confined to Eskimo and Aleut loanwords. But Alaskan Indian words were entering English simultaneously. These will be discussed in the next chapter.)

In 1876, Delmonico's Restaurant in New York City began serving a dessert consisting of sponge cake topped with ice cream, the whole covered with a thick layer of meringue. The concoction was then baked just long enough to brown the meringue without melting the ice cream. Initially called "Alaska-Florida," the dessert became more famous as *baked Alaska*.[13]

Other loan terms appeared that incorporated *Alaska*. The naturalist John Muir recorded *Alaska cedar* in 1880. "The steep slopes on which they grow allow almost every individual tree, with its peculiarities of form and color, to be seen like an audience on seats rising above one another—. . . and the airy, feathery, brownish-green Alaska cedar."[14]

Alaska cypress and *Alaska pine* followed, both by 1897.[15] Still other such loan terms are *Alaska blackfish, Alaska cod, Alaska goose, Alaska grayling* (1890), *Alaska longspur,* and *Alaska pollack.* Later would come *Alaskan malamute* (1938), originally a powerful sled dog, and *Alaska time* (1945), the time of the tenth time zone west of Greenwich, which includes central Alaska.[16]

A related word is *alaskite* (1889), a light-colored granite. And in 1902, a Sears, Roebuck & Co. catalogue was offering the *alaska,* a rubber overshoe with a high front. "This is the only style of Alaska that will correctly fit a wide extension soled shoe."[17]

The bountiful animal life of Alaska enabled naturalists to bring back the descriptions—and names—of other distinctive Alaskan animals. Describing Eskimo boots, Frederick Whymper wrote in 1868, "Their boots vary in length, and in the material used for the sides, but all have soles of 'maclock,' or sealskin, with the hair removed."[18] Frequently cited as the first source of *mukluk,* or Eskimo boot (see below), this quotation appears to refer more pertinently to the hides used in making it. The typical raw material of mukluks came from the *makluk,* great bearded seal—Eskimo *maklak.*

The *malamute,* a large Eskimo dog raised originally for drawing sleds, received its name from the *Malimiut,* Eskimos who first bred such dogs, and was noted in 1898.

The *Atka mackerel* is a black-banded mackerel named after Atka, an island in the Aleutians near the fishing grounds for this fish. Its name was recorded by Smithsonian naturalist Henry W. Elliott in 1886 during a tour of Alaska. "Among the sea-weed that floats in immense rafts everywhere throughout the Aleutian passes, the 'Yellow-fish,' or 'Atkha mackerel,' is very abundant."[19]

In 1899, Rowland Ward mentioned the *Kodiak bear*—a variety of grizzly bear that is the world's largest living land carnivore—in a book on big game. "Even more gigantic is the Kadiak bear . . . of Kadiak Island, Alaska."[20]

In 1898, the *Medicine Hat News* (Alberta, Canada) carried a piece of doggerel including a definite reference to *mukluk:*

Her parkee, made of Caribou, it is a lovely fit.
And she's all right from muck-a-luck unto her dainty mit.[21]

Mukluk is derived from the Eskimo *maklak* (see above).

After the gold rush of 1899–1902, Alaska seemed to fade in the national consciousness. The territory's population actually dropped between 1910 and 1920. For the next two decades, population and industry grew unspectacularly. A government attempt during the depression to portray Alaska as the land of opportunity for jobless men fizzled.

World War II rekindled national interest in Alaska. The United States developed military bases in the territory and built the fifteen-hundred-mile Alaska highway from British Columbia into Alaska. Alaska's coming of age politically in 1959 as a state was reinforced in the 1970s by an oil boom that pumped billions of dollars into the state's economy. Alaska moved far beyond its former status as an intriguing but out-of-the-way possession of the United States.

Yet the borrowing of English loanwords from Eskimo and Aleut has declined sharply in this century. Apart from the three loanwords—*alaska* (overshoe), *Alaskan malamute, Alaska time*—mentioned earlier, few others can be named. *Anorak,* Eskimo *annoraaq,* a hooded pullover jacket, appeared during the early 1920s. "He was habited . . . in anorak and skin breeches and mukluks," stated *Chamber's Journal of Popular Literature* in 1924.[22] A few years later appeared the geological word *pingo* (1928), meaning a low hill or mound pushed up by the pressure of freezing water, from the Eskimo *pinguq.* These two loanwords come through European sources and are non-Alaskan in origin.

Why have so few Eskimo and Aleut loanwords entered English in the twentieth century? The reasons may be similar to those behind the decline in the adoption of northern American Indian loanwords into English. Over the years, visitors and settlers became less dependent on the specialized knowledge of the earlier inhabitants of Alaska. Objects new to whites had mostly been named in English by the early twentieth century. Finally, the predominance of English rendered the speaking of Eskaleut tongues less common and less influential.

But there are signs that the potential of Eskaleut languages for enriching English has not been exhausted. Gordon Hempton of Seattle, for example, identifies himself on his stationery as "The Sound Tracker." He has frequently backpacked the Pacific Northwest wilderness, carrying sound-recording equipment, in search of the naturally noise-free places that are becoming rarer in the modern world. "In such a setting you feel at peace," he said in 1990. "Things begin to make sense again. . . . There's a letting go. . . . You see yourself as part of the planet." Hempton's term for this phenomenon is the Eskimo word *seuketat* (see'-u-ka-tat), meaning "ear of the animal."[23]

CHAPTER TEN

Words along the Fiery War Trail

ON NOVEMBER 10, 1855, BOSTONIANS IN FROCK coats or hoopskirts and shawls traipsed into their city's bookstores all day long. The nation's leading poet, Henry Wadsworth Longfellow, had finally delivered to an impatient public *The Song of Hiawatha*. Longfellow was the author of a dozen books (not including textbooks), had served as a professor at Harvard, and enjoyed transatlantic fame as an authority on European languages and as a man of letters.

Hiawatha sold more than 4,000 copies to literati on the first day of publication. But the 316-page poem quickly reached a vaster audience, selling 50,000 copies in its first year. An estimated one million copies were sold during the author's lifetime; the poem became a familiar sight in parlors and classrooms throughout the country.

"I have at length hit upon a plan for a poem on the American Indians, which seems to me the right one, and the only," Longfellow had commented during composition of the poem. "It is to weave together the beautiful traditions into a whole."[1] Nevertheless, some critics called the result a hodgepodge. They pointed out, for example, that the episodes of the poem came largely from Ojibwa legends but that the historic Hiawatha was a Mohawk or an Onondaga medicine man. The closeness of the poem's meter and style to the Finnish epic *Kalevala* bothered other critics.

Yet Longfellow had studied Indian legends closely. He

wrote about Indians in circumstantial detail. As if to heighten the authenticity of his poem, he appended a "Vocabulary" of 130 of the Indian names and words used in it. Among the words are some still current, such as *Maskenozha* (maskinonge, pike), *Pemican* (pemmican), *Puggawaugun* (pogamoggan), and *Wabeno* (an Ojibwa shaman). Other still-current Indian loanwords in the poem—such as *totem, wampum,* and *wigwam*—were too well-known for Longfellow to list separately.

The chief weakness of the poem for the modern reader is its sentimentality, as in repeated expostulations to "Minnehaha, Laughing Water." Both the content and the sing-song meter of *Hiawatha* have lent themselves to devastating parodies. Readers put off by the poem's flaws, however, miss some of the purest nature poetry of that era, as well as somber hints of what awaited Indians and whites during the rest of the nineteenth century.

> Fiercely the red sun descending
> Burned his way along the heavens,
> Set the sky on fire behind him,
> As war-parties, when retreating,
> Burn the prairies on their war-trail;
> And the moon, the Night-Sun, eastward,
> Suddenly starting from his ambush,
> Followed fast those bloody footprints,
> Followed in that fiery war-trail.[2]

By the time of *Hiawatha*'s publication, U.S. territory had officially reached the shores of the Pacific. England yielded the Oregon country to the United States in 1846. The United States conquered the Spanish Southwest from Mexico two years later. Meanwhile, the California gold rush of 1848–49 flooded the future state with prospectors and settlers.

By the middle of the nineteenth century, about 360,000

Indians were living west of the Mississippi. Almost a fourth of them had been driven from the East, looking for new homes where they might live unmolested. These refugees joined other Indians, representing scores of diverse cultures and languages. Together, they comprised peoples more varied than those of modern Europe.

A resource the western Indians shared, however, was the apparently boundless lands that whites coveted. And the West beckoned easterners with more than just the prospect of gold or their own farmsteads. It represented the ideal of a new and expansive life. "We go eastward," Henry David Thoreau said in 1851, "to realize history and study the works of art and literature, retracing the steps of the race; we go westward as into the future, with a spirit of enterprise and adventure."[3]

Despite government pledges to Indians securing their lands, whites thronged west in ever-increasing numbers. No force could stem this movement of people, soon sped by railroads that developed into the world's largest inland transportation network. Inevitably, Indians defended themselves against the invasion. Many had mastered the horse and the white man's rifle. A number of tribes traditionally engaged in warfare, following a warrior's code that glorified heroism in battle— training that prepared them well for the struggle over their homelands. The U.S. Army would find itself severely challenged as it moved to protect beleaguered and often provocative settlers.

So the Indian wars, with all their savagery, erupted throughout the West. This warfare made later-nineteenth-century Americans more acutely aware of Indians than Americans had been since early colonial times. "No span of years in the nation's past has produced as many famous figures and as many historic encounters between Indians and whites as the period from 1846 to 1890," wrote frontier historian Robert M. Utley. "In this brief time, the names of John Ross of the Cherokee Nation; Sitting Bull and Red Cloud, spokesmen respectively for the Hunkpapa and Oglala Sioux; Mangas Coloradas, Cochise, and Geronimo, Apache leaders; and Chief Joseph of the Nez Percé, became house-hold words."[4]

Sometimes eastern whites responded with outrage to notable massacres or displacements of Indians. Well-meaning groups in the East struggled to understand the western Indians and to persuade the government to have them treated with benevolence, if not necessarily fairness. Eastern clergymen and journalists visited the western Indians and reported on their plight. Travel writers described the wonders and peoples of western lands. Scientists, often employed by the government, classified the new plants and animals to be found in the western half of the continent. Westerners themselves offered their colorful views in a growing number of newspapers.

New Indian loanwords and loan terms poured into English at an accelerating rate. Almost half these loans are of non-Algonquian origin, most from the languages of the western Indians. That fraction becomes over half when compound terms including already familiar loanwords such as *squaw* and *moose* are left out.

These new words and terms will not be presented here according to the chaotic events of the Indian wars. A regional approach more clearly reveals the significance of the borrowings.

PACIFIC NORTHWEST

By the mid-nineteenth century, Chinook influences (see chapter 8) still loomed large in the Pacific Northwest. The region's enormous yield of fish, fur, and timber attracted traders from Europe and from Indian tribes as far inland as the

Great Plains. Chinook Jargon enabled the polyglot people coming together to communicate with one another.

The mercantile significance of the Pacific Northwest Indian languages enriched the English vocabulary by the end of the nineteenth century with some twenty new loanwords and loan terms. An obvious example is the *Chinook*—a warm, dry wind blowing eastward from the Rocky Mountains toward the Great Plains. The word is recorded as a noun in 1860 and as a verb in 1890: "We worked three days getting the sheep to ground part clear of snow; they done well for two days, but it chinooked for a few hours and then froze a heavy crust" (quoted in the *Oregon Historical Quarterly*).[5] The term *Chinook licorice,* denoting a silky blue-colored herb, followed in 1893.

Salmon played a major part in the economy of Chinooks and other Indians of the region. Indians would canoe fresh, dried, or salted salmon to the port of Astoria, where it brought six dollars per hundred pounds. The *Chinook salmon,* or king salmon, is the largest species, growing to about three feet long. "We notice that P. B. Macy & Co. have received a supply of Chenook salmon, by the Sea Gull," noted the *San Francisco Picayune* in 1851.[6] *Sockeye salmon,* also known as blueback or red salmon, is the most valuable salmon for food. Its name, recorded in 1869, comes by folk etymology from Salish (dialectal) *suk-kegh.* (Salish, a contributor of words to Chinook Jargon, is a family of languages spoken in the northwestern United States and British Columbia.) Another fish name from a Salish language is *kokanee* (1875), a small landlocked form of sockeye salmon.

Beset by pestilence and white encroachment, northwestern Indians looked back to their traditions of prosperity and elegance. *Potlatch,* literally in Chinook Jargon to make a potlatch gift, cited in chapter 8 as a verb, is noted as a noun by 1861. The Chinook Jargon *high-muck-a-muck,* literally "plenty to eat," earlier recorded in abbreviated form, is rendered in full in 1856 with the meaning "important person."

One of the achievements of Indians in the region and northward that has always fascinated visitors is the *totem pole*. The first, or Ojibwa, part of the term was recorded much earlier, in 1609 (see chapter 2). The naturalist John Muir traveling through Alaska used the new term in 1879. "The carved totem-pole monuments are the most striking of the objects displayed here. The simplest of them consisted of a smooth, round post fifteen or twenty feet high and about eighteen inches in diameter, with the figure of some animal on top."[7]

But Indians faced unsettling influences from the outsider, *cheechako* (1897)—Chinook Jargon from Lower Chinook *chee* (new) + Nootka *chako* (come). Despite laws and agreements, whites often traded whiskey to the Indians. And the Tlingit-speaking Hootsnoowoos ("great den of bears") Indian tribe responded with their own molasses-based brew that an American soldier taught them how to make. One entire village became so drunk on it that Muir said he could hear the howling of the villagers half a mile away. This drink became popular in the Northwest under the name *hoochinoo*, a variant of Hootsnoowoos (also spelled "Kootznahoos").[8] A writer in the *Puget Sound Argus* observed in 1877, "I have frequently seen soldiers go to the Indian ranch for their morning drink of Kootznehoo."[9] The name was shortened to the more familiar *hooch* by 1897.

A common punishment for brawls resulting from too much hoochino was confinement in the *skookum-house*—Chinook Jargon "powerful" from Chehalis (a Salishan language) *skukm* (an evil spirit) + *house*. "It was only after much *waw-waw* (parley) and sundry threats of the skookum house (jail) . . . that one of them was got to undertake to carry him" (1873).[10]

Specialized Pacific Northwest and northern Pacific food

words include *geoduck,* a large, edible clam, from Puget Salish (1883), *wokas,* a yellow water lily with edible seeds, from
Klamath (1878), and *quisutsch,* the edible silver salmon, from a
native name in Kamchatka and Alaska (1886).

Proper names are prominent in Indian loan terms from
the Northwest and Alaska during the same period. The *Kamloops trout* (1896) echoes the Indian name of Kamloops, British Columbia. *Sitka spruce* (1879) includes the name of the
former capital of Russian America. The *Nootka cypress* (1892)
bears witness to the Indian people of that name.

From *Oregon,* a name of obscure Indian origin, came *Oregon
grape* (1851), *Oregon robin* (1860), *Oregon ash* (1869), *Oregon
cedar* (1872), *Oregon alder* (1874), and *Oregon crab apple* (1884).

CALIFORNIA

The Indians of California to the south belonged to an amazingly complex—but fragile—array of tribes. A reliable esti-
mate places the number of languages once spoken among
them at more than one hundred, most mutually unintelli-
gible. The region is said to have been home to a greater
variety of languages than any other part of the country, or
possibly world, of comparable size.[11]

But California Indians suffered notably from the invasion
of whites, mainly Spanish and American. Pestilence vied
with the depredations of miners and settlers to push the
Indians close to annihilation. The small number of surviving loanwords from the California Indian languages testi-
fies both to the cultural havoc among the Indians and to the
failure of whites to develop meaningful communication with
the original inhabitants of California (a Spanish name).

Abalone comes from an extinct language of the Costanoan
Indians, who lived on the California coast (hence their Span-
ish-derived name). The original word *aulon* yielded the Spanish plural *abulones.* A form of that was recorded in a book

called *Eldorado* in 1850. "The *avelone,* which is a univalve, found clinging to the sides of rocks, furnishes the finest mother-of-pearl."[12]

Another word from the Indians of California is *chuckwalla* (1869), which denotes a large harmless lizard in the southwestern United States. Its name comes from Cahuilla of the Uto-Aztecan language family, through Spanish. The *Shasta daisy* (1893) received its name from two-mile-high Mount Shasta in northern California, in turn named for the mountain-dwelling Shasta Indians.

THE SOUTHWEST

Among the high cultures of the Southwest, the Hopis enjoyed a relatively calm relationship with the U.S. government. One reason was that bitter conflicts with earlier Spanish rulers made U.S. authority look almost inviting by contrast. Religious devotion further helped the Hopis survive, and three loan terms from their language bear witness to the centrality of religion in their culture.

The *kiva* is an underground room where Hopis hold religious services and other important meetings. This loanword, derived from Hopi *kíva,* from *ki* (house) + unidentified element, occurs in an observation in 1871: "Found pieces of pottery and arrowheads. Also saw a 'kiver' or underground 'clan room.'"[13]

The Kachina Cult highlights Hopi worship. *Kachina* derives from Hopi *kachi* (life or spirit) + *na* (father). It primarily refers to supernatural beings who visit the Hopis during the first part of the year to control the weather and provide a link between gods and people. Additionally *Kachina* refers to the masked spirit-impersonators at religious ceremonies. *Kachina dolls* portray the Kachinas. The word seems first to have been transcribed into English in 1873 as *Cachina* in a government survey of the West.[14]

The Hopis' Navajo neighbors did not escape so lightly in their early dealings with the U.S. government. During the 1860s, government troops under Kit Carson pacified the Navajos in a campaign still resented by the Indians. A rare Navajo loanword from the nineteenth century is *hogan* (1871)—denoting a practical dwelling made of logs and sticks covered with earth, from Navajo *hooghan,* hogan, home. It is no accident that this loanword refers to a more mundane aspect of culture than the loanwords from the "less troublesome" Hopis: whites related more comfortably to the latter.

Nearly all the other still-current Indian loans from the Southwest deal with the natural history of that region. *Gila trout* (1852) and *Gila woodpecker* (1858) are named after Arizona's Gila River, which harks back to an Indian tribe of that name. The *Gila monster* (1877) is one of only two known venomous lizards in the world. The name of the *saguaro* or *sahuaro* (1856), a giant cactus whose blossom is the Arizona state flower, comes from American Spanish but probably has a Piman origin.

According to David J. Weber, historian of the Hispanic Southwest, *Texas* is derived, through Spanish, from a Caddo word, meaning "friends" or "allies," that the Spanish and then Americans adopted as *Tejas* or *Texas.*[15] Shortly after the admission of Texas to the Union in 1845, the state's name was being used in connection with several manmade and natural objects. The *Texas* is the structure on a riverboat that contains the pilothouse and officers' quarters (1853). It received its name from the labeling of Mississippi steamboat cabins after states, the officers' cabin being the largest. Other datable terms incorporating the state name are the *Texas fever tick* (1866) and *Texas bluegrass* (1882). About thirty other terms now also incorporate *Texas.*

Even before Arizona achieved statehood in 1912, its possibly Pima or Papago name was being applied to various objects: *Arizona ruby* (1893), a type of garnet, and *Arizona pine* (1897). The mineral *arizonite* (1909) is named for its locality.

THE MIDWEST

It might seem strange that whites did not borrow more words from the languages of the vigorous native peoples they encountered in the nation's central prairies and woodlands. In fact, the warlike nature of several Midwest tribes had a chilling effect on white intruders, with the struggle of subduing the Indians taking precedence over that of understanding them.

The Fox people, speaking an Algonquian language, lived in what is now Wisconsin. They battled neighbors such as the Chippewa and Illinois tribes, then stoutly resisted French and American incursions. A surviving loanword from Fox designates a dwelling once common in the upper Great Lakes region and later in much of the West—the *wickiup* (1852), a frame hut covered with bark, brush, or matting. In western usage, *wickiup* came to refer to any rude hut. The word derives from Fox *wiikiyaapi* (house) and is cognate with *wigwam*.

Several of the Midwest loan terms feature tribal names. *Menominee whitefish* (1884), including the same name as the tribe in Wisconsin, is a food fish occurring in lakes of the northern United States and Canada. *Arkansas* derives through French from the Quapaw tribe of the Sioux, who called themselves *Ugakhpah*—"downstream people." The name became attached to a variety of objects such as the *Arkansas goldfinch* (1858), *Arkansas* (sharpening) *stone* (1869), and *Arkansas kingbird* (1870). Also note *Arkansas toothpick* in chapter 8.

Perhaps more than any other tribal name, *Kickapoo* has been employed for non-Indian purposes. It appears as a place-name in at least eight states. It has been borrowed by western border rangers during the Civil War, splinter political parties in Oklahoma, and fraternal orders and lodges.[16]

The historical Kickapoos were, according to western historian John Upton Terrell, the most warlike of the Indians. Their Algonquian name is *Kiwigapawa,* which means "he moves about."[17] This designation is apt. The Kickapoos started out around Wisconsin, but they ranged widely in search of booty—from the Great Lakes to Mexico and from the Great Plains to New York, Pennsylvania, and Georgia. Eventually white pressure forced the Kickapoos to retreat westward and southward. But the Kickapoos never surrendered, some establishing themselves as far away as the Mexican province of Chihuahua.

It was in association with patent medicine, however, that *Kickapoo* became a household word in the United States. Operating out of a building in New Haven, Connecticut, known as "The Principal Wigwam," the Kickapoo Indian Medicine Company was sending more than one hundred medicine shows throughout the United States by 1880. These shows featured performers, such as singers and dancers, along with purported doctors who hawked the medicines. Indians of various tribes, touring with the shows in full regalia, were billed as "pure-blooded Kickapoos." Their alleged medicines, made of herbs and barks sometimes laced with rum, promised relief from many ailments. One example was Sagwa, going for fifty cents or one dollar a bottle, which was supposed to cure consumption as well as "all ills that afflict the human body."[18] Sold out in 1910, the Kickapoo Company had given an already eminent tribe added, if meretricious, fame.

THE EAST

Borrowing from Indian languages continued in the East. But the new loanwords and loan terms tended to be different from those in the rest of the country. Nineteenth-century easterners were seeing much less of Indians than were settlers and others journeying to western lands. And for the most part, objects in the East native to the United States had already been named, in contrast to discoveries still turning up in the West. Not surprisingly, the most common sources of new Indian loanwords and loan terms in the East were place-names of Indian origin or already existing loanwords combined with other words.

Henry David Thoreau introduced the verb *honk* to describe the clangorous sound of migrating Canada geese. "I was startled by the *honking* of geese flying low over the woods, like weary travellers," he wrote in *Walden* (1854).[19] It seems likely that Thoreau, a connoisseur of Indian speech, adopted this expressive word from Wampanoag or Narragansett *honck,* gray goose, the Canada goose. (It has been suggested, however, that Thoreau may simply have coined the word as onomatopoetic.)

Other new words and terms reveal a growing sophistication. For example, *Saratoga trunk* (1858), from the Saratoga Springs resort center in New York State, designates a large traveling trunk. The resort's name is possibly of Mohawk origin, meaning "springs (of water) from the hillside." *Saratoga chip* (1876)—the original name of that basic American junk food, the potato chip—originated in the resort. According to tradition, a patron at Moon Lake Lodge there in 1853 complained that his French-fried potatoes were not thin enough. An irritated chef sliced some potatoes paper-thin, fried them crisply, and delighted the fussy diner.[20] The chips became a featured item on the restaurant's menu and subsequently won national acceptance.

The emergence of *Tammany* as a political term had its roots in colonial history. The Sons of Tammany was founded in the late eighteenth century as a fraternity of patriots dedicated to American independence. It borrowed its name from *Tamanend,* "the affable," a seventeenth-century Delaware chief (flourished 1682–1700) celebrated for his friendliness to whites.²¹ Tammany Societies in New York, Philadelphia, and other major American cities typically held convivial monthly meetings. Members listened to speeches, dined, drank toasts, watched Indian dances, and smoked the *Calumet* of peace and friendship. The Indian theme of the organization was borne out by appropriate terminology for its structure: members were *braves;* leaders were *sachems* (ruled by a *Grand Sachem*); and subgroups were *tribes.* Meetings were held in a building called a *wigwam* at the "going down of the sun."²²

The New York society rose beyond the others to become a political machine called Tammany Hall after its headquarters on Madison Avenue. In the later 1860s, the political boss William M. Tweed used Tammany Hall to gain control of the city and allegedly loot it of millions of dollars. By 1871, *Tammany* or *Tammany Hall* had become a term for a group seeking control of a city through corruption or bossism—a far cry from the naively patriotic organization that gave it birth. Tammany continued to be a power in New York City politics until a reform movement ended its power in the 1960s.

New York's Chautauqua Lake, with an Indian name of uncertain origin, furnished English with a more positive loanword. From the town named for the lake comes the word *chautauqua* (1873), referring to an assembly or traveling institution that combines education with entertainment. Theodore Roosevelt called the original Chautauqua Institution "the most American thing in America."²³ The Chautauqua Literary and Scientific Circle, established in 1878, is reputed to be the world's first book club. A summer festival still held at Chautauqua has attracted some of the nation's most distinguished writers, artists, and thinkers. *Chautauqua muskellunge,* a linguistically related term, refers to a variety of game fish found chiefly in the Ohio and St. Lawrence river drainages.

A touchstone of social sophistication, the *tuxedo* was named after a country club in Tuxedo Park, New York. This town's Algonquian name probably means "round-foot-he-has," that is, "wolf."[24] "The low-roll, silk-faced sack, variously called the 'Cowes' coat, the 'Tuxedo' coat, and the Dress Sack, is undoubtedly popular," advised the *Sartorial Art Journal* in 1889.[25] A *tuxedo sofa* is an upholstered sofa with slightly curved arms and back.

The *Manhattan,* a cocktail made of vermouth and whiskey, became another mark of sophistication by 1890. It was named after the city, in turn bearing the name of an Indian tribe that once inhabited the New York City area; the name is from Proto-Algonquian *menahanwi* (unattested), "isolated thing in water," or "island."

Meanwhile, the northern New England states, less urban, furnished some interesting new loanwords for objects from natural history. Among them is *Sebago salmon* (1883), a landlocked salmon named after Sebago Lake in Maine, with an Abenaki name meaning "big lake."[26] Another is *monadnock* (1893), a rocky mass or mountain that has survived erosion to stand isolated on a plain—named after New Hampshire's Mount Monadnock, from a southern New England Algonquian name meaning "isolated mountain." (Note the apparent relationship with *Manhattan.*)

Compared with borrowings earlier in the century, *Canada* occurs much less often in late-nineteenth-century loan terms. "This was an interesting botanical locality [near the Penobscot River]," wrote Thoreau in a piece published in 1858, "for one coming from the South to commence with; for many plants which are rather rare, and one or two which are not found at all, in the eastern part of Massachusetts, grew abundantly between the rails,—as Labrador tea, Kalmia glauca, Canada blueberry (which was still in fruit, and a second time in bloom)."²⁷ *Canada lyme grass* occurs by 1894 and *Canadian hemlock* by 1897.

Among the new eastern and western loan terms employing already familiar Indian loanwords are several including *squaw: squaw vine* (1850), *squawberry* (1852), *squaw huckleberry* (1857), *squaw winter,* a brief period of wintry weather in autumn (1861), *squaw dance,* one in which women choose their partners (1864), *squaw man,* a white man married to an Indian woman (1866), and *squawfish* (1881). It is noteworthy that the word *squaw,* today often regarded as disparaging, was being applied to Indians for whom this Algonquian word was not native.

Throughout this period of cultural ferment, western Indians found themselves increasingly hemmed in. The defeat of Sitting Bull in 1881 and Geronimo in 1886 signaled the end of effective Indian resistance to white domination. But white settlers were the true victors, rather than the thinly spread U.S. troops. Flocking westward, the settlers preempted resources that supported traditional Indian life—grasslands, forest, and game animals. Then, in 1885, professional hunters finished off the last great herd of buffalo, a mainstay of Plains Indian economics and culture.²⁸

Simultaneously, the U.S. government was formalizing Indian defeats by reducing the last Indian landholdings to enclaves in the vast domain over which they once held sway. The government's reservation system was intended both to contain and to "civilize" the Indians. By the mid-1880s, about a quarter of a million Indians lived on 187 reservations. Indian Bureau agents administered these units and distributed government aid to the inhabitants, often pilfering much of it for their own advantage.

What did the government mean by its policy of introducing civilization? Indians were supposed to farm or practice crafts rather than hunt. They were supposed to look to the government for guidance rather than to their chiefs. They were supposed to exchange their ancestral ceremonies and religion for white customs and faith. The government wanted the Indians to act, think, and be like whites. This policy, repugnant though it may now look, was endorsed by sincere friends of the Indians among eastern whites. They saw no future for Indians in trying to follow a traditional way of life against overwhelming white pressure. Only adaptation to white civilization could save the Indians, argued these well-meaning idealists.

A main target of the Indian Bureau agents was the Indian languages. After the Civil War, Congress had authorized the establishment of an Indian Peace Commission. "In the difference of language to-day," that influential body said, "lies two-thirds of our trouble." It called for schools in which Indian children could learn English to replace "their barbarous dialects."[29] The commission felt, in short, that the adoption of English was the key to breaking down tribal cultures and thus assimilating the Indians into U.S. society.

In 1888, Indian Commissioner J. D. C. Atkins moved briskly to achieve this goal. He ordered that the entire curriculum of Indian schools be conducted in English, with a ban on Indian vernacular. When the administrators of Indian church schools protested, he granted an exception only for oral instruction in morals and religion. Even to some advocating the "civilizing" of Indians, this seemed too harsh. Atkins replied that forcing Indians to give up their native languages was no more cruel than making them give up the scalping knife and tomahawk.[30]

The late nineteenth century marked a fateful turning point in Indian culture and white-Indian relations. A last desperate attempt of western Indians to unite in a mystical religious movement, the Ghost Dance, failed with the massacre at Wounded Knee in 1890. Indian morale plummeted. By 1900, the U.S. Indian population had dropped to its lowest point in recorded history—137,000, according to the Census

Bureau. At about the same time, effective discourse between Indians and whites almost vanished.

Indians began to appear before the American public primarily as stereotypes, like the cigar-store Indians that had become common in city streets. The Kickapoo medicine shows, already noted, turned traditional Indian herbal lore into ballyhoo. In 1883, "Buffalo Bill" Cody founded his Wild West show, which toured the United States and Europe. This extravaganza offered mock battles with Indians, spectacular displays of sharpshooting, and feats of horsemanship. Cody recruited real Indians for his shows, with the great Sitting Bull as a star attraction for a while. But the acts bore little relationship to Indian life.

Friends of the Indian deplored such travesties. The commissioner of Indian affairs protested in 1889 that Wild West shows corrupted Indian participants and stirred up unrest on reservations. Nevertheless, performances continued well into the twentieth century. These shows, along with pulp western novels, also introduced in the 1880s, served as substitutes for contact with real Indian culture.

Meanwhile, verbal borrowing from the Indians peaked during the same period. Approximately 200 new datable and still-current Indian loanwords and loan terms entered the English language during the second half of the nineteenth century—a record number for a half-century period. "Our changed conditions and the spread of our people far to the south and far to the west," wrote Mark Twain in 1878, "have made many alterations in our pronunciation, and have introduced new words among us and changed the meanings of many old ones."[31] He referred, of course, to Spanish influence, among others, but the Indian influence was second to none.

The Indian contribution to English parallels the tragic but interculturally fruitful collision between two quite different peoples. Despite the Indian wars, whites and Indians had been trading, negotiating, hunting, and conversing with each other. They encountered each other constantly both in friendly and in warlike relationships. Utley has described the frontier not as a line along which whites advanced their civilization but as "zones of ethnic interaction."[32] When most of the Indians had been confined to reservations and subjected to a systematic campaign of "civilization," that interaction all but disappeared.

LOANWORDS AND LOAN TERMS FROM THE SECOND HALF OF THE NINETEENTH CENTURY

1850–1859

abalone 1850	zebra opossum 1855
Allegheny vine 1850	campoody 1856
mahala 1850	high-muck-a-muck 1856
Missouri currant 1850	saguaro (or sahuaro) 1856
mooseflower 1850	tucket 1856
squaw vine 1850	caribou moss 1857
allocochick 1851	catawba (grape) 1857
Chinook salmon 1851	squaw huckleberry 1857
chumpa 1851	wahoo (Dakota) 1857
lunge (longe) 1851	Arkansas goldfinch 1858
maypop 1851	Canada blueberry 1858
Oregon grape 1851	Gila woodpecker 1858
Gila trout 1852	Missouri skylark 1858
husky (dog) 1852	papoose board 1858
squawberry 1852	pocan 1858
wickiup 1852	Saratoga trunk 1858
Texas (structure on river-boat) 1853	Texas millet 1858
upland moccasin 1853	corn pone 1859
woodland caribou 1853	piki 1859
honk 1854	raccoon fox 1859

1860–1869

Chinook (wind) 1860
chuck (inlet) 1860
midewiwin 1860
Oregon robin 1860
possum haw 1860
moosemise 1861
musquaw 1861
potlatch (n.) 1861
pride of Ohio 1861
squaw winter 1861
tyee salmon 1863
marrow squash 1864
squaw dance 1864
pogonip 1865

squaw man 1866
Texas fever tick 1866
raccoonberry 1867
squash beetle 1867
Hubbard squash 1868
moose tick 1868
raccoon dog 1868
Arkansas stone 1869
chuckwalla 1869
coho 1869
coon oyster 1869
Oregon ash 1869
sockeye salmon 1869

1870–1879

Arkansas kingbird 1870
Mississippian (geol.) 1870
hogan 1871
kiva 1871
Susquehanna salmon 1871
Oregon cedar 1872
punky 1872
salt-marsh terrapin 1872
chautauqua 1873
Chesapeake Bay retriever
    1873
cocashweed 1873
Erian (geol.) 1873
kachina 1873
skookum-house 1873

totemistic 1873
Oregon alder 1874
unakite 1874
Canadianism 1875
kokanee 1875
pac or pack 1875
Appalachian tea 1876
Dakota (geol.) 1876
Keweenawan (geol.) 1876
painted terrapin 1876
red-bellied terrapin 1876
Saratoga chip(s) 1876
skunk bear 1876
Washoe process 1876
cui-ui 1877

1870–1879 (continued)

diamondback terrapin 1877
Gila monster 1877
hominy grits 1877
hoochinoo 1877
sacalait 1877
tiswin (or tizwin) 1877

toboganner 1878
wokas 1878
cottonmouth moccasin
   1879
Sitka spruce 1879
totem pole 1879

1880–1889

Mohawk (skating) 1880
logan 1881
poke salad 1881
squawfish 1881
totemist 1881
haddo 1882
striped skunk 1882
Texas bluegrass 1882
geoduck 1883
oquassa (fish) 1883
paho 1883
punkwood 1883
Sebago salmon 1883
winninish (winnonish)
   1883
beshow 1884
chinquapin perch 1884
hickory elm 1884
hickory pine 1884
Hohokam (culture) 1884
mattowacca 1884
Menominee whitefish 1884
Michigan grayling 1884

Oregon crab apple 1884
possum oak 1884
quoddy 1884
Sitka cypress 1884
skunk porpoise 1884
toboggan slide 1884
Wyandot(te) (fowl) 1884
mugwumpery 1885
mugwumpian 1885
tupelo gum 1885
zunyite 1885
Keewatin (geol.) 1886
mugwumpism 1886
quisutsch 1886
Manitoba maple 1887
squaw hitch 1887
Virginia poke 1887
sieva bean 1888
uintaite 1888
death camas 1889
mugwump (v.) 1889
tegua 1889
tuxedo 1889

1890–1899

Algonkian (geol.) 1890
koshare 1890
Manhattan cocktail 1890
moosecall 1890
skunkery 1890
Massachusetts ballot 1891
sipapu 1891
squash borer 1891
Uto-Aztecan 1891
choctaw (skating) 1892
missey-moosey 1892
Nootka cypress 1892
taconite 1892
Arizona ruby 1893
canader (canoe) 1893
Chinook licorice 1893
Conestoga (brogan) 1893
coonroot 1893
hickory poplar 1893
monadnock 1893
Shasta daisy 1893
stogy or stogie (cigar) 1893
Canada lyme grass 1894
Iowan (geol.) 1894

Kansan (geol.) 1894
muskie or musky 1894
skunk spruce 1894
Wisconsin (geol.) 1894
chebog 1895
poke milkweed 1895
pone (lump) 1895
bogan 1896
Canada pea 1896
Illinoian (geol.) 1896
Kamloops trout 1896
Arizona pine 1897
Canadian hemlock 1897
cheechako 1897
hard-bark hickory 1897
hickory oak 1897
hooch 1897
king nut hickory 1897
Klondike (source of wealth)
    1897
Shasta cypress 1897
Shasta red fir 1897
skunky 1897
muskrat weed 1897–98

CHAPTER ELEVEN

Indianisms in Current English

"THE GROUND ON WHICH WE STAND IS SACRED ground. It is the dust and blood of our ancestors. On these plains the *Great White Father* at Washington sent his soldiers armed with *long knives* and rifles to slay the Indian. Many of them sleep on yonder hill where Pahaska—*White Chief of the Long Hair*—so bravely fought and fell," declaimed Chief Plenty Coups of the Crow Nation in 1909 at Little Bighorn council grounds, Montana.[1]

Plenty Coups spoke before what was expected to be the last great Indian council. The U.S. Indian population was believed to be plummeting. And, in the opinion of the nation's most prominent chiefs assembled in the council, Indian culture itself was on the brink of disappearing. Those sentiments account for Plenty Coups' elegiac tone and the perhaps self-conscious Indian cast of his comments.

"A few more passing *suns* will see us here no more," Plenty Coups went on, "and our dust and bones will mingle with these same prairies. I see as in a vision the dying spark of our *council fires,* the ashes cold and white. I see no longer the curling smoke rising from our *lodge poles.* I hear no longer the songs of the women as they prepare the meal. The antelope have gone; the *buffalo wallows* are empty. Only the wail of the coyote is heard. The white man's *medicine* is stronger than ours; his *iron horse* rushes over the buffalo trail. He talks to us through his *whispering spirit.*"[2]

The terms italicized heighten the uniquely Indian flavor of Plenty Coups' speech. Translations of the less obvious expressions follow:

> *long knives* = swords
> *White Chief of the Long Hair* = Gen. George A. Custer
> *suns* = days or years
> *council fires* = ceremonial fires kept burning during a council
> *medicine* = magical power
> *whispering spirit* = telegraph or telephone

Such terms can be classified as *Indianisms,* English words or phrases that translate expressions in Indian languages. In this chapter, the term will be extended to include English words or phrases specifically related to the Indians. The Indianisms presented here are a significant contribution to English, and their history reflects Indian-white cultural relations as much as loanwords and loan terms adopted directly from Indian languages.

Most Indianisms coined in the early seventeenth century pertain to corn (maize), among the most historically American of plants. First cultivated in Mexico at least seven thousand years ago, corn spread from its point of origin to much of North and South America. High civilizations such as the Aztecs and smaller societies such as the New England woodland Indians cherished this grain as a staple and often literally as a gift of the gods. Corn enabled Indians to enjoy a reliable food supply with leisure for pursuits beyond the gathering of food.

The early European colonists found corn no less vital to their well-being. Jamestown settlers at first made the mistake of trying to grow European wheat in their New World environment. When that crop failed, only the purchase of corn from Powhatan's Indians saved the settlers from starvation.

The Pilgrims fed themselves initially with corn they found in caches left by local Indians. This discovery tided the New Englanders through their sickness-ridden first winter. Subsequently the Pilgrims harvested enough corn from their own first planting of twenty acres to provide each person with two pounds of cornmeal every day. (The Pilgrims, like the typical English farmers many had been, ate heartily when they could.) Like the Jamestown settlers, the Pilgrims would have perished without corn.

Yet corn had been known to Europeans since Columbus introduced it to them in the later 1400s. He had also brought back with him the Taino (Arawakan) word *maize* for the plant. This word entered the English vocabulary during the sixteenth century (see chapter 5). But settlers preferred to use the more familiar, and perhaps comforting, Old English word for cereal grains in general, *corn*. The settlers commonly added *Indian* to qualify terms relating to this particular kind of grain.

The number of early Indianisms referring to corn highlights its crucial importance to the settlers. *Indian meal* (cornmeal) was noted in 1609 and *Indian corn* itself in 1617. *Indian maize,* though redundant, followed in 1637. The word *Indian* had acquired the secondary meaning of Indian corn by 1639, since *Indian harvest* by then meant a harvest of that crop. By 1654, corn bread was known as *Indian bread.* "The want of English graine . . . proved a sore affliction to some stomacks, who could not live upon Indian Bread," lamented Edward Johnson in *Wonder-working Providence of Sion's Saviour in New England.*[3]

Indian pudding did not apparently appear in print until 1722. That classic New England dessert made of cornmeal, milk, sugar, butter, molasses, and spices was not named after the Indians but after the Indian corn that is its main ingredient. Most of the ingredients, in fact, did not even originate with the Indians.

Several Indianisms from the era show an appreciation of other aspects of Indian culture. *Longhouse,* denoting a communal Indian dwelling often over one hundred feet long, made its appearance in printed English by 1643. *Indian doctor* for medicine man was recorded in 1670. *Calumet,* a French word designating the ornamental ceremonial pipe typically smoked on religious or state occasions, was adopted into English by 1665.

The few other Indianisms from the latter seventeenth century generally reflect a harrowing period of uprisings and burnt villages. King Philip's War (1675–76) inflicted the greatest amount of damage on New England of all the wars in that region's history, destroying all or most of nearly fifty towns. Dread of renewed Indian attacks lay behind negotiations between a Massachusetts major and a Mohawk chief in 1680 to keep Mohawk war parties west of the Hudson River. We learn how "meeting wth ye Sachem the[y] came to an agreem+ and buried two axes in ye Ground; one for English and another for y^mselves: which ceremony to them is more significant than all Articles of Peace the Hatchet being a principal weapon wth y^m."4 And bitterness against King Philip's warriors persisted well after the war. *Redskin* first appeared, in a derogatory context, in 1699. "Ye first Meetinge House was solid mayde to withstande ye wicked onsaults of ye Red Skins."5

During the eighteenth century, expressions relating to Indian culture continued to filter into English as whites penetrated more deeply into the wilderness. For example, twenty-one-year-old Virginia major George Washington employed the term *council fire*—occurring in Plenty Coups' speech—while on a mission in 1753 to observe French maneuvers near Lake Erie. The youthful officer noted in his diary, "[A Seneca chief] told me that at this Place a Council Fire was kindled, where all their Business with these People was to be transacted."6

But the majority of Indianisms in this period, apart from those incorporating the word *Indian,* reflect continuing conflict between two very different cultures. The eighteenth century was comparatively barren of Indian loanwords and loan terms as well, at least partly because of bad relations between whites and Indians. Cultural misunderstandings certainly did much to inflame white-Indian relations. It would be apparent from Indianisms alone that the two peoples had difficulty understanding basic customs of each other. This mutual ignorance led to insults that became embedded in the English vocabulary.

The Indians, for example, had a concept of gift-giving quite different from that of the whites. In 1764, the expression *Indian gift* appeared in a history of Massachusetts. "An Indian gift is a proverbial expression, signifying a present for which an equivalent return is expected."[7] Later the term was corrupted to mean, more commonly, a gift that is taken back.

But Indians regarded the bestowing of gifts as a means of establishing and maintaining a friendly relationship, one that called for reciprocal gifts. Whites found this significance hard to understand, brought up as they were on the principle that giving is more blessed than receiving. The Indian cultural expectation of a return for a gift ironically fed the common white perception of Indians as guileful.

Indians, on the other hand, found some white customs just as baffling. For example, James Adair, in his 1775 *History of the American Indians,* first noted the Indian use of *forked tongue* to characterize the speech of lawyers in Anglo-Saxon courts. According to Adair, the Indians saw the lawyers as "hired speakers, who use their squinteyes and forked tongues like the chieftains of the snakes (meaning rattlesnakes) which destroy harmless creatures."[8] This term, of course, came to be used more broadly to express an Indian view of whites as deceitful.

Indians fought on behalf of both the English and the French

during more than seventy years of warfare ending in 1763, then on both sides of the American Revolution. Throughout, clashes between settlers and Indians heightened a white view of Indians as bloodthirsty. *Red man* in 1725 and *half-breed* in 1760 emphasized the racial distinction between whites and Indians. Indianisms beginning with *war* convey the terror whites felt at Indian hostilities. Thus *war dance* occurred in 1711. "The Baron de Graffenried . . . was still alive but supposed only reserved for a more solemn execution, to be tomahawked and tortured at their first publick War Dances."9 *War whoop* followed by 1739.

The latter half of the eighteenth century saw a still-greater influx of martial Indianisms: *warpath* (1755), *war song* (1757), *war hatchet* (1760), *war pole* (1775), *war club* (1776), and *war post* (1779). The flavor of these terms can be judged from a contemporary passage in Adair: "When the leader begins to beat up for volunteers, he goes three times round his dark winter-house, contrary to the course of the sun, sounding the war-whoop, singing the war-song, and beating the drum." Adair noted the grim return to the *war pole* the day after a successful raid, when warriors went to their leader's dwelling and circled "his red-painted war-pole, till they have determined concerning the fate of the prisoners."10 The war pole received a slash for each scalp taken or was used to display the scalps.

Despite the hard edge of so many eighteenth-century Indianisms, one of the gentlest originated at this time. *Indian summer* was mentioned by J. Hector St. John Crèvecoeur in 1778. "A severe frost succeeds [the autumn rains] which prepares it [the earth] to receive the voluminous coat of snow which is soon to follow; though it is often preceded by a short interval of smoke and mildness, called the Indian Summer."11 This period of mild weather in late autumn or early winter was known in Europe by such names as St. Martin's Day, All-hallow summer, or Old Wives' summer.

Several theories seek to explain the substitution of *Indian summer* in U.S. usage. In 1832, the *Boston Transcript* suggested that the name arose because this time of year occurs when "Indians break up their village communities, and go to the interior to prepare for their winter hunting."[12] Some people more romantically derive the name from the similarity of the season's haze to the smoke from Indian fires. Others offer the explanation that Indians forewarned whites about the short-lived respite before winter or suggest simply that Indian summer is most noticeable in regions once inhabited by Indians.

Indian summer is a fleeting—and haunting—time of the year. Whatever its origins, the expression probably derives its staying power from a common nineteenth-century and early-twentieth-century impression of Indians as a dwindling people, transient as the interlude named after them.

Among President Thomas Jefferson's reasons for sponsoring the Lewis and Clark Expedition of 1804–6 was his wish to replace mere impressions of the far-West Indians with more objective data. He directed the expedition not only to explore the vast region opening up to the United States but also to communicate with the Indians inhabiting it. The expedition encountered some of the continent's most prominent tribes—among them the Blackfeet, Mandan, Nez Percé, Shoshone, and Sioux tribes. Despite hardships and some hostility from Indians, members of the expedition brought back a wealth of Indian artifacts and descriptions of Indian customs and languages.

The expedition journals include the Indianism *medicine* to describe one of the most subtle Indian concepts. This hitherto unusual specialized term covers a wide range of activities, from medical care to feats of magic. It commonly implies supernatural power. How did *medicine* come to acquire this special sense? The *Oxford English Dictionary* theorizes that native peoples "usually regard the operation of medicines as due to what we should call magic." Outsiders, the *OED* suggests, would often hear the words for magic when applied to medicine in the ordinary sense. *Medicine* then would be regarded in the primary sense of a term for magic in general.

The artist George Catlin plausibly argued that the term is French in origin. "These Indian doctors," he wrote in 1867, "were called by the Frenchmen, who were the first traders on the frontiers, '*Médecins*,' the French word for physicians; and by a subsequent frontier population, '*Medicine Men*'; and all mysteries, '*Medicine*,' as synonymous with mystery."[13]

In 1805, the Lewis and Clark journals indicated the mysteriousness of this word. "It is probable that the large river just above those great falls . . . has taken its name *Medicine River* from this unaccountable rumbling sound, which like all unaccountable things with the Indians of the Missouri is called *Medicine*." A shamanistic aspect of the word appeared in 1805 in *medicine dance*. "A Buffalo Dance (or Medeson) for 3 nights passed in the 1st Village, a curious Custom. . . . All this is to cause the buffalow to Come near So that they may Kill them."[14]

Essential equipment for a *medicine man*, recorded earlier in 1801, included the contents of a *medicine bag*, which could contain some odd items, such as those described by Lewis and Clark in 1805. "The Chief then directed his wife to hand him his medison bag which he opened and showed us 14 fingers . . . of his enemies which he had taken in war."[15] The contents of such bags varied according to regions, however, and more often included herbs, quartz crystals, cups, rattles, wands, and other objects of magical significance. A medicine man or *medicine woman* (1834) might practice the art in a *medicine lodge* (1808).

Further occurrences of *medicine* were numerous throughout the nineteenth century. A *medicine iron* (1846) was a gun. A *medicine dog* (1846) was a horse. A *medicine buffalo* (1848) was an ox. The *medicine line* (1910) was the U.S.-Canada border. This mystery-evoking Indianism also occurs in a number of place-names such as Medicine Bow, Wyoming; Medicine Lake, Montana; Medicine Lodge, Kansas; Medicine Mound, Texas; and Medicine Park, Oklahoma.

At the same time, new martial Indianisms reflected the many conflicts that broke out as whites spread through Indian territories. The term *brave* to designate an Indian warrior was noted in 1819. "Their warriors are called braves, to which honour no one can arrive, without having previously plundered or stolen from the enemy."[16] This use of *brave* came directly from French *brave,* implying courage with perhaps a lingering hint of the word's probable Latin origin in *barbarus,* barbarous.

And specific *war* phrases continued to enter English. *War feast* in the sense of a ceremonial consumption of part of slain enemies appeared by 1809. The use of feathers from the golden eagle, or *war eagle,* was cited in 1817. "These offerings are propitiatory, either for success in war or in hunting, and consist of various articles, of which the feathers of the war eagle are in greatest estimation."[17] Some tribes held that these feathers lacked medicine if a wearer had not captured the eagle (from a blind) and killed it with his bare hands. John Charles Frémont described in 1845 the impressive sight of *warbonnets* made with feathers—"Indians . . . with the long red streamers of their war bonnets reaching nearly to the ground."[18] James Fenimore Cooper put the Indianisms *war paint* and *scalplock* into circulation, if he did not originate them, in *The Last of the Mohicans* in 1826.

During the nineteenth century, legends about the Indian grew. It became hard to distinguish between expressions actually translated from Indian languages and those that authors put into the mouths of stage Indians. When talking with whites, some Indians almost certainly used these artificial Indianisms to conform to stereotype.

Paleface, for example, may be a white coinage. One of its earliest—and non-Indian—citations was G. A. McCall's *Letters from Frontiers* (1822). "[At a masquerade ball, a man dressed as] an Indian chief . . . thus accosted him,—'Ah, Paleface! what brings you here?'"[19] Cooper either coined or gave currency to *happy hunting ground,* for the afterlife. "A young man has gone to the happy hunting grounds."[20] The next recorder of this expression, in 1836, was another major author, Washington Irving—adding to its literary aura.

The true provenance of the noun or quasi-adjective *heap,* meaning "plenty" or "a lot," is similarly in question. In his journals in 1832, Irving quoted an Indian guide as saying, "'Look at these Delawares,' say the Osages, 'dey got short legs—no can run—must stand and fight a great heap.'" By 1871, Mark Twain, on a trip in the West, ridiculed the expression. "Mph! stove heap gone!" he quoted an Indian saying in camp. "I will explain that 'heap' is 'Injun-English' for 'very much,'" Twain added. "The reader will perceive the exhaustive expressiveness of it in the present instance." The linguist Beverly Olson Flanigan cited *heap* in this sense as a likely example of American Indian Pidgin English.[21]

Widely accepted Indianisms sprang from this jargon. "With the Anglo-Saxon settler, trapper, or scout, [the Indian] spoke a much reduced jargon sometimes based on Indian vocabulary and structure, such as the Chinook jargon, but more often based on English structure," noted another linguist. "This language, stripped of inflections and much of its power and subtlety, became the language of communication when Indian and Englishman met, although neither spoke it elsewhere. It was a pidgin."[22]

A common example of such pidgin may be the salutation *How!* An early reference to it came from the travel writer

John Bradbury in 1817. "We were interrupted by one of the chiefs crying 'How,' signifying amongst the Indians 'Come on,' or 'let us begin.'" Some authorities believe the expression is originally Sioux; others say it is of uncertain origin. Flanigan has suggested that *How!* probably represents an abbreviated form of the white man's own "How do you do?" or "How do ye?" Whatever its source, *How!* arguably became the most stereotypical, and hackneyed, Indian expression in the nineteenth century.[23]

From the East came a curious though not so widespread pidgin-based Indianism noted by that student of the Indian, Henry David Thoreau. On an excursion into Maine in 1846, he referred to the midges, or *no-see-ums* (he used the spelling *no-see-ems*), that joined other insects to make travel in the woods almost impossible at the wrong time of the year. On another trip to Maine in 1857, he resumed his complaint with a pun on the insect's Latin name, which he gives. "Here . . . I was molested by the little midge called the No-see-em (Simulium nocivum, the latter word is not the Latin for no-see-em), especially over the sand at the water's edge, for it is a kind of sand-fly."[24]

An enduring Indianism of much broader application, one that recalls the tradition of white-Indian trading, is *buck*— slang for one dollar. This word is shortened from *buckskin,* which was long the unit of exchange between Indians and whites. The *OED* recorded *buck* in the sense of dollar by 1856. But a reference, in John Heckewelder's early-nineteenth-century book on the Indians, to an itinerant preacher's sales pitch for a religious book suggests that the actual monetary value of a buck may have been fixed by 1818. According to Heckewelder, the preacher gave the book's price as "only one buck-skin or two doe-skins a piece," which, Heckewelder added in a footnote, was "of the value of one dollar."[25]

With the twentieth century, the borrowing of Indianisms precipitously declined—just as did the absorption into English of both Eskimo-Aleut and Indian words. Almost surely, the same principle was at work. There was no longer enough contact between the Indians and the prevailing white culture to promote intercultural exchanges on the scale of the borrowings of the nineteenth century.

One relatively new Indianism, however, reflects the increasing white interest in Indian religions. Significantly, the recorder was an anthropologist seeking to capture the subtleties of Indian culture that still eluded whites after centuries of contact. In 1922, Ruth Benedict examined one of the various traditions among many Indian groups across the country of seeking spiritual guidance through a solitary vigil—the *vision quest*. "Three patterns of wide distribution are sometimes taken to characterize the vision quest of the Plains: (1) The infliction of self-torture; (2) the lack of a laity-shamanistic distinction; (3) the attaining of a guardian spirit," she wrote.[26] Today the vision quest is practiced not only by Indians following their own traditions but also by many whites drawn to the Native American outlook.

And the mythic quality of the Indian in American life persists in recent idiom. In 1989, *Newsweek* magazine reported that commercial pilots had a nickname for small, private airplanes flying in congested areas. The pilots called them *Indians*.[27]

ADDITIONAL INDIANISMS

bannerstone 1881—
perforated stone of uncertain use
big chief 1861
big knife 1774—settler
blanket Indian 1859—
Indian who retains or resumes tribal costume or customs

breech cloth 1793
burden strap 1879
council
coup 1832—the striking or touching of an enemy in warfare
coupstick 1876—stick used for coup
firewater 1757

Ghost Dance 1890—cult and dance of Plains Indians

Great Father 1796—U.S. president

Great Spirit 1703—chief deity

Great White Father 1909—U.S. president

Honest Injun 1892—honestly

long knife 1750—settler

moon 1665—month

parfleche 1827—rawhide or bag made of it

peace belt 1758—strand of wampum symbolizing a desire for peace

peace pipe 1760

pipestone 1761—stone used for tobacco pipes

Praying Indian 1652 member of Massachusetts Christian Indians living in six villages

reservation 1782

scalp dance 1791

scalp yell 1792

sleep (n.) 1670—unit of measurement indicating number of nights a journey would take

smoke signal 1873

stick-dice 1903—Indian game

Sun Dance 1849—rite of Plains Indians

sweat lodge 1848

talking leaves—book or newspaper

thunderbird 1875

travois 1847—sledge consisting of two poles joined together and dragged by a horse

Ugh!—grunt of assent

CHAPTER TWELVE

The Twentieth Century and Beyond

THE LOUISIANA PURCHASE EXPOSITION OF 1904 focused world attention on St. Louis. Fifteen vast exhibition halls, among other buildings, occupied more than twelve hundred acres of manicured grounds in the host city, celebrating the hundredth anniversary of the purchase. Nations around the world sent paintings and sculptures, examples of advanced technology, and representatives to explain the fine points of their exhibits. Not omitted were picturesque examples of culture in its early stages, gathered in a "Congress of Races" by W. J. McGee, chairman of the Smithsonian Institution's department of anthropology. Along with artifacts, McGee arranged living groups of peoples classified as primitive: Ainus from Japan, Pygmies from Africa, natives from Patagonia—and representatives of several North American Indian groups including Sioux, Arapaho, and Oneida peoples.

The outdoor section of the exhibit displayed these peoples on a hillside, with each demonstrating native skills. At the top of the hill was a two-story U.S. government Indian school with students practicing trades such as cooking and blacksmithing. To the majority of the three million visitors who filed past the exhibit, these earnest Indians may have seemed close to the government's official goal for them: learning to participate in American civilization.

Yet the exhibit, as the historian Frederick E. Hoxie has

observed, marked a diminution in the government's Indian program. It was certainly a comedown from the Philadelphia Centennial Exposition of 1876, in which an optimistic Indian exhibit seemed to point to unlimited progress. "Positioned in the center of a bizarre anthropological curio shop," said Hoxie of the Indians in St. Louis, "and described as an element of the 'white man's burden,' the tribesmen seemed best suited for a life of manual labor. In 1876, journalists had dwelt on the Indian's future; a visitor to the Indian exhibit in St. Louis called it 'The Last Race Rally of the Indians.'"[1]

Speeches given by Plenty Coups, cited in the previous chapter, and other chiefs at the "Last Great Council" of 1909 indicate that many Indians too were developing a pessimistic view of their status. Chief Two Moons of the Cheyennes spoke of his happiness at attending the council "because our old chiefs are fast dying away, and our old Indian customs soon will pass out of sight." Mountain Chief of the Blackfeet declared that the council "shows that the Government is greater than the Indian." Chief White Horse of the Southern Yankton Sioux wistfully confessed to fellow chiefs that his wish was "that the Indians will come to be like the white people, and be able to invent things, but the thought comes to me that this will be impossible."[2]

Did Indian demoralization play a part in the decline of word borrowing? In the adoption of Indian words into English, 1910 stands as a watershed—an end to the frequent linguistic borrowing that prevailed in the nineteenth century and into the early twentieth century. The overall number of Indian loanwords and loan terms entering English remained high between 1900 and 1909 but then diminished. Further, the number of loanwords coming *directly* from Indian languages (as distinguished from secondary terms often taken from Indian-derived place-names) was greater in that earlier decade than in any of the six decades afterward.

But Indian words continued entering English at least throughout the first three-quarters of this century, if at a slower pace. Although Indians had faded as a threat and in many cases even as a consideration in a rapidly developing United States, they still represented the wilderness and unspoiled past of North America. The Boy Scouts of America, incorporated in 1910, and other popular youth organizations beginning around the same time reaffirmed the tradition of Indians as resourceful masters of woodcraft. Anyone who has experienced the Indian-tinged ceremonies in scouting such as those of the Order of the Arrow, a Scout camping fraternity within the Boy Scouts, can testify to its emotional impact. The fire-lit sacred circle in the forest, the throbbing drums, and the ritual incorporating Indian words have left a permanent impression on young participants.

The rise of the movies as popular entertainment early in this century touched a much wider public. Indians on the silver screen often appeared as savages opposing the progress of civilization. But hundreds of movies also portrayed the American Indian as deeply involved with nature, often to the point of being doomed because of an inability to adapt to a changing environment. The "Noble Anachronism," as this kind of movie Indian has been dubbed, struck a deep chord in the audiences of an America steadily becoming more urban.[3]

Portrayals of the Indian as master (or child) of nature reinforced historical trends in the verbal borrowing of the twentieth century. About half the datable loans so far in this century pertain to nature and the outdoors. A number made their debut in publications such as *Outing* magazine and the book *Barn Doorways and Byways*.

Among these newer Indian loans is *moccasin telegraph,* the grapevine, recorded in *The Conquest of the Great Northwest* in 1908. "Word of the white woman ran before the advancing traders by 'moccasin telegraph.'"[4] *Squaw wood* was noted in

Outing magazine in 1914 as an expression for kindling wood or the dead branches easily gathered at the base of a tree. *Chum salmon* (1902) is yet another Chinook Jargon name for a kind of salmon (from Chinook Jargon *cam,* meaning mixed colors, spotted, striped)—the dog salmon, abundant in streams of the Pacific Coast.

The wilderness-haunting *Sasquatch* was named by the Salish Indians. This humanlike creature, also known as Bigfoot, supposedly stands about eight feet tall or more, is covered with hair, and has a fetid odor. It is extremely shy and avoids human contact so diligently that it has never been captured or distinctly photographed. *Maclean's Magazine* of Canada first published the name in 1929, observing that the Sasquatch was "rarely seen and seldom met."[5] But this apparent product of Indian lore enjoys fame, especially in Canada and the U.S. Northwest, with search parties going out year after year in quest of evidence for its existence.

Place-names of Indian origin additionally furnished many outdoors or sports-related terms to the English vocabulary in the twentieth century. The *Sunapee trout* (1900) is a brilliantly colored char of Sunapee Lake, New Hampshire. The *Tahoe trout* (1902) is a large cutthroat trout found in Lake Tahoe on the California-Nevada boundary and in the surrounding region. The *Pismo clam* (1913), a large clam widely used for food, was named after Pismo Beach, California. The name of *cuttyhunk* (1916), a kind of linen fishing line suitable for deep-sea sport fishing, came from Cuttyhunk Island, Massachusetts. The *Klamath weed* (1922) is a yellow-flowered St. John's-wort named after the Klamath River of California and Oregon. The *Adirondack chair* (1948) is a kind of wooden slant-back lawn chair named after New York State's Adirondack (Mountains) resort area, where it first became popular. The *Malibu board* (1962), a kind of surfboard, is named for Malibu Beach, California, a favorite location for surfing. (For etymologies, see glossary 1.)

Texas excels as the main single U.S. source of words arising from Indian-derived place-names. Among eight newer *Texas* words are *Texas leaguer* (1905), *Texas longhorn* (1908), and *Texas tower* (1954). *Tex-Mex* (1949) is especially significant as a description of the international blend of cultures that has developed along the Texas-Mexico border, including a spicy cuisine.

Indians continue to be trivialized in this century by stereotypes of ferocity on the one hand and by humorous references or associations on the other. The use of *Apache* to mean ruffian came from France, with a first publication as an English word in this sense in Britain's *Westminster Gazette* in 1902, which commented on "the leader of the band of roughs in Paris known as 'Apaches.'" *Apache dance,* in the sense of a violent duet dance of the Parisian underworld, was noted in English by 1914; the term was subsequently applied to more moderate versions of this dance.[6] More recently, the U.S. Apache helicopter gunship and Tomahawk cruise missile, aided by the Kiowa scout helicopter, played a devastating role in the Persian Gulf War of 1991.

Several Native American loans have been introduced in whimsical contexts. The poet M. C. Davies wrote in 1924 of the *Appaloosa,* a breed of rugged saddle horse with white rump: "They find death in a dramatic flare: Trying to ride the apaloochy mare."[7] This distinctive breed of horse received its name obscurely—perhaps after the Opelousa, a Louisiana tribe, though it is associated with the Nez Percé Indians and the Palouse River of the Northwest. The *Eskimo Pie,* a chocolate-covered ice cream bar with a smiling Eskimo child pictured on the wrapper—still to be found in supermarket freezers—was noted in 1928 but dates back to 1921. (See chapter 9 for background on the Indian etymology of *Eskimo.*) *Siwash,* originally referring to an Indian of the Northwest, won wider fame through the humorous writings of George Helgeson Fitch, whose *At Good Old Siwash*

(1911) and other fiction established *Siwash* as a jocular term for a provincial college.

Two major English writers who lived for years in the United States showed their sensitivity to this country's idioms by apparently introducing Native American words in their writing. In his *Songs from Books* (1912), Rudyard Kipling wrote, "Shaman, Ju-ju or Angekok, Minister, Muk-a-muk, Bonze."[8] Here he introduced into print Chinook Jargon *muckamuck* in the sense of eminent person (specifically, in this case, priest) and included *angakok,* the Eskimo term for shaman (see chapter 9). D. H. Lawrence, who spent several years in the Southwest, presented *squash blossom* in 1923, musing in *Birds, Beasts, Flowers:* "The fig, the horseshoe, the squash-blossom. Symbols."[9] The squash blossom is a distinctive southwestern Indian motif in art, as well as a Hopi woman's hairstyle with a large loop of hair over each ear.

Some borrowing from Indian languages, however, is apparent mainly to specialists in various fields. Dr. Don R. Egolf, the U.S. National Arboretum's shrub specialist, develops new breeds of shrubs that are sold commercially. Egolf chose American Indian tribal names for twenty-three new varieties of crape myrtles—including the Tuskegee, Apalachee, Comanche, Osage, Sioux, Yuma, Chippewa, Hopi, Pecos, Zuni, Natchez, and Shoshone. "I want something American that would be associated with the National Arboretum," he explained in 1987.[10]

It will have become apparent that, with extremely rare exceptions, the loans from Indian languages throughout history have been nouns. Albert Marckwardt, the authority on the history of English, believes that this limitation indicates "in a sense the most superficial type of borrowing." Yet he has also observed that some borrowed nouns have been transformed into verbs. He cites *caucus, powwow, tomahawk, hickory, skunk* (slang), *wigwam,* and *mugwump* (he might have added *siwash*)—with several of these verbal forms in more common use than others. Some of the Indian loans, he also noted, "show a strong tendency toward the attachment of derivative prefixes and suffixes." *Mugwump,* for example, has acquired suffixes leading to *mugwumpery, mugwumpian, mugwumpish,* and *mugwumpism.*[11]

Marckwardt finds that the versatility of the Indian loans is further increased by the readiness with which they have entered compound-word constructions. *Hickory* alone has lent itself to about thirty-two combinations and *raccoon* to about twenty-five combinations. This compounding, suggests Jack Weatherford, anthropologist and author of *Native Roots,* may have been stimulated by a similar practice in many Indian languages (see chapter 3).

Curiously, an exclusive or near-exclusive borrowing of nouns is paralleled in a reverse situation—the historical flow of Spanish loanwords into Nahuatl, the language of the Aztecs. James Lockhart, the authority on Nahuatl, has discovered three stages in the passage of Spanish loans into Nahuatl:

•During the first few decades after the conquest, Nahuatl-speakers borrowed proper names only.
•During the second stage (1540–50 to about 1640–50), the words the Nahuatl-speakers borrowed consisted of hundreds or even thousands of nouns, with virtually no verbs.
•During the current third stage, Nahuatl-speakers have borrowed verbs and speech particles as well as nouns, with a deep influence of Spanish idiom and grammar.[12]

Lockhart views the three-stage pattern of Nahuatl borrowing as associated with overall cultural change. "When one surveys the whole process," he wrote, "it is evident that the stages correspond to the increasing frequency and intensity of contact between Nahuas [Aztecs] and Spaniards. . . . Linguistic phenomena prove to be the most sensitive indicator the historical record contains of the extent, nature, and trajectory of contact between the two populations."[13] His findings are in keeping with the thesis of this book.

But the English borrowing of Native American words would seem to have been frozen at Lockhart's Stage 2—presumably because English-speakers did not fall under the political domination of Native Americans as Nahuatl-speakers did under the Spanish. That limitation, however, does not trivialize the Native American impact on the English language. Indian loans are indispensable to the English vocabulary. These words not only name uniquely American phenomena but also link the modern people of North America to the continent's most distant human past. The significance of Indian nouns, even excluding place-names, goes well beyond their numbers and part of speech.

Yet few of the nouns among the estimated fifteen to twenty thousand new words and usages currently enlarging the English vocabulary each year are of Indian origin.[14] Do circumstances in North America no longer call for new Indian loanwords? The answer to this question is complex, since the nation and the American Indian's status have passed through a series of dramatic and sometimes turbulent changes in this century. There are several salient reasons for diminished borrowing from Indian languages.

First, Indians have been the nation's most underprivileged minority. Reservation Indians have the lowest per-capita income and life expectancy of all minority groups. Alcoholism, suicide, and violent death are rampant among the most needy Indian groups. The first Americans, it has been said, are also the poorest.

Unsuccessful or insufficient government programs have much to do with this record of poverty and misery. One of the worst government mistakes was the Indian Allotment Act, introduced by Senator Henry L. Dawes of Massachusetts and passed by Congress in 1887. Most tribal Indians at that time had already been confined to reservations. The object of the Dawes Act was to parcel out among individual Indians the tribal lands held collectively according to Indian tradition. In this plan, the lands were to be divided among Indian families or individuals in parcels of 40 to 160 acres. Title to the parcels was to be assigned within twenty-five years to recipients judged "competent." The object was to develop personal initiative among Indians and to enable them to join white society as self-sufficient farmers and ranchers. Through inexperience at handling private property, however, thousands of Indians in fact sold their property to non-Indians. Indian landholdings went from more than 140 million acres in 1886 to less than 50 million acres at the ending of the plan in 1934. Other programs since then, some endorsed by Indian groups, have failed to solve the Indian's economic distress. The demoralizing poverty experienced by many Indians curtailed the expression—and possibly the transmission—of their culture.

Second, the attrition among Indian languages was noted in chapter 3. Many have disappeared, leaving no possibility of any new borrowing from their vocabularies. Even in tribes retaining ancestral languages, English has typically become the dominant language. Government schools long fostered the use of English as a way of assimilating Indians, and the need of many Indians to negotiate their way in white society led many to master English for practical reasons—often to the neglect of native languages. "As Indians learn English," noted the anthropologist William L. Leap, "and English becomes the language used for communication between Indians and whites, loanword incidence declines, and Indian-English type English varieties emerge—Indian Englishes rather than standard English becoming the primary form that the tribes learned and shared within their communities."[15]

A third factor behind diminished borrowing is that starting with Thomas Harriot, a primary reason for borrowing from Indian languages was to name plants, animals, and Indian artifacts or customs new to whites. But in time, such phenomena received names. "Most [English borrowings from American Indian languages] pertain to plants and animals native to North America," noted the linguist William Bright, "like *persimmon* or *skunk,* or to objects and institutions characteristic of American Indian culture, like *tepee* and *kachina.* By the end of the nineteenth century, since Anglo-Americans had expanded throughout the continent, English had pretty much borrowed all the terms of this kind that it had need for."[16]

Fourth, the change from a rural to an urban culture made traditional Indian cultures, and words, less relevant to the experiences of many Americans. "I think that the climax era of the nineteenth century [in the borrowing of Indian loanwords]," wrote Jack Weatherford, "probably came because the frontier between Indians and the settlers was the real focus of American life at that time. Now the focus has moved on to urban areas in this century, and consequently we borrow more words from urban subcultures."[17]

Finally, a reason related to the above is the condition of white-Indian communication—central for the borrowing of loanwords and loan terms. One who sees a loss in this respect is the Reverend Stanislaus Maudlin, OSB, executive director of the American Indian Culture Center at Blue Cloud Abbey in Marvin, South Dakota. In reply to a query on white-Indian relations in 1991, Father Maudlin wrote:

Communication, as I think of it, must be mutual. Even in my lifetime, I've seen a diminution of communication. The diminution has come about, I think, because the majority culture does not any longer need the minority.

If you do not need a person, or persons, you do not listen to him/her; you do not take on his or her feelings and expressions. What you have called cultural contact is lost.

Even fifty years ago, when I was a young priest on the Crow Creek Reservation, life together and interdependence were evident. The life of Indian and non-Indian was centered in the land. Food and fuel came directly from the earth. All living was procured by labor-intensive effort.

Then technology took over. Division began, and interdependence was not needed. People now depend more on machines than on each other. Here in South Dakota, after the Indian People asked for it, there had to be a special YEAR OF RECONCILIATION [1990]. It has not yet produced interdependence, but it has raised the consciousness of the majority to the presence of the minority.[18]

Powwows across the country are drawing many Indians together for an exchange of views and for cultural renewal. Non-Indians attending these gatherings can get a sense of the variety of Indian activities in the nation today. Cooking fry bread, booths stacked with crafts, demonstrations of traditional skills such as flint knapping, and performances in the dance circle offer a panorama of Indian cultures.

One remarkable outgrowth of the powwows beginning in 1987 is the American Indian Dance Theatre, with representatives from some twenty tribes. Members perform ceremonial and seasonal dances that give an overview of the essential role that dance plays in Indian cultures. Accompanying the dances are players of traditional musical instruments made from hollowed logs, clay pots, gourds, deer hooves, shells, bone, and hide. The company has gone on tours across the United States, Europe, North Africa, and the Middle East, and it has appeared on U.S. public television.[19]

The ethnomusicologist David P. McAllester, a pioneer in developing university programs for the study of American Indian music and dance, regards the current expressions of these arts as holding promise for greater Indian-white verbal communication. "There are lots of native teachers about with devoted students," he said in 1991, "and an increasing number of native writers being read by wide audiences. There are singers publishing tapes with native words written and translated in the casette notes. I'm studying R. Carlos Nakai, Navajo-Ute flute player and composer of New Age music. He has an international audience (eighteen concerts in Germany, Martha Graham Co. using his music). In his voluminous notes he uses some Navajo words, like *hózhó*, that could well pass into the language at large."[20]

Literature by Native American authors may be the most fertile source for new Indian loans. *Publishers Weekly* in 1991 described the blossoming of Native American fiction and memoirs. The magazine quoted Mary Mulligan, buyer for Denver's huge Tattered Cover Bookstore, who stated that the publication of Native American books had grown almost half again during the preceding four-year period. Most of the new books were coming from university presses, though a substantial number were being issued by trade publishers. Gerald Vizenor, a Chippewa writer and university professor, was quoted as saying that much of the audience for this literature came from the increasing number of Native Americans who attended universities. The magazine observed that university courses in Native American literature were also introducing a mainstream audience to Native American writing.[21]

The *Oxford English Dictionary,* along with other major dictionaries, monitors the writing and speech of Native Americans as a potential source of new loans. In the late twentieth century, the *OED* was collecting a rising number of previously unfamiliar words from the writings of Indian authors (with movies being considered another possible source after the Lakota dialogue of *Dances with Wolves*). The *OED* furthermore was gleaning coinages from the Indian Englishes noted above by Leap. In 1991, a member of the dictionary's editorial staff expressed the hope that some of these words would appear in future editions of the *OED*.[22]

But with or without a renewed infusion of loanwords and loan terms, the Indian element in the English vocabulary continues to be vital to the language, as well as a continual reminder of the abiding influence of the Indian. Thoreau celebrated the Indians again and again in his writings. He assembled a collection of more than nine hundred Indian artifacts and accumulated some twenty-eight hundred pages of notes on Indian lore, possibly for a book on Indians he died too soon to write. While on a tour through the Maine wilderness in 1853, he listened with awe one night as his guide conversed with another Indian in their native tongue. "These were the sounds that issued from the wigwams of this country before Columbus was born," Thoreau later mused. "They have not yet died away; and with remarkably few exceptions, the language of their forefathers is still copious enough for them. I felt that I stood, or rather lay, as near to the primitive man of America that night, as any of its discoverers ever did." It is not surprising that the final two words of the dying Thoreau were *moose*—one of the earliest Indian loanwords in English—and *Indian*.[23]

LOANWORDS AND LOAN TERMS FROM THE TWENTIETH CENTURY

1900–1909

Canada anemone 1900	coon cat 1901
Cree potato 1900	Niagara green 1901
pattypan squash (or pattypan) 1900	Apache (ruffian) 1902
	bayou bass 1902
Sunapee trout 1900	chum (salmon) 1902
Canada bluegrass 1901	Klondike (solitaire) 1902
Canadian hemp 1901	mackinaw coat 1902

1900–1909 (continued)

orenda 1902
Siwash (jargon) 1902
Tahoe trout 1902
Comanchean (geol.) 1903
coony 1903
Texas umbrella tree 1903
Siwash (v.) 1904
totemite 1904
quahog (v.) 1905
Texas leaguer 1905
coon shouter 1906
chum salmon 1907
dwarf chinquapin oak 1907
keekwilee-house 1907

mahala mat 1907
mohawk weed 1907
catalpa worm 1908
moccasin telegraph 1908
mountain caribou 1908
Texas longhorn 1908
arizonite 1909
Canada lily 1909
Nebraskan (geol.) 1909
shawneewood 1909
squaw currant 1909
Texas sparrow 1909
Texas star 1909
turban squash 1909

1910–1919

giant chinquapin 1910
Oregon jay 1910
Siwash (small college) 1911
muckamuck (or muck-
   etymuck) 1912
coontail 1913
Pismo clam 1913
toboggan chute 1913

Apache dance 1914
squaw wood 1914
squaw cabbage 1915
cuttyhunk 1916
Eskimoid 1918
hog-nosed skunk 1918
mugwumpish 1918

1920–1929

coon grape 1920
coonhound 1920
Klamath weed 1922

squash blossom 1923
Appaloosa 1924
pima (or pima cotton) 1925

1920–1929 (continued)

Geechee 1926
illinium 1926
possum belly 1926

Eskimo Pie 1928
Sasquatch 1929

1930–1939

Siberian husky 1930
Canada mayflower 1931
giant sequoia ca. 1931
alabamine 1932
Michigan bankroll 1932
Yuma point 1932
Canadian bacon ca. 1934
Chicago (cards) 1934
Idaho (potato) 1934
Oregon myrtle 1934
Maine coon 1935
quahogger 1935

Allegheny spurge ca. 1936
oka 1936
possum grape 1936
acorn squash 1937
Eskimo potato 1937
illite 1937
squashberry 1937
Okie 1938
oklabar 1938
Tennessee Walking Horse
    1938

1940–1949

Manhattan clam chowder
    1940
metasequoia 1941
Quonset (hut) 1942
Canadian football 1944
Michigan (cards) 1944

butternut squash 1945
Oklahoma (cards) 1945
Adirondack chair 1948
buttercup squash 1949
Tex-Mex 1949

1950–1959

Yukon time 1950
Quebec ca. 1952

coon cheese 1953
Texas tower 1954

1960–1969

Appalachian dulcimer 1962   Oregon lily 1964
Malibu board 1962

1970–1979

skunk works ca. 1974
spaghetti squash 1975

canola 1979

1980–1989

canola oil 1986

Epilogue

ONE WINTER MORNING AS I STRODE TO WORK, A glint from between the roots of a maple tree caught my eye. With my jackknife blade, I pried a sliver of stone from the frozen ground. It turned out to be an Indian point of iron quartz slightly more than an inch long. Possibly four thousand years ago (the style indicated), its maker had designed the point for felling small game to augment the nuts, berries, and limited crops that sustained New England woodland Indians of that time.

I wondered about the Indian who had fashioned the point. Was he aiming at a squirrel or a bird? Did he hope that sympathetic magic would cause the red of the stone to seek out the red of an animal's blood? Was he successful? Such speculations arose as I held the point in the palm of my hand—slim, sharp, forever poised to fly from an unknown hunter toward an unknown target.

Indian loanwords in English embody a magic similar to the stone points with which the American earth is sown. The origins of both are often mysterious. They are freighted with implied significance. They display an esthetic appeal beyond their intended use. But unlike the points, Indian loanwords have never ceased traveling in the books and minds of English-speaking peoples.

Fortunately, the loanwords spring from a rich historical background. This book has examined that background to discover how and why certain loanwords were selected from the vast word hoards of Indian groups. The fluctuations of such borrowing, it has been argued, closely reflect the crucial historical events and stages in the European settling of this continent.

Perhaps a greater awareness of the Indian influence on our vocabulary will heighten an awareness of the Indian's lasting cultural impact in other ways. Much more remains to be learned from and about the primal American.

GLOSSARY 1

English Loanwords from the North American Indian Languages (North of Mexico)

THE FOLLOWING LOANWORDS AND LOAN TERMS HAVE been gleaned from *Webster's Third New International Dictionary* (1971) and its supplements, *6,000 Words* (1976) and *12,000 Words* (1986). The date of first recorded use, where known, accompanies each entry, with the source of that date. (See abbreviations below for sources.)

   •*Etymologies,* where known, follow—the style of which varies with the sources. With compound terms, *only* the etymology of the Indian element is given.

   •*Pronunciations* for the more obscure words, indicated between slant lines, are simply phonetic. See an authoritative dictionary for the subtleties of pronunciation.

   •The concluding brief *definitions* are offered mainly for purposes of identification, not as a substitute for dictionary definitions.

ABBREVIATIONS

AHD I	*American Heritage Dictionary,* First Edition
AHD III	*American Heritage Dictionary,* Third Edition
DAE	Craigie, William A., and James R. Hulbert, eds. *Dictionary of American English on Historical Principles*
DARE	Cassidy, Frederic G., ed. *Dictionary of American Regional English*

DC	*Dictionary of Canadianisms on Historical Principles*
Harder	Harder, Kelsie. *Illustrated Dictionary of Place Names*
M	Mathews, Mitford M. *A Dictionary of Americanisms*
OED	*Oxford English Dictionary*
RH II	*Random House Dictionary of the English Language: Second Edition*
6,000 Words	*6,000 Words: A Supplement to Webster's Third New International Dictionary*
Stewart	Stewart, George R. *American Place-Names*
12,000 Words	*12,000 Words: A Supplement to Webster's Third New International Dictionary*
W 9	*Webster's Ninth New Collegiate Dictionary*
W 10	*Merriam-Webster's Collegiate Dictionary,* Tenth Edition
W III	*Webster's Third New International Dictionary*

abalone \A-buh-LOH-nee\ 1850 (OED) Costanoan (a language of California from San Francisco Bay to Monterey) *aulon,* which gave rise to the Spanish plural *abulones;* a large, edible shellfish

acorn squash 1937 (M) Narragansett *askútasquash* (AHD III); an acorn-shaped, dark-green winter squash

adirondack blackfly - from *Adirondack* Mountains in northeastern New York, from *Adirondack* Indians, perhaps from Mohawk *hatiróntaks,* literally "they eat trees" (W III); common blackfly

Adirondack chair 1948 (M) (etym. above); wooden slant-back lawn chair named after New York State's *Adirondack* Mountains resort area, where it first became popular

alabama (genus of moths) - Muskogean name of a tribe of the Creek confederacy; a genus of moths

Alabama terrapin (or turtle or slider) - (etym. above) + Virginia Algonquian *torope;* a freshwater tortoise

alabamine 1932 (OED) (etym. above); chemical element now called *astatine*

Algoman (or Algomian or Algomic) - from Canadian place-name

coined from *Alg*onquin plus *goma* ("waters" in Ojibwa); geologic formation

Algonkian (geol.) 1890 (OED) Algonquian; geologic time division

alleghanyite - probably Delaware, from *Alleghany* County, N.C., from *Allegheny* Mountains; a manganese mineral

Alleghenian - probably Delaware, from *Allegheny* Mountains, range of the Appalachian system in eastern United States; a biogeographic zone

Allegheny (or Alleghany or Allegany) - (etym. above); geologic system

Allegheny barberry - (etym. above); American barberry

Allegheny spurge (or Allegheny mountain spurge) ca. 1936 (W 10) (etym. above); kind of low herb or subshrub

Allegheny vine (or fringe) 1850 (M) (etym. above); climbing fumitory

allocochick \A-luh-kuh-CHIK\ 1851 (M) Yurok *otl* human beings + *we-tsik* their dentalium shells (W III); Indian shell money in northern California

animikean \uh-NIM-uh-KEE-n\ (geol.) - from Chippewa placename *animiki:* thunder (intended as translation of "Thunder Bird Bay" in Ontario, Canada) (Harder); geologic formation

animikite \uh-NIM-uh-KIGHT\ - (etym. above); silver mineral named after Canadian region where it was discovered

Apache \uh-PASH\ (ruffian) 1902 (OED) from name of the Athabaskan people; ruffian (originally referring to a member of the Parisian underworld)

Apache (color) - (etym. above); sienna brown

Apache dance 1914 (OED) (etym. above); violent duet dance of the Parisian underworld

Apache \uh-PACH-ee\ devil dance - (etym. above); ceremonial dance of Apache Indians

Apache pine - (etym. above); three-leaved pine of Arizona and New Mexico

Apache plume - (etym. above); an evergreen shrub

apachite - named after *Apache* Mountains in Texas (etym. above); kind of rock

apishamore 1804 (DC) modif. of Ojibwa *apishamon,* "something to lie down on" (W III); saddle blanket usually made of buffalo hide

Appalachian - from the *Appalachian* Mountains in the eastern United States, from the Muskogean name of the *Apalachee* tribe of Florida; mountain-making episode of geologic history

Appalachian dulcimer (or dulcimore) 1962 (W 10) (etym. above); American folk instrument with three or four strings, held on lap and played by plucking or strumming

Appalachian tea 1876 (DARE) (etym. above); leaves of either of two shrubs (one of them yaupon) used as tea

Appaloosa 1924 (M) perhaps from the *Opelousa,* a Louisiana tribe; a breed of rugged saddle horse with white rump

arapahite - named for its discovery on land owned by *Arapaho* tribe, probably of Pawnee etymology; a basic basalt rock

Arizona ash - possibly Pima or Papago; an ash tree of the southern United States and Mexico

Arizona cardinal - (etym. above); large cardinal that ranges from Arizona to Mexico

Arizona crested flycatcher - (etym. above); flycatcher of southern Arizona desert

Arizona cypress - (etym. above); timber tree found mainly in Arizona

Arizona gourd - (etym. above); calabazilla or prairie gourd

Arizona hooded oriole - (etym. above); hooded oriole of southwestern United States and Mexico

Arizona jay - (etym. above); blue and gray jay of Arizona and New Mexico

Arizona longleaf pine - (etym. above); Apache pine

Arizona pine 1897 (DAE) (etym. above); Arizona longleaf pine, timber tree of Arizona and nearby regions

Arizona ruby 1893 (M) (etym. above); ruby-colored pyrope garnet of southwestern United States

Arizona sycamore - (etym. above); tree of Arizona and nearby regions

Arizona walnut - (etym. above); short tree with edible nut in southwestern United States

Arizona white oak - (etym. above); an oak of Arizona and Mexico

arizonite 1909 (OED) (etym. above); metallic mineral found in Arizona

Arkansas goldfinch 1858 (M) French variant of *Ugakhpah* or *Quapaw,* meaning "downstream people," tribe of the Sioux; a small goldfinch of the southwestern United States

Arkansas kingbird 1870 (M) (etym. above); a kingbird of the western United States

Arkansas soft pine - (etym. above); lumber of any of several soft pines

Arkansas stone 1869 (OED) (etym. above); stone from Arkansas used as whetstone, or whetstone made from that stone

Arkansas toothpick 1836 (M) (etym. above); bowie knife or long pointed sheath knife

Arkie - (etym. above); migrant worker, especially from Arkansas

arkite - (etym. above); kind of rock found in Arkansas

asimina \uh-SIM-uh-nuh\ - from AmerF *assimine* papaw, modif. of Illinois *rassimina* (W III); the genus of shrubs and small trees including the papaw

assapan \A-suh-PAN\ 1612 (Smith—see chap. 2) Virginia Algonquian; the American flying squirrel

assi - Creek *ássi* short for *ássi-lupútski,* "small leaves" (W III); yaupon (which see)

atamasco lily (or atamasco) 1629 (M) Virginia Algonquian *attamusco* (AHD III); plant of southeastern United States having a long stem and white-to-pinkish flower

atikokania - named after *Atikokan* River in Ontario, Canada, Algonquian?; genus of Precambrian fossils

Atokan (geol.) - from *Atoka* County, Okla., Creek; geologic time division

Attapulgite - Seminole, from *Attapulgus* Creek, Ga.; fibrous clay mineral

babiche 1806 (OED) Micmac; thread or thong made of rawhide or the like

baggataway (or bagataway) 1767 (Henry, 77) Ojibwa *pa-ka-atowe,* "he plays lacrosse" (RH II); lacrosse

balsam hickory 1785 (M) Virginia Algonquian *pocohiquara,* drink made of pressed hickory nuts; tree with small sweet nut and aromatic wood

barren ground caribou 1829 (DC) Micmac (AHD III), "shoveler of snow," any of several caribou of Barren Grounds of North America and Greenland

bayou 1763 (W 10) [1710–20, RH II] French *bayouque, bayou,* perhaps from Choctaw *bayuk* (AHD III); creek or sluggish stream

bayou bass 1902 (DARE) (etym. above); largemouth black bass

bayou lake - (etym. above); swampy offshoot of a lake, small bay, lagoon, or the like

beshow \buh-SHOW\ 1884 (M) Makah *bishowk* (W III); sablefish

big shellbark hickory - Virginia Algonquian *pocohiquara,* drink made of pressed hickory nuts; hickory resembling the shagbark but having a larger nut

black Cayuga - ultimately from Iroquoian name of tribe; Cayuga duck

black cohosh 1828 (DARE) Eastern Abenaki; a bugbane, or plant with flowers distasteful to insects

black hickory 1787 (M) Virginia Algqonquian *pocohiquara,* drink made of pressed hickory nuts; any of several hickories

black quahog - Narragansett *poquaûhock* (Williams—see chap. 4); a North Atlantic clam with a shell darker in color than that of the quahog

black titi - possibly Timucuan; tree found in southern United States, buckwheat tree

black tupelo - probably Creek *'topilwa: íto* (tree) + *opilwa* (swamp) (AHD III); black gum tree blue cohosh 1821 (M) Eastern Abenaki; perennial herb used medicinally

bogan 1896 (DC) apparently shortening of *pokelogan,* possibly of Indian origin; inlet or marshy place branching from a stream or lake

bogue 1814 (DARE) from Louisiana French from Choctaw *bok,* creek, stream, river (RH II); a bayou, stream, or waterway

broom hickory 1813 (M) Virginia Algonquian *pocohiquara,* drink made of pressed hickory nuts; a pignut hickory formerly used in broommaking

brown hickory - (etym. above); a pignut hickory

bush-tailed opossum - Virginia Algonquian *aposoum* (AHD III); an Australian marsupial

busk (festival) 1759 (M) Creek *púskita,* fast or fasting (W III); Creek festival of first fruits

buttercup squash 1949 (DARE) Narragansett *askútasquash* (AHD III); a kind of turban squash

butternut squash 1945 (W 10) (etym. above) named after its color; a smooth winter squash

camas \KA-muhs\ (or camass or quamash) 1805 (M) Chinook Jargon *kamass* (W 10); plant of lily family

camas rat 1849 (M) (etym. above); pocket gopher that feeds on the camas

camassia (or quamassia) - (etym. above); genus of herbs with edible bulbs

campoody 1856 (DARE) Paiute from Spanish *campo,* camp, from Latin *campus,* field (W III); an Indian village in the Southwest

Canada anemone 1900 (DARE) apparently from Huron-Iroquoian *kanata,* village or community (Harder); woodland herb with white flowers

Canada balsam 1806 (DARE) (etym. above); oleoresin from the balsam fir used as a transparent cement

Canada birch - (etym. above); sweet birch

Canada blueberry 1858 (Thoreau—see chap. 10) (etym. above); low shrub with sweet, bluish-black fruit

Canada bluegrass 1901 (M) (etym. above); wire grass

Canada buffalo berry - (etym. above); a kind of buffalo berry (named for its location in buffalo country)

Canada field pea - (etym. above); field pea widely grown in the United States and Canada for forage and food

Canada fleabane - (etym. above); horseweed

Canada ginger - (etym. above); wild ginger

Canada goose (or Canada) 1676 (DAE) (etym. above); the common wild goose

Canada hare - (etym. above); the varying hare of North America

Canada hemp - (etym. above); Indian hemp

Canada jay 1772 (DC) (etym. above); kind of jay in northern and western North America, moosebird or whisky jack

Canada lily 1909 (M) (etym. above); meadow lily

Canada lyme grass 1894 (DAE) (etym. above); a wild rye

Canada (or Canadian) lynx 1836 (Back, 494) (etym. above); a North American lynx

Canada mayflower 1931 (DARE) (etym. above); false lily of the valley

Canada mint - (etym. above); a common wild American mint

Canada moonseed 1785 (DAE) (etym. above); a woody vine of eastern North America with small white flowers

Canada pea 1896 (DARE) (etym. above); tufted vetch

Canada pitch - (etym. above); resin of hemlock spruce

Canada plum 1848 (M) (etym. above); a native plum of northeastern North America

Canada porcupine 1787 (DC) (etym. above); the porcupine of northeastern North America

Canada rockrose - (etym. above); frostweed

Canada root 1828 (DARE) (etym. above); butterfly weed

Canada snakeroot 1832 (M) (etym. above); wild ginger

Canada sweet gale - (etym. above); sweet fern

Canada tea - (etym. above); wintergreen

Canada thistle 1799 (M) (etym. above); a Europeanized thistle naturalized in the United States and Canada

Canada turpentine - (etym. above); Canada balsam

Canada violet 1821 (M) (etym. above); perennial herb with violet-streaked white flowers

Canada warbler 1844 (DAE) (etym. above); a common warbler of northern North America

Canada wild rye - (etym. above); a wild rye

Canada wormwood - (etym. above); aromatic weedy herb found chiefly in Canada

Canada yew - (etym. above); ground hemlock

canader 1893 (OED) (etym. above); canoe (British usage)

Canadian (geol.) - (etym. above); geologic time division

Canadian bacon ca. 1934 (W 10) (etym. above); cured bacon from the loin of a pig

Canadian burnet - (etym. above); a common herb of eastern North America

Canadian football 1944 (W 10) (etym. above); game resembling both American football and rugby

Canadian goldenrod 1836 (M) (etym. above); a large goldenrod of eastern North America

Canadian goose 1806 (DAE) (etym. above); Canada goose

Canadian hemlock 1897 (DAE) (etym. above); eastern hemlock

Canadian hemp 1901 (DAE) (etym. above); Indian hemp

Canadian holly 1785 (M) (etym. above); mountain holly

Canadianism 1875 (OED) (etym. above); Canadian expression

Canadianize 1829 (OED) (etym. above); to make Canadian

Canadian moonseed 1785 (DAE) (etym. above); Canada moonseed or yellow parilla

Canadian pondweed - (etym. above); waterweed

Canadian red pine - (etym. above); red pine

Canadian rig - (etym. above), kind of oil-well rig

Canadian small reed - (etym. above); bluejoint

Canadian warbler - (etym. above); Canada warbler

Canadian waterleaf - (etym. above); woodland herb with purplish white flowers canadine - (etym. above); crystalline alkaloid found in root of goldenseal

canadol - (etym. above); a petroleum substance named after its extraction from Canadian petroleum

canola 1979 (W 10) (etym. above) formed from *Can*ada *o*il—*l*ow *a*cid; a rape plant with seeds low in erucic acid (a kind of fatty acid) that are the source of canola oil, or short for canola oil

canola oil 1986 (W 10) (etym. and acronymic formation above); an edible vegetable oil obtained from the seeds of canola

cantico (or kantikoy) 1612 (Strachey—see chap. 2) modification of Delaware *kəntka,* "to dance" (W III); a dancing party

carcajou 1703 (OED) Canadian French from Montagnais *kùakuàtsheu* (AHD III); wolverine

caribou 1605 (Rosier—see chap. 2) Micmac (AHD III) perhaps originally "shoveler of snow"; the animal

caribou moss 1857 (DC) (etym. above); reindeer moss

carideer - caribou (etym. above) and reindeer; a hybrid of the two animals

cassina (or cassena) 1587 (Hakluyt—see chap. 1) American Spanish from Timucua *kasine* (AHD III); yaupon (which see)

cassioberry 1753 (OED) *cassina* (etym. above) + *berry;* yaupon or either of two other plants

Catahoula hog dog - from name of a parish in Louisiana, Indian of uncertain origin (Harder); larger houndlike dog used in hunting and in herding wild hogs

catalpa 1731 (Catesby—see chap. 6) Creek *katalpa* from *ka*-(head) and *talpa** (wing) (from the shape of it flowers—"head with wings"); any of various flowering trees with heart-shaped leaves and white flowers

catalpa sphinx (moth) - (etym. above); a large American hawk moth

catalpa worm 1908 (M) (etym. above); larva of the catalpa sphinx

catawba (wine) 1846 (M) from the *Catawba* Indian tribe, perhaps of Shawnee origin (RH II); a light dry wine

---

*/λ/ is a sound rather like *lth* in the English word *wealth.*

catawba (grape) 1857 (OED) (etym. above); reddish North American grape

catawba rhododendron 1813 (M) (etym. above); a pink-flowered rhododendron

catawba tree 1832 (M) by folk etymology from *catalpa* (Harder); either of two kinds of catalpa

catoctin - from *Catoctin* Mountain, Maryland and Virginia, Algonquian meaning "speckled rock" (Harder); kind of hill or ridge rising above an eroded plain

?caucus 1763 (Adams—see chap. 6) probably from Latin *caucus,* drinking vessel, rather than from an Indian language; political group

cawquaw 1787 (DC—under "Canada porcupine") Cree *kaakwa* (W III); Canada porcupine

Cayuga duck - ultimately from Iroquoian name of tribe; American breed of ducks like but slightly smaller than Peking ducks

cayugan (geol.) - (etym. above); geologic time division

cayuse 1841 (OED) from *Cayuse* Indians; native range horse

chautauqua 1873 (M) Iroquoian name (Stewart) of uncertain origin; an assembly or traveling institution that combines education with entertainment

chautauqua muskellunge - (etym. above) + Canadian French *maskinongé* from Ojibwa *maashkinoozhe* (AHD III); kind of muskellunge found mainly in the Ohio and St. Lawrence river drainages

chautauquan (geol.) - (etym. above); geologic time division

chebacco boat 1823 (M) Algonquian from former parish name in Ipswich, Mass., where it originated; narrow-sterned boat once used in Newfoundland fisheries

chebog \CHUH-BOG\ 1895 (M) probably Natick (W III); menhaden

cheechako (or chechako or cheechaco or chechaqua) 1897 (M) Chinook Jargon: Lower Chinook *chee* (just now, new) + *chako* (come) (RH II); in Alaska and northern Canada, newcomer or tenderfoot

chemawinite \chuh-MAW-wuh-NITE\ - from *Chemahawin, Chem-*

ayin. Indian name of Hudson Bay post; fossil resin like amber found near the post

Cherokee - from the name of the Iroquoian people but perhaps ultimately Creek; tile red, moderate reddish orange

Cherokee rose 1823 (M) (etym. above); a Chinese climbing rose

Chesapeake Bay retriever (or dog) 1873 (M) Algonquian name of village possibly meaning "big-river-at," transferred by English to the bay (Stewart); large sporting dog developed in Maryland

Chesapeake canoe - (etym. above); special craft used on Chesapeake Bay

Chicago (cards) 1934 (M) Algonquian "garlic field" (Harder); method of playing contract bridge

Chicago acid - (etym. above); a crystalline acid used in making dyes

Chicago blue - (etym. above); any of several shades of blue dyes

Chicago piano - (etym. above); pom-pom (kind of automatic gun)

Chicago pool - (etym. above); a kind of pool (game)

Chicago style - (etym. above); a method of butchering animal carcasses

Chickasaw plum 1760 (M) from the Muskogean name of the tribe; an American shrub or small tree with red or yellowish cherrylike fruit

chicken terrapin (or tortoise or turtle) - Virginia Algonquian *torope;* edible aquatic turtle

chikee (or chickee) \chi-KEE\ - Mikasuki (a Muskogean language) *čikî,* dwelling (RH II); a stilt house of the Seminole Indians

chindi (or chindee) - Navajo *chindi* (W III); a Navajo evil spirit of the dead

Chinook \shuh-NOOK\ (wind) 1860 (M) Chehalis (Salishan) Tsinúk (W III); warm moist wind of the Pacific coast

Chinook Jargon 1840 (OED) (etym. above); pidgin based on Chinook combined with Nootka and other Indian, English, and French words

Chinook licorice 1893 (M) (etym. above); blue-flowered herb found on Pacific coast

Chinook salmon 1851 (M) (etym. above); king salmon

chinquapin \CHINK-uh-PIN\ (or chincapin or chinkapin) 1612 (Smith—see chap. 2) Virginia Algonquian *chechinkamin*, chestnut (AHD III); any of several trees including several related to the chestnut

chinquapin oak 1785 (M) (etym. above); either of two North American chestnut oaks

chinquapin perch (fish) 1884 (M) (etym. above); white crappie (sunfish)

chipmunk (or chipmonk or chitmonk) 1832 (M) *chitmunk*, apparently from Ojibwa *ačitamo·nʾ*, headfirst (RH II); the animal

chittam (or chittem or chittim) bark - perhaps of Muskogean origin (W III); the bark of the cascara buckthorn

chittamwood (or chittimwood) 1843 (M) (etym. above); one of the buckthorns

chivey \SHI-vee\ - probably Natick (W III); Menominee whitefish

choctaw (language) 1839 (M) from the Muskogean name of the language; strange or incomprehensible language

choctaw (skating) 1892 (OED) (etym. above); a maneuver in fancy skating

choctaw beer - (etym. above); bootleg beer made in the southwestern United States

chogset 1842 (M) Algonquian akin to Pequot *cachauxet* (W III); cunner (a kind of marine fish)

choupique (or choupic) 1763 (M) through American French, Choctaw *shupik* (W III); bowfin

chuck (woodchuck) - an anglicization of a word presumed from a southern New England Algonquian language, compare Narragansett *ockqutchaun*, woodchuck (RH II); the animal

chuck (inlet) 1860 (DC) Chinook Jargon for any of various bodies of water; inlet, harbor

chuckwalla (or chuckawalla) 1869 (M) American Spanish *chacahuala*, from Cahuilla, a Uto-Aztecan language (AHD III); a large harmless lizard of the southwestern United States and Mexico chum (salmon) 1902 (W 10) Chinook Jargon *cam,* spotted, striped, from Lower Chinook (AHD III); Pacific salmon with specks on its back

chumpa 1851 (M) perhaps from Choctaw *chumpa,* purchase (W III); faggot of pine kindling

chum salmon 1907 (W 10) (see etym. for *chum* above); Pacific salmon

chunkey (or chunky) 1709 (Lawson, p. 57) perhaps modification of Catawba *chenco* (W III); Muskogean game played with a staff and a stone bowl

cibolero 1844 (M) from Spanish for "buffalo," after Spanish *Cíbola,* land of the Zuñis in New Mexico and Arizona, from Zuñi *šíwona* (W III); buffalo hunter

cisco 1848 (OED) Canadian French *ciscoette,* from Ojibwa *bemidewiskawed,* "the (fish) with oily skin" (AHD III); any of several freshwater fishes resembling the whitefish

cocash \kuh-KASH\ 1828 (DAE) Algonquian (W III); a North American herb, horseweed

cocashweed 1873 (DARE) (etym. above); a golden ragweed

Cochise - from *Cochise* County, Ariz., after Apache chief *Cochise* (Harder); prehistoric culture of southeastern Arizona and New Mexico

cockarouse (or cockerous) 1612 (Smith—see chap. 2) Virginia Algonquian; a person of importance among American colonists

coho (or cohoe or coho salmon or cohoe salmon) 1869 (OED) probably of native origin (DC); silver salmon

Cohonina - from the name *Cohonina* (W III) Indian?; prehistoric Indian culture in northwestern Arizona

cohosh 1789 (W 10) Eastern Abenaki (AHD III); any of several medicinal plants

Comanchean (geol.) 1903 (W 9) from *Comanche,* Texas—Spanish from Ute *kimanči* (AHD I); geologic formation

comanchero - Spanish from Ute *kimanči* (AHD I); a trader with Indians in the nineteenth century

Conestoga (wagon) 1717 (W 10) from *Conestoga,* Pa. (named after an Iroquoian tribe that became extinct in 1763), where the wagon was first made; a heavy covered wagon

Conestoga (brogan) 1893 (OED) (etym. above); kind of heavy shoe

Connecticut chest - from the Mohican *Quonehtacut* or the like (Harder), perhaps "at the long tidal river" (W III); chest made in seventeenth- and eighteenth-century Connecticut, with sunflower and tulip designs on it

Connecticut warbler 1812 (M) (etym. above); large wood warbler that breeds in north-central North America and winters in Brazil

coon (n.) 1742 (M) short for Virginia Algonquian *aroughcun* (see chap. 2); raccoon

coon (v.) 1834 (M) (etym. above); to crawl or creep along

coon bear - (etym. above); giant panda

coon bug - (etym. above?); black and white Australian bug

coon cat - 1901 (W 10) (etym. above); a large long-haired domestic cat, or cacomistle, or coati

coon cheese 1953 (W 10) (etym. above); probably from offensive slang *coon*, black person; a cheddar cheese usually coated with black wax

coon dog - 1833 (M) (etym. above); dog trained for raccoon hunting

cooner - (etym. above); coon dog

coon grape 1920 (DARE) (etym. above); fox grape with a strong scent that reminds some people of a coon or fox scent

coonhound 1920 (M) (etym. above); large black-and-tan hound developed for hunting raccoons

cooniness - (etym. above); caginess, canniness

coon oyster 1869 (DARE) (etym. above?); small or undersized oyster

coonroot 1893 (DARE) (etym. above); from Virginia Algonquian *puccoon* (which see); bloodroot

coon's age 1843 (M) short for Virginia Algonquian *aroughcun*, raccoon; very long time

coon shouter 1906 (DARE) (etym. above, used offensively of a black); one who sings like a blackface minstrel coonskin 1818 (M) (etym. above); hide of raccoon or article of clothing made from it

coon song 1844 (M) (etym. above); ragtime song of the nineteenth century related to songs of the southern blacks

coon-striped shrimp - (etym. above); large shrimp found off U.S. Pacific coast

coontail 1913 (DARE) (etym. above); hornwort

coontie (or comptie) 1791 (M) Florida Creek *kuntí*, arrowroot (AHD III); an arrowroot or the starch produced from it

coony 1903 (M) short for Virginia Algonquian *aroughcun*, raccoon; cagey or canny

corn pone 1859 (M) Virginia Algonquian *poan, appoans,* cornbread (AHD III); johnnycake or corn pone

cottonmouth moccasin 1879 (DARE) Natick *mohkussin* (AHD I); water moccasin

cous \KOWS\ (or cowish) 1806 (DARE) perhaps Nez Percé *kowish* (W III); herb of northwestern United States with edible roots

coween \kuh-WEEN\ - Algonquian (W III); old-squaw, a common sea duck

crab-eating opossum - Virginia Algonquian *aposoum* (AHD I); a South American opossum

crab-eating raccoon - Virginia Algonquian *aroughcun* (see chap. 2); a South American raccoon

Cree potato (or turnip) 1900 (DARE) from name of Indian people, ultimately probably from Ojibwa (W III); breadroot, a food plant of the U.S. West

crescent terrapin - Virginia Algonquian *torope* (AHD I); a common North American turtle with a yellow crescent behind each eye

croton bug ca. 1842 (OED) from *Croton* (name of early Indian chief) River; kind of cockroach supposedly introduced into New York City through *Croton* River water

cui-ui \KWEE-WEE\ 1877 (M) Northern Paiute *kuyui* (AHD III); a freshwater sucker found only in Nevada

cultus (or cultus cod) 1849 (DC) Chinook *cultus*, worthless (W III); lingcod cushaw \kuh-SHAW\ 1588 (Harriot—see chap. 1) possibly Virginia Algonquian; any of several kinds of winter squash with curved neck

cuttyhunk 1916 (M) from *Cuttyhunk* Island, Mass., of uncertain Indian origin (W III); a twisted linen fishing line suitable for deep-sea fishing

Dakota (geol.) 1876 (M) from the *Dakota* territory after the Siouan people; geologic time division

Dakota millet - (etym. above); foxtail millet or other kind of millet

death camas 1889 (M) Chinook Jargon *kamass;* any of several western plants that are poisonous to livestock

diamondback terrapin 1877 (M) Virginia Algonquian *torope* (AHD III); any of several terrapins found along the Atlantic and Gulf coasts

dockmackie 1817–18 (M) probably from American Dutch, perhaps of Mahican origin (AHD III); shrub of eastern North America with clusters of white flowers

dormouse opossum - Virginia Algonquian *aposoum* (AHD I); any of several small phalangers that resemble mice

dowitcher (or dowitch) 1841 (M) perhaps Iroquoian (RH II); longbilled snipelike shore bird

dwarf Canadian primrose - apparently from Huron-Iroquoian *kanata,* village or community; mistassini (which see)

dwarf chinquapin oak 1907 (DARE) Virginia Algonquian *chechinkamin,* chestnut (AHD III); a small shrubby oak

Erian (geol.) 1873 (OED) Iroquoian, from Lake *Erie;* geologic time division

Eskimo (color) - French *Esquimaux* from Montagnais *ayashkimew,* Micmac (AHD III); rustic brown, a moderate reddish brown

Eskimo curlew 1813 (M) (etym. above); New World curlew that breeds in northern North America and winters in South America

Eskimo dog 1774 (DC) (etym. above); work-dog used in Arctic regions

Eskimoid 1918 (OED) (etym. above); resembling the Eskimo

Eskimology - (etym. above); the study of Eskimo culture or language

Eskimo Pie 1928 (etym. above); trademark ice cream bar with chocolate shell

Eskimo potato 1937 (DARE) (etym. above); Alaskan plant with starchy edible root

Eskimo purchase - (etym. above); an Eskimo tackle for catching seals

eulachon (or eulachan or oolachan) 1806 (M) Chinook Jargon *vlâkân* (AHD III); candlefish

foothill death camas - Chinook Jargon *kamass;* an herb of the western United States that is poisonous to cattle

four-eyed opossum - Virginia Algonquian *aposoum* (AHD I); any of various South American opossums

gahe - Apache; masked dancers representing mountain spirits in Apache ceremonies (see *Apache devil dance*)

Geechee 1926 (OED) Muskogee, from *Ogeechee* River, Ga.; dialect containing words of African origin spoken by descendants of slaves in vicinity of river

geoduck \GOO-ee-DUK\ (or goeduck or goeyduc, etc.) 1883 (OED) Puget Salish; large edible clam from Pacific coast of Northwest

giant chinquapin 1910 (DARE) Virginia Algonquian *chechinkamin,* chestnut (AHD III); a chinquapin

giant sequoia ca. 1931 (W 10) from Cherokee leader *Sequoyah* (1760?–1843); big tree, the California evergreen, noble fir

Gila \HEE-luh\ monster 1877 (M) from *Gila* River, Ariz., named after Indian tribe; one of only two known venomous lizards in the world

Gila trout 1852 (DARE) (etym. above); bonytail

Gila woodpecker 1858 (M) (etym. above); large red-crowned wood-pecker of southwestern North America

golden chinquapin - Virginia Algonquian *chechinkamin,* chestnut (AHD III); a Pacific coast tree with evergreen leaves

Grant (or Grant's) caribou - Micmac (AHD III); a small caribou of the Alaska peninsula

grassy death camas - Chinook Jargon *kamass;* a death camas of the northwestern United States

gray squeteague - of Algonquian origin (AHD III); gray trout hackmatack 1792 (M) perhaps from Western Abenaki (AHD III) *hakmantak;* tamarack, common juniper, balsam poplar (different word from the Nahuatl homonym)

haddo 1882 (DARE) Nisqualli *huddoh* (W III); humpback salmon

hako \HAH-koh\ - Pawnee (W III); Pawnee ceremony representing union of heaven and earth

hammock hickory - Virginia Algonquian *pocohiquara,* drink made of pressed hickory nuts; a Florida tree

hard-bark hickory 1897 (M) (etym. above); mockernut

hardy catalpa - Creek *catalpa* from *ka-*(head) + *talpa* (from the shape of its flowers—"head with wings"); western catalpa

hawok \HAH-WAHK\ - Maidu *howok* (W III); Indian money of California

heishi \HEE-SHEE\ (or heishe) - Navajo, literally "shell" (12,000 Words); bead made of disk-shaped shell or other materials

hiccan (or hican) Virginia Algonquian *pocohiquara* + American French *pacane* from Illinois *pakani;* the nut of hickory-and-pecan hybrid

hickory (n.) 1612 (Smith—see chap. 2) Virginia Algonquian *pocohiquara,* drink made from pressed hickory nuts; American tree of the genus *Carya*

hickory (v.) 1842 (M) (etym. above); to give a whipping to

hickory acacia - (etym. above); an Australian acacia

hickory bark beetle (or borer) - (etym. above); a small beetle that burrows under the bark of hickories

hickory borer - (etym. above); any of various beetles whose larvae live in hickories

hickory elm 1884 (M) (etym. above); rock elm

hickoryhead - (etym. above); ruddy duck

hickory horned devil 1816 (OED) (etym. above); a caterpillar with greenish body, red head, and four anterior spines

hickory midge - (etym. above); a gallfly that forms galls on the leaves of various hickories

hickory nut 1802 (OED) (etym. above); nut of hickory tree

hickory oak 1897 (DARE) (etym. above); canyon live oak

hickory pine 1884 (M) (etym. above); bristlecone pine or table-mountain pine

hickory poplar 1893 (DARE) (etym. above); tulip tree

hickory shad 1800 (M) (etym. above); shad with stomach like a hickory nut

hickory shirt 1836 (OED) (etym. above); a shirt made of strong twilled cotton fabric with vertical stripes and used especially as a work shirt

hickory shuckworm - (etym. above); grub that feeds on the developing fruits of the hickory and pecan

hickory wattle - (etym. above); a kind of acacia

high-muck-a-muck 1856 (OED) Chinook Jargon *hayo makamak,* "plenty to eat" (AHD III); important person, bigwig

hoary puccoon 1612 (Smith—see chap. 2) Virginia Algonquian *poughkone* (RH II); a perennial herb with hairy foliage

hogan 1871 (M) Navajo *hooghan;* a usually earth-covered Navajo dwelling

hog and hominy 1776 (DARE) Virginia Algonquian *uskatahomen,* probably "that which is ground" (RH II); poor fare

hog-nosed skunk 1918 (M) Massachusett *squnck;* a large stocky skunk of southwestern North America

Hohokam 1884 (M) Pima *huhukam,* "ancient one" (W III); a prehistoric desert culture of the southwestern United States

hominy 1612 (Smith—see chap. 2) Virginia Algonquian *uskatahomen,* probably "that which is ground" (RH II); hulled and dried kernels of corn, boiled for food

hominy grits 1877 (DARE) (etym. above); ground usually white meal of dried and hulled corn kernels boiled and served as a breakfast food or side dish

honey possum - Virginia Algonquian *aposoum* (AHD I); a long-muzzled phalanger of Australia

honk 1854 (Thoreau—see chap. 10) perhaps from Wampanoag or Narragansett *honck,* gray goose, the Canada goose; call of Canada goose

hooch 1897 (W 10) short for *hoochino,* from *Hootsnoowoos,* a Tlingit tribe that distilled liquor illegally, from Tlingit *xutsnuuwú* (AHD III); cheap or bootleg liquor

hoochinoo 1877 (M) (etym. above); hooch

Hopi (color) - Hopi *hópi,* "peaceable" (AHD III); French beige

Hopi Way - (etym. above); Hopi code of behavior depicted in annual ceremonial cycle

how (greeting) 1817 (Bradbury—see chap. 11) perhaps of Indian origin; a traditional salutation

Hubbard squash 1869 (DARE) Narragansett *askútasquash* (AHD III); any of various green winter squashes

huskanaw (n.) 1692 (Ewan, 66) Algonquian akin to Natick *wiskenoo,* "he is young" (W III); initiation rite for Indian youths of Virginia

huskanaw (v.) - (etym. above); to put through a huskanaw

husky 1852 (OED) from *husky* dog, *husky* breed, from *Eskimo*— French *Esquimaux* from Montagnais *ayashkimew,* Micmac (AHD III); dog developed for pulling sleds

Idaho (potato) 1934 (W 10) coined name with an invented Indian meaning, or possibly Kiowa Apache; elongated potato suitable for baking and grown especially in Idaho

Idaho fescue - (etym. above); a tall meadow grass of western North America

Idaho white pine - (etym. above); western white pine or its wood

illinium 1926 (OED) from *Illinois,* from French for *Illini,* a confederation of peoples in the Midwest, of Algonquian origin; chemical element 61, now called *promethium*

Illinoian (geol.) 1896 (OED) (etym. above); geologic time division

Illinois gooseberry - (etym. above); Missouri gooseberry

Illinois nut 1781–82 (OED) (etym. above); pecan

illite 1937 (OED) (etym. above); any of a group of clay minerals

Indian moccasin 1844 (DC) Natick *mohkussin* (AHD I); stemless lady's slipper

Indian poke 1784 (M) Virginia Algonquian *pocan,* pokeweed; American hellebore

Indian puccoon - Virginia Algonquian *poughkone* (RH II); hoary puccoon

Indian wickape - Eastern Abenaki *wikɘpi,* inner bark used for cordage (AHD III); fireweed

Indian wickup (or wicopy) - same as above

Iowa crab (or crab apple) - from French *ayoés,* ultimately from Dakota *ayúxba* (AHD III), an Indian people; a wild crabapple of the western United States with pink flowers

Iowan (geol.) 1894 (M) (etym. above); geologic time division or the glacial drift of it

iruska \uh-ROO-skuh\ - Pawnee, literally "the fire is in me" (W III); dance of a fire-handling society of the Pawnees

islay \IZ-ligh\ - from Salinan, a California language; a California wild plum

kachina (or katcina, etc.) 1873 (Dockstader—see chap. 10) Hopi *katsina;* supernatural being, masked impersonator of a supernatural being, or kachina doll

kachina doll - (etym. above); a doll representing a kachina

Kamloops trout (or Kamloops) 1896 (M) from city in British Columbia, with Indian name *kahm-o-loops,* either "the meeting of the waters" or "the meeting place" (Harder); large rainbow trout found in western streams and lakes

Kansan (geol.) 1894 (OED) from *Kansa,* in the old Siouan language, "people of the south wind" (Harder); geologic time division

Kansas gay-feather - (etym. above); a perennial herb with spikes of purplish flowers

Kansas horse plague - (etym. above); contagious equine disease

Kansas thistle - (etym. above); buffalo bur

Kayenta - from *Tyende* Creek, Ariz., from Navajo for "where they fell into a pit" (Stewart); of or belonging to the northern Arizona branch of the Anasazi culture

keekwilee-house \KEEK-wuh-lee\ 1907 (DC) Chinook Jargon *keekwilee,* "below" (W III); earth lodge partly below ground level, used by Indians of Northwest Coast of North America

Keewatin (geol.) 1886 (OED) Cree, from the *Keewatin* district of the Northwest Territories; geologic time division

Kentucky bass (or black bass) - Wyandot *ken-tah-teh,* "land of tomorrow" (Harder); spotted black bass

Kentucky bluegrass (or blue) 1849 (M) (etym. above); a grass grown for pasturage and lawns

Kentucky cardinal - (etym. above); cardinal bird

Kentucky coffee tree 1785 (M) (etym. above); tall North American tree the seeds of which were used as a coffee-bean substitute

Kentucky flat - (etym. above); large flatboat formerly used on rivers to carry produce and stock to market

Kentucky green - (etym. above); a dark yellowish green

Kentucky jean 1835 (M) (etym. above); a homemade jean with a cotton warp and a wool weft

Kentucky rifle 1832 (W 10) (etym. above); a long-barreled rifle widely used on the frontier

Kentucky warbler 1811 (OED) (etym. above); a warbler of the eastern United States

Kentucky windage - (etym. above); windage correction in aiming a firearm

Keweenawan (geol.) 1876 (OED) Ojibwa, from *Keweenaw* Point, Mich.; geologic time division

king nut hickory 1897 (M) Virginia Algonquian *pocohiquara,* drink made of pressed hickory nuts; big shellbark tree resembling the shagbark

kinkajou 1796 (OED) French *quincajou,* probably a blend of Ojibwa and Montagnais words (AHD III); an arboreal animal of Central and South America also called *honey bear*

kinnikinnick \KIN-uh-kuh-NIK\ (kinnikinic, etc.) 1796 (OED) Unami (Delaware language) *kələkkəniïkkan,* literally "item for mixing in," kinnikinnick (AHD III); mixture of bark and dried leaves for smoking

kisi - Hopi; a bower of branches for keeping snakes before a snake dance

kiva 1871 (M) Hopi *kíva, ki* (house) + unidentified element; a

Pueblo Indian room, partly underground, used for ceremonial and other purposes

Klamath \KLAM-uth\ weed 1922 (M) Chinook *tlamatl,* name of sister tribe of the Modocs (Harder), word probably from *Klamath River* in Oregon and California; a yellow perennial St. John's-wort

Klondike 1902 (M) from region in Yukon Territory, Canada, of obscure Indian origin; a kind of solitaire

Klondike (source of wealth) 1897 (OED) (etym. above); a source of valuable material or wealth

klootchman 1837 (OED) Chinook Jargon *klootshman,* from Nootka *lotssma,* woman or wife (W III); Indian woman of northwestern North America

kokanee \koh-KA-nee\ (or kokanee salmon) 1875 (OED) Shushwap (Salish) (RH II); a small landlocked sockeye salmon

koshare 1890 (OED) Keresan (W III); a Pueblo Indian clown society

koyemishi \koh-YEM-shee\ - Zuñi; a Zuñi Indian clown society

large tupelo - probably Creek *'topilwa: íto* (tree) + *opilwa* (swamp) (AHD III); tupelo gum, a swamp tree in the southeastern United States

little spotted skunk - Massachusett *squnck;* any of several kinds of skunk found in the southwestern United States and Mexico

logan 1881 (M) possibly American Indian (see *pokelogan*); pokelogan or a usually stagnant or marshy place branching from a stream or lake

Louisiana muskrat - Algonquian, probably influenced by *musk* and *rat;* a kind of muskrat found in the marshes of Louisiana

lunge (or longe) 1851 (OED) Canadian French *maskinongé* from Ojibwa *maashkinoozhe* (AHD III); lake trout, muskellunge

lye hominy 1821 (M) Virginia Algonquian *uskatahomen,* probably "that which is ground" (RH II); hominy prepared from grain soaked in lye to remove hulls

mackinaw (or mac or mack) 1822 (M) from Ojibwa *michilmachinak,* "island of the large turtle," referring to nearby *Mackinac* Island; a heavy woolen blanket in solid colors or stripes distributed by the U.S. government to the Indians mackinaw boat 1812 (M) (etym. above); flat-bottomed boat with pointed prow formerly used on the upper Great Lakes

mackinaw cloth - (etym. above); heavy cloth completely or partly of wool, usually heavily napped and felted for warmth

mackinaw coat 1902 (M) (etym. above); a short, usually double-breasted and belted coat of mackinaw or similar heavy fabric

mackinaw trout 1840 (M) (etym. above); lake trout

macock \MAY-cok\ (or maycock) 1588 (Harriot—see chap. 1) Algonquian?; kind of melon or squashlike plant that Indians of eastern North America cultivated

mahala 1850 (M) Yokuts word for "woman," *moxelo* (Yawelmani dial.) old woman (RH II); in the West, Indian woman

mahala mat 1907 (M) (etym. above), so called because of its use by women for making mats; a low shrub of the U.S. Pacific coast

Maine coon 1935 (W 10) short for Virginia Algonquian *aroughcun*; a breed of large long-haired domestic cat with full tail, coon cat

Malibu board 1962 (OED) from *Malibu* Beach, Calif., probably Chumash (Stewart); fiberglass-covered surfboard about ten feet long

mananosay \man-uh-NOH-say\ (or maninose) 1709 (Lawson, 162) probably Algonquian (W III); soft-shell clam

mango-squash - Narragansett *askútasquash* (Williams—see chap. 4); chayote, fruit of a West Indian vine

Manhattan clam chowder 1940 (M) from a tribe of Algonquian-speaking Indians, may mean "isolated thing in water" (AHD I); soup made with clams, tomatoes, other vegetables, and seasonings

Manhattan cocktail 1890 (OED), (etym. above); a cocktail made of sweet vermouth, whiskey, and a dash of bitters

Manitoba maple (box elder) 1887 (DC) probably Cree or Ojibwa (Harder), from *Manitoba,* Canada; box elder

manitou (or manitu or manito) ?1588 (Harriot—see chap. 1) French from Ojibwa *manitoo* (AHD III); supernatural power that permeates the world

mankato (geol.) - Siouan "blue earth" (Harder), from *Mankato,* Minn.; geologic time division map terrapin (or turtle) - Virginia Algonquian *torope* (AHD III); small aquatic turtle of the central and eastern United States marked by delicate yellow tracings

maracock 1612 (Smith—see chap. 2) Virginia Algonquian; maypop, a passionflower

marrow squash 1864 (M) Narragansett *askútasquash* (Williams—see chap. 4); vegetable marrow, any of several summer squashes

maskinonge or maskalonge, var. of muskellunge (which see)

Massachusetts ballot 1891 (M) Algonquian "big-hills-at" (Stewart); kind of election ballot

Massachusetts fern - (etym. above); a delicate shield fern of the eastern United States

Massachusetts trust - (etym. above); a kind of unincorporated business organization

massasauga (or massasauga rattler) 1835 (OED) Algonquin, from the *Missisauga,* a river of southeast Ontario, Canada (AHD III); a small rattlesnake

matchcoat 1612 (Smith—see chap. 2) Virginia Algonquian *matshcore* probably influenced by *coat* (partly W III); a mantle or similar loose covering worn by Indians

mathemeg 1787 (OED) Cree *mâthemek* (W III); a kind of northern catfish

mattowacca 1884 (M) probably Algonquian (W III); fall herring

maycock - variant of *maracock* (which see)

maypop 1851 (W 10) - variant of *maycock* (which see)

meadow death camas - Chinook Jargon *kamass;* a death camas that grows mainly in wet grasslands

menhaden \men-HAY-d'n\ 1643 (Williams—see chap. 4) possibly blend of Narragansett *munnawhatteaûg* and English dialectical *poghaden* (probably Algonquian) (AHD III); fish also called *mossbunker* or *pogy*

menhaden oil - (etym. above); oil obtained from the menhaden and used in paint, varnish, inks, etc.

Menominee whitefish (or Menomini) 1884 (M) Algonquian, from

the *Menomini* people; small whitefish found in lakes of northern United States and Canada

Meramec (geol.) - from an Indian tribal name meaning "cat fish" (Harder), *Meramec* River, Mo.; geologic time division

mesabite \muh-SAH-bight\ (mineral) - Indian word of uncertain origin, *Mesabi* Range, Minn.; a mineral

metasequoia 1941 (OED) from Cherokee leader *Sequoyah* (1760?–1843); a genus of trees including the dawn redwood

Michigan (cards) 1944 (M) Indian word of uncertain origin; a kind of card game

Michigan bankroll 1932 (M) (etym. above); a roll of paper money with a large bill on the outside of small-denomination or counterfeit bills

Michigan grayling 1884 (OED) (etym. above); a fish that is a variety of the arctic graying and occurs only in northern Michigan

Michigan rummy - (etym. above); a kind of card game

mico \MEE-koh\ 1737 (M) Muskogee *miko* (W III); a Muskogean chief

midewiwin \muh-DAY-wuh-win\ 1860 (DC) (or mide or midewin) Ojibwa *midêwin* (W III); a once powerful secret society among the Ojibwas and neighboring Indians

Milwaukee brick - Algonquian, probably "a good spot or place" (Harder); a pale orange-yellow to yellow

Minnesota (swine breeds) - Dakota, perhaps "the waters reflect the weather" (Harder): *Minnesota number one, Minnesota number two*

Minnesotaite - (etym. above); a kind of mineral

missey-moosey 1892 (M) Algonquian, alteration of *moosemise;* American mountain ash

Mississippi (culture) - Indian "great water," common to several languages (Harder); of a culture pattern in the Mississippi drainage system dating A.D. 1300–1700

Mississippi (game) - (etym. above); a kind of game played on an oblong table with a cue and balls

Mississippian (geol.) 1870 (OED) (etym. above); geologic time division

Mississippi catfish (or cat) - (etym. above); blue catfish or flathead catfish

Mississippi kite 1811 (M) (etym. above); a small kite (the bird)

Missourian (geol.) - Algonquian, perhaps meaning "river of the big canoes"; geologic time division

Missouri currant 1850 (M) (etym. above); buffalo currant

Missouri gooseberry - (etym. above); a shrub of the central United States or its berry

Missouri gourd - (etym. above); prairie gourd

Missouri grape - (etym. above); a kind of grape of the central and southern United States

Missouri skylark 1858 (OED) (etym. above); Sprague's pipit

mistassini - from Lake *Mistassini,* Quebec, Canada, Cree "great stone" (Harder); a dwarf primrose of northern and alpine America

mistonusk - Cree *mĭstanask* broad (W III); American badger

mobile terrapin - *Mobile,* Ala., of Indian origin + Virginia Algonquian *torope* (AHD III); an edible terrapin of the southern United States

Mobilian - (etym. above); a pidgin based on Choctaw and formerly a lingua franca in the southeastern United States

moccasin (or moccasin or moc) 1609 (Lescarbot—see chap. 2) Algonquian, compare Natick *mohkussin* (AHD I); a heelless shoe of soft leather, a kind of pit viper, argus-brown color

moccasin flower 1680 (M) (etym. above); any of several lady's slippers

moccasin telegraph 1908 (M) (etym. above); the grapevine

mockernut hickory 1810 (M) Virginia Algonquian *pocohiquara,* drink made of pressed hickory nuts; a smooth-barked North American hickory or its nut

mocock \muh-KOK\ (or mocuck) 1779 (OED) Algonquian, akin to Ojibwa *makak* box (W III); box or basket, as of birch bark, for keeping food

Mohawk 1880 (OED) Narragansett *mohowaúg* (AHD III), man-eaters; a maneuver in fancy skating, Tuscan brown color mohawk weed 1907 (M) (etym. above); a bellwort of eastern North America

Mohock 1711–12 (Swift—see chap. 6) (etym. above); an aristocratic ruffian of the early eighteenth century

Mohockism - (etym. above); unruly behavior as of the Mohocks

monadnock 1893 (OED) from Mount *Monadnock,* N.H., Abenaki "at the most prominent island-mountain," used for a lookout (Harder); a hill or mountain of resistant rock surmounting a peneplain

Monongahela (a whiskey) 1805 from the *Monongahela* River valley in Pennsylvania and northern West Virginia, from Delaware, probably "high-banks-falling-down" (Stewart); American whiskey, specifically, rye whiskey made in western Pennsylvania

mooneye cisco - Canadian French *ciscoette,* from Ojibwa *bemidewiskawed,* "the (fish) with oily skin" (AHD III); bloater, a small but common cisco

moose 1605 (Rosier—see chap. 2) (1603 is claimed by some) Eastern Abenaki *mos;* the animal

mooseberry 1789 (DC) (etym. above); the hobblebush or its fruit, the cranberry bush

moosebird 1832 (M) (etym. above); Canada jay

moosebush 1784 (M) (etym. above); hobblebush

moosecall 1890 (M) (etym. above); an instrument used by hunters to call moose

moose elm 1810 (etym. above); slippery elm

mooseflower 1850 (M) (etym. above); trillium

moose fly 1834 (OED) (etym. above); horsefly

moose maple 1839 (M) (etym. above); mountain maple

moosemise 1861 (DC) (etym. partly above); missey-moosey or American mountain ash

moose tick 1868 (OED) (etym. above); winter tick

moosetongue - (etym. above); willow herb

moosewood 1778 (M) (etym. above); striped maple, leatherwood, or hobblebrush mountain caribou 1908 (DC) Micmac (AHD III); a large caribou found from British Columbia to Alaska

mountain hickory - Virginia Algonquian *pocohiquara*, drink made of pressed hickory nuts; a large Australian timber tree

mouse opossum - Virginia Algonquian *aposoum* (AHD I); dormouse opossum or opossum of the genus *Marmosa*

muckamuck (v., eat) 1838 (M) Chinook Jargon hayo *makamak*, "plenty to eat" (AHD III); eat

muckamuck (n., food) 1847 (M) (etym. above); food

muckamuck (or mucketymuck) (big shot) 1912 (OED) (etym. above), short for *high-muck-a-muck, high-muckety-muck;* an important, sometimes overbearing, person

mugwump (n.) 1832 (M) Massachuset *mugguomp, mummugguomp,* war leader (AHD III); a person of importance or one who acts independently, especially in politics

mugwump (v.) 1889 (OED) (etym. above); adopt the position of a mugwump

mugwumpery 1885 (M) (etym. above); the views and practices of mugwumps

mugwumpian 1885 (M) (etym. above); of, suggesting, or being a mugwump

mugwumpish 1918 (OED) (etym. above); having the characteristics of mugwumpery

mugwumpism 1886 (M) (etym. above); independent action in politics

mummichog (or mummachog or mummychog) 1643 (Williams— see chap. 4) Narragansett *moamitteaûg;* a killifish of the Atlantic coast

murine opossum 1796 (OED) Virginia Algonquian *aposoum* (AHD I); any of several arboreal opossums in South and Central America

muskeg (or maskeg or maskeeg) 1775 (DC) Cree *maske'k* (RH II); a swamp or bog formed by the accumulation of sphagnum moss, leaves, and decaying matter

muskeg moss - (etym. above); any of various mosses that thrive on muskeg muskellunge (or muskallunge, etc.) 1789 (M) Canadian French *maskinongé* from Ojibwa *maashkinoozhe* (AHD III); a large food and game fish of the pike family in the northern United States and southern Canada

muskie (or musky) 1894 (W 10) (etym. above); muskellunge

muskie weed - (etym. above); an aquatic plant

muskrat (or muskrat beaver) 1607 (Percy) or 1612 (Smith—see chap. 2) Algonquian, given by Smith as *mussacus,* probably influenced by *musk* and *rat;* the animal

muskrat potato - (etym. above); wapatoo

muskrat weed 1897–98 (OED) (etym. above); tall meadow rue

musk terrapin - Virginia Algonquian *torope* (AHD I); musk turtle, musk tortoise

musquash 1612 (Smith—see chap. 2) (see *muskrat* for etymology); muskrat

musquash root 1807 (M) (etym. above); spotted cowbane

musquashweed 1767 (M) (etym. above); tall meadow rue

musquaw 1861 (OED) Algonquian; black bear

namaycush \NAM-ee-KUSH\ 1743 (DC) Cree *namekos* (AHD III); lake trout

Nantucket pine tip moth - *Nantucket* Island, Mass., from Indian word of uncertain meaning; a small reddish-brown silver-marked moth that attacks various pines

Nantucket sleighride (etym. above); run in a whaling boat attached to a harpooned whale

Narragansett (a domestic turkey) - from *Narragansett,* R.I., from name of tribe; a domestic turkey developed in Rhode Island

Narragansett pacer 1777 (OED) (etym. above); an extinct breed of American pacing saddle horses

nasaump \nuh-SOMP\ 1643 (Williams—see chap. 4) Narragansett *nasàump,* cornmeal mush; hominy

Naumkeag (n.) (or Naumkeag machine or scourer) probably from *Naumkeag,* old name for Salem, Mass., shoe manufacturing city (W III), Algonquian "fishing-place-at" (Stewart); machine for smoothing shoe soles or heels

Naumkeag - (v.) (etym. above); to buff a shoe bottom in the manufacture of shoes

Naumkeager - (etym. above); operator of a Naumkeag machine

Navaho (color) - American Spanish *Navajó,* originally a place name from Tewa *navahū* large arroyo with cultivated fields (AHD III); strong-to-vivid orange

Navaho blanket (or rug) 1834 (M) (etym. above); blanket woven by the Navajos with geometric designs of symbolic meaning

Navajo stitch - (etym. above); a coiled basketry stitch

Nebraskan (geol.) 1909 (OED) Siouan "flat or spreading water" (Stewart); geologic time division

netop \NEE-top\ 1612 (Smith—see chap. 2) akin to Narragansett *nétop,* friend, companion (AHD I); "friend," used by colonists in greeting Indians

Niagara 1841 (OED) Iroquoian from *Ongiaahra,* an Indian town (Harder); an overwhelming flood

Niagara green 1901 (M) (etym. above); a light bluish-green

Niagaran (geol.) - (etym. above); geologic time division

nocake 1634 (Wood—see chap. 4) Algonquian, akin to Narragansett *nokehick,* parched cornmeal (W III); Indian corn parched and pounded into a powder

Nootka cypress (or Nootka Sound cypress) 1892 (M) from *Nootka* Sound, Vancouver Island, British Columbia, from the Wakashan people of that name; yellow cedar

northern muskellunge - Canadian French *maskinongé* from Ojibwa *maashkinoozhe* (AHD III); Chautauqua muskellunge

nutmeg hickory 1832 (OED) Virginia Algonquian *pocohiquara,* drink made of pressed hickory nuts; a hickory of the southern United States and Mexico with a nutmeg-shaped fruit

Ochoan (geol.) - Indian? from *Ochoa,* locality in southeastern New Mexico; geologic time division

oconee \uh-KO-nee\ bells - from *Oconee* River in Georgia from Muskogean name of a tribe (Harder); a stemless perennial herb

Ogeechee lime - Muskogean, "river of the Yuchis," from Indian tribe that lived along its banks (Harder); the drupe of a tupelo of the southern United States, or tree whose fruits are Ogeechee limes

Ohioan (geol.) - Iroquoian "river-fine" (Stewart); geologic time division

Ohio buckeye 1810 (M) (etym. above); a buckeye that occurs mainly in the central United States

Ohio curcuma - (etym. above); goldenseal

Ohio horsemint - (etym. above); a perennial mint

oka 1936 (DC) from Algonquian *Oka,* village in Quebec, Canada, where it is made; a cheese made by Trappist monks in Quebec

Okie (or Oakie) 1938 (OED) from *Oklahoma* State from Choctaw "red people" from *okla* (people) + *humma* or *homma* (red) (Harder); a migrant agricultural worker, especially one from Oklahoma

oklabar 1938 (OED) *Okla*homa (etym. above) + *bar;* a breed of domestic fowl

Oklahoma (or Oklahoma gin) 1945 (OED) (etym. above); a form of gin rummy

Oklahoma plum - (etym. above); a low shrub with red fruit

old-squaw 1838 (M) Massachusett *squà,* younger woman (AHD III); a common sea duck

Oneota - from *Oneota,* village in eastern Minnesota, Indian?; of a culture of the Upper Mississippi phase of the Mississippi culture pattern (Indian)

Ontario violet - Iroquoian; a pale purplish-blue

opossum 1610 (M) Virginia Algonquian *aposoum* (AHD I); the animal

opossum mouse 1832 (OED) (etym. above); any of several small Australian phalangers

opossum rat - (etym. above); any of several small South American marsupials

opossum shrimp 1844 (OED) (etym. above); a small crustacean that carries its eggs in a pouch between its legs

opossum tree - (etym. above); opossum wood or liquidambar

opossum wood - (etym. above); silver bell (tree) or an Australian timber tree oquassa \oh-KWAH-suh\ 1883 (OED) Eastern Abenaki, from *Oquassa* Lake in Maine; small, dark-blue lake trout

Oregon alder 1874 (M) Indian of uncertain origin; red alder

Oregon ash 1869 (OED) (etym. above); a timber tree of western North America

Oregon balsam - (etym. above); an oleoresin or mixture of rosin and turpentine

Oregon balsam fir - (etym. above); Douglas fir

Oregon boat - (etym. above); an iron shackle attached to the foot and ankle of a prisoner to prevent escape

Oregon box - (etym. above); a low evergreen shrub of western North America

Oregon cedar 1872 (OED) (etym. above); Port Orford cedar

Oregon char - (etym. above); Dolly Varden, a large char of western North America

Oregon cliff brake - (etym. above); a North American fern with wiry light-brown stripes

Oregon crab apple - 1884 (M) (etym. above); a small tree of western North America

Oregon fir (or Oregon Douglas fir) 1904 (M); Douglas fir

Oregon grape (or Oregon holly grape) 1851 (OED) (etym. above); either of two shrubs native to the Pacific coast

Oregon graperoot - (etym. above); berberis, the dried roots of certain barberries

Oregon Jargon - (etym. above); Chinook Jargon

Oregon jay 1910 (DC) (etym. above); a crestless jay of northwestern North America

Oregon larch - (etym. above); western larch or noble fir

Oregon lily 1964 (OED) (etym. above); an herb of western North America with orange-red purple-spotted flowers

Oregon maple - (etym. above); a large-leaved maple of the Pacific coast of North America

Oregon myrtle 1934 (M) (etym. above); California laurel

Oregon oak (or Oregon white oak) - (etym. above); an oak of western North America, called also Garry oak

Oregon pine 1845 (M) (etym. above); Douglas fir

Oregon robin 1860 (M) (etym. above); varied thrush

Oregon triton - (etym. above); a large whelk of the Pacific coast of North America

orenda 1902 (OED) coined by an ethnologist from the supposed Huron cognate of a Mohawk word; the invisible power Iroquois Indians believed pervaded all animate and inanimate natural objects

Osage (Osage orange) - from the Siouan tribal name; Osage orange

Osage orange (or apple) 1817 (OED) (etym. above); an ornamental American tree with orangelike fruit, or coloring matter extracted from the wood of the tree

Osagian (geol.) - (etym. above); geologic time division

Oswego bass 1758 (OED) Iroquoian name, from the *Oswego* River of New York; largemouth or smallmouth black bass

Oswego tea 1752 (OED) (etym. above); a North American mint also called *bee balm*

ouananiche \WAH-nuh-NEESH\ (or ouananiche salmon) 1808 (DC) Canadian French *ouananiche* from Montagnais *wananish* diminutive of *wanans,* salmon (W III); small landlocked salmon of Canada

pac or pack 1875 (M) (shortened from *shoepac,* which see); shoepac, or sheepskin or felt shoe worn inside a boot or overshoe in cold weather

Pacific cultus - Chinook *cultus,* worthless (W III); lingcod

Pacific terrapin - Virginia Algonquian *torope* (AHD I); an aquatic mud turtle sold as terrapin

paha - Dakota *pahá* hill (W III); a hill or ridge of glacial origin topped with loess, found especially in northeastern Iowa

paho (or baho) 1883 (M) Hopi *páʻho* (RH II); prayer stick of the Hopi Indians

painted terrapin (or turtle or tortoise) 1876 (OED) Virginia Algonquian *torope* (AHD I); painted turtle or tortoise, found chiefly in the eastern part of the United States

papoose (or pappoose) 1634 (Wood—see chap. 4) Narragansett *papoòs,* child; an Indian infant or very young child papoose board 1858 (M) (etym. above); cradleboard

papooseroot 1815 (OED) (etym. above); blue cohosh

Patayan \PAHD-uh-YAHN\ - Walapai *pataya,* ancient people, pertaining to a culture of western Arizona dating from about 700 to 1200

pattypan squash 1900 (W 10) Narragansett *askútasquash* (Williams—see chap. 4); cymling, a summer squash having a scalloped edge

Patuxent (geol.) - from the Algonquian name of an Indian people; geologic time division

Pawnee (color) - from the Siouan name of the Indian people; a light grayish-yellowish brown

peag \PEEG\ (or peage or peak) 1634 (OED) shortening of *wampumpeag* (which see); wampum

pearl hominy - Virginia Algonquian *uskatahomen,* probably "that which is ground" (RH II); a hominy milled to pellets of medium size

pecan 1712 (W 10) (or 1612?) North American French *pacane* from Illinois *pakani* (AHD III); the tree or the nut it produces

pecan brown - (etym. above); golden chestnut (the color)

pecan carpenter worm - (etym. above); a worm that bores in the wood of the pecan, oak, and hickory

pecan nut casebearer - (etym. above); a grub that feeds on various hickories and walnuts

pecan scab - (etym. above); a fungal disease of the pecan

pecan weevil - (etym. above); a weevil that attacks hickory and pecan nuts

pekan \PEK-uhn\ 1760 (OED) Canadian French *pékan* from Eastern Abenaki *pékané;* fisher (the carnivorous animal)

pembina (or pimbina) 1760 (DC) Cree *m'pimina'na* (RH II); cranberry tree

pemmican (or pemican) 1743 (Isham, 156—see chap. 6) Cree *pimihkaam* (AHD III); trail food made of dried meat pounded fine, mixed with fat and dried fruits or berries

Pensacola snapper - from *Pensacola* Bay, Fla., from Choctaw *panshi* (hair) + *okla* (people), long-haired people (Harder); gray snapper

persimmon 1612 (Smith—see chap. 2) Algonquian, akin to Cree *pasiminan,* dried fruit (AHD I); any of various tropical trees with edible orange-red fruit

pickaway anise - perhaps from *Pickaway* County, Ohio, from folk etymological form of *piqua,* apparently the name of a Shawnee subtribe (Harder); hop tree

pig hickory - Virginia Algonquian *pocohiquara,* drink made of pressed hickory nuts; pignut hickory

pignut hickory 1705 (M) (etym. above); a hickory bearing pignuts (which are bitter flavored)

piki \PEE-kee\ 1859 (M) Hopi; maize bread baked in thin sheets by Indians of the southwestern United States

pima (or pima cotton) 1925 (W 10) from *Pima* County, Ariz., where it was developed, from the *Pima* people; a very strong high-grade cotton

pipe tomahawk - Virginia Algonquian *tamahaac* (AHD III); a tomahawk with a bowl in the head for use also as a pipe

pipsissewa 1789 (M) perhaps Eastern Abenaki *kpi-pskwáhsawe,* woods flower, pipsissewa (AHD III); an evergreen herb whose leaves have been used as a tonic and diuretic

piskun \PIS-kuhn\ 1805 Blackfoot; a steep cliff used for driving a large number of buffalo to their slaughter

Pismo \PIZ-moh\ clam 1913 (M) from *Pismo* Beach, Calif., probably from Chumash word for tar or for mustard plant that grows nearby (Harder); an edible thick-shelled clam of the southern Pacific coast of North America

Piute \PIGH-yoot\ - probably from *Paiute* Indian people; a brilliantly colored cutthroat trout in California

pocan (or pocan bush) 1858 (M) Virginia Algonquian skin to *puccoon;* pokeweed

pocosin \Puh-KOH-sin\ (also pocoson or pocosen) 1634 (OED) possibly Virginia Algonquian (AHD III); chiefly South Atlantic United States; a swamp in an upland coastal region, also called *dismal*

Podunk 1841 (Read—see chap. 8) Natick "swamp (or miry place) -at" (Stewart), name of two New England meadows, then used by a southern newspaper as a term for an inconsequential town; a small, unimportant, and isolated town

pogamoggan ca. 1787 (DC) Ojibwa *pakama·kan* (RH II); club with knobbed head

pogonip 1865 (M) Shoshone *pakenappeh* (AHD III), thundercloud (RH II); ice fog

pogy (or pogie) ca. 1847 (W 10) alteration of dialectal *poghaden,* perhaps of Eastern Abenaki origin (AHD III); menhaden

poison camas - Chinook Jargon *kamass;* a common perennial death camas

poison sego - Southern Paiute *sigh'o* (AHD III); death camas

poke (tobacco) 1634 (OED) Virginia Algonquian akin to *puccoon* (AHD III); tobacco

poke (pokeweed) 1708 (M) Virginia Algonquian akin to *puccoon* (AHD III); a tall North American plant with blackish-red berries

pokeberry 1774 (M) (etym. above); pokeweed or the berry of it

pokelogan (or pokeloken) 1818 (DC) Algonquian; stagnant inlet or marshy place branching off from a stream or pond

poke milkweed 1895 (OED) Virginia Algonquian akin to *puccoon* (AHD III); a milkweed of the eastern United States with leaves resembling those of the pokeweed

pokeroot 1687 (M) (etym. above); pokeweed

poke salad 1881 (OED) (etym. above); the cooked young shoots of pokeweed

pokeweed 1751 (OED) (etym. above); a tall North American plant with blackish-red berries

pokeweed family - (etym. above); a family of chiefly tropical herbs including the pokeweed

pone (or pone bread) 1605 (Rosier—see chap. 2) Virginia Algonquian *poan, appoans,* corn bread (AHD III); johnnycake or corn bread

pone (lump) 1895 (M) (perhaps etym. above); lump or swelling possum (n.) 1613 (Whitaker—see chap. 2) Virginia Algonquian *aposoum* (AHD III); opossum

possum (v.) 1822 (OED) (etym. above); to play possum or hunt opossum

possum belly 1926 (M) (etym. above); storage space beneath the flooring of a vehicle

possum fruit (or apple) - (etym. above); persimmon

possum grape 1936 (M) (etym. above); chicken grape, another grape resembling the chicken grape, or marine ivy

possum haw 1860 (M) (etym. above); bearberry or the plant withe rod

possum oak 1884 (M) (etym. above); a tall water oak of the southeastern United States

possum-trot plan - (etym. above); a plan of a house in two parts with a breezeway between

possumwood - (etym. above); persimmon, the wood of the sandbox tree, or opossum wood

potlatch (or potlach) (n.) 1861 (M) Chinook Jargon from Nootka *p'achitl,* "to make a potlatch gift" (AHD III); a ceremonial feast in the Pacific Northwest at which gifts are liberally bestowed

potlatch (v.) 1847 (M) (etym. above); to hold or give a potlatch, sometimes used figuratively

Pottawattomi (or Pottawattami) potted - from *Potawatomi* tribe, Algonquian; preserved in a closed pot, jar, or can; made easily understandable by abridgment or glamorization; literally or figuratively canned

powitch - Chinook Jargon from Chinook -*páuč* (W III); Oregon crab apple

powwow (n.) 1605 (Rosier—see chap. 2) Narragansett *powwaw,* shaman; a council or meeting of Indians, an Indian shaman, or a gathering in general

powwow (v.) 1642 (Lechford—see chap. 4) (etym. above); to hold a powwow

powwow doctor - (etym. above); one who heals by incantation or magic pride of Ohio 1861 (M) Iroquoian, "river-fine" (Stewart); the common American shooting star

puccoon 1612 (Smith—see chap. 2) Virginia Algonquian *poughkone* (RH II) related to Algonquian *pak* blood (?); any of several plants, including the bloodroot, whose roots yield a red dye

pukeweed 1848 (M) variation of *pokeweed?* (which see); Indian tobacco—in the sense of an American wild lobelia

pung 1825 (OED) short for *tom-pung* from an Algonquian language of southern New England (AHD III), cognate with *toboggan;* a low one-horse box sleigh

punk (decayed wood) 1618 (M) Virginia Algonquian *pungnough,* in Strachey with the sense of something burnt to a powder; wood that is so decayed as to be very dry, crumbly, and useful for tinder

punkie (or punky) (biting midge) 1769 (M) of North American Dutch origin from Munsee (Delaware language) *ponkw·s* (AHD III); any of several biting flies, biting midge, or no-see-um

punkwood 1883 (OED) (for etym. see *punk* above); rotten wood

punky (adj., of decayed wood) 1872 (M) perhaps alteration (influenced by Delaware *punk,* fine ashes, powder) of *spunk;* of or like *punk,* decayed wood

pygmy possum - Virginia Algonquian *aposoum* (AHD I), mouse opossum

quahog (or quahaug or quohog or quohaug) (n.) 1643 (Williams—see chap. 4) Narragansett *poquaûhock,* an edible clam of the Atlantic coast of North America

quahog (v.) 1905 (M) (etym. above); to dig quahogs

quahogger (or quahauger) 1935 (M) (etym. above); one who digs quahogs

Quebec (letter *q*) ca. 1952 (W 10) from *Quebec,* Canada, from Algonquian "where the river narrows" (Harder); a communications code word for the letter *q*

Quebec deal (etym. above); timber of any width and three inches or more in thickness

Quebec standard deal - (etym. above); a deal board three inches by eleven inches by twelve feet quickhatch 1683 (DC) East Cree *kwi'hkwaha'ke'w* (RH II); wolverine

quinnat salmon (or quinnat) 1829 (OED) Chinook *ikwanat* (AHD III); Chinook salmon

quisutsch 1886 (Elliott, 94) native name in Kamchatka and Alaska (W III); silver salmon

quoddy 1884 (M) from Passama*quoddy* Bay from the Micmac name of the Indian people; an open sloop-rigged sailboat

Quonset 1942 (OED) from *Quonset* Point, R.I., from Algonquian "long-place" (Stewart); *trademark,* a prefabricated portable hut having a semicircular roof of corrugated metal that curves down to form walls

raccoon (or racoon) 1608 (Smith—see chap. 2) Virginia Algonquian *aroughcun;* raccoon

raccoonberry 1867 (M) (etym. above); the fruit of the mayapple

raccoon dog 1868 (M) (etym. above); member of the canine family in eastern Asia and Japan with facial markings like the raccoon's

raccoon family - (etym. above); a family of carnivorous animals consisting of raccoons, coatis, cacomistles, kinkajous, and sometimes the pandas

raccoon fox 1859 (M) (etym. above); cacomistle, a small mammal of the southwestern United States

raccoon grape 1834 (M) (etym. above); fox grape or a shrub chiefly of the southeastern United States

raccoon oyster 1834 (OED) (etym. above); coon oyster (which see)

raccoon perch - (etym. above); yellow perch

red-bellied terrapin (or turtle) 1876 (OED) Virginia Algonquian *torope* (AHD I); a terrapin of the tributaries of Chesapeake Bay

redheart hickory - Virginia Algonquian *pocohiquara,* drink made of pressed hickory nuts; shagbark hickory

red hickory - (etym. above); mockernut or pignut

red puccoon - Virginia Algonquian *poughkone* (RH II); bloodroot

red titi - probably Timucuan (W III); leatherwood, the tree of the southeastern United States and South America roanoke 1624 (Smith—see chap. 2) Virginia Algonquian *raw-ranoke*, shell money, probably from *rarenawok*, smoothed shells (W III); wampum

Roanoke bell - (etym. above); Virginia cowslip

rock opossum - Virginia Algonquian *aposoum* (AHD I); a rock wallaby

sacalait 1877 (OED) Louisiana French from Choctaw *sakli*, trout (taken as *sac* [sack] + *a* [for] + *lait* [milk]) (RH II); white crappie, warmouth, killifish

sachem 1622 (Morton—see chap. 4) Narragansett *sâchim*, chief (AHD I); a chief of an Indian tribe or a member of the ruling council of the Iroquois confederacy

sachemship 1651 (M) (etym. above); the office or authority of a sachem

sagamité \suh-GAH-muh-TAY\ 1665 (OED) Canadian French of Algonquian origin (W III); hulled corn or a thin porridge of hulled corn

sagamore 1605 (Rosier—see chap. 2) Eastern Abenaki *sàkama* (AHD I); a subordinate chief or war chief of Indians on the northern Atlantic coast, sachem

saguaro (or sahuaro or suwarro) 1856 (OED) American Spanish probably of Piman origin (AHD III); a very large cactus of the southwestern United States and Mexico

salal 1805 (M) Chinook Jargon *sallal* from Chinook *sálal* (AHD III); a small evergreen shrub native to the Pacific coast of North America with edible purple-black berries

salt-marsh terrapin 1872 (M) Virginia Algonquian *torope* (AHD I); diamondback terrapin

samp 1643 (Williams—see chap. 4) Narragansett *nasàump*, corn-meal mush; cornmeal mush

sand squeteague - of Algonquian origin (AHD III); a weakfish of the Gulf of Mexico

Sangamon (geol.) - from *Sangamon* River and County, Ill., from Ojibwa probably "the outlet" (Harder); division of geologic time sannup 1628 (Levett—see chap. 4) Massachussett *sanomp* (RH II); a married male Indian

Saratoga (cards) - possibly Mohawk "springs (of water) from the hillside" (Harder); a variation of the card game Michigan

Saratoga chip (or potato) 1876 (M) (etym. above); potato chip

Saratoga chop - (etym. above); a boneless shoulder chop of lamb rolled and skewered

Saratoga cocktail - (etym. above); a cocktail consisting of brandy, sweet vermouth, bitters, and sometimes a fruit juice

Saratoga spittlebug - (etym. above); a bug that feeds on pines in the northern United States

Saratoga trunk 1858 (W 10) (etym. above); a large traveling trunk usually with a rounded top

saskatoon 1800 (DC) Cree *misa'skwato'min* derivation of *misa'skwat* (literally, "that which is solid wood") with *-min* berry (RH II); a shrub of northwestern North America with edible dark-purple fruit

Sasquatch 1929 (M) Salish *se'sxac* wild men (12,000 Words); Bigfoot

Schenectady putter - from Mohawk village of *Schaunactada* (Harder); a golf putter in which the shaft is fastened near the center of the head

scoke 1778 (M) New England Algonquian language, compare Eastern Abenaki *skókimin* pokeberry (RH II); pokeweed

scup 1848 (M) short for Narragansett *mishcuppaûg;* a porgy of the northern Atlantic waters important as a food fish

scuppaug 1643 (Williams—see chap. 4); see above

Scuppernong (grape) 1811 (OED) from *Scuppernong,* small river in North Carolina from Southern Algonquian for "bay-tree-at" (Stewart); a cultivated variety of the muscadine grape with sweet yellowish fruit

Scuppernong (wine) 1825 (OED) (etym. above); white aromatic wine made from Scuppernong grape

seapoose (or sea puss or sea purse) 1650 (M) Unquachog *seépus,* river (RH II); a dangerous swirling of undertow or an undertow along shore

Seawanhaka \suh-WAHN-uh-kuh\ boat - from *Seawanhaka* yacht club, Oyster Bay, Long Island, perhaps from *Siwanoy* for "great bay of the island of shells" (from Ashley in Heller, *Names*); a kind of flat broad sailboat

Sebago salmon 1883 (M) from *Sebago* Lake, Maine, from Abenaki for "big lake" (Harder); landlocked salmon

sego lily \SEE-goh\ (or sego) 1846 (W 10) Southern Paiute *sigho'o* (AHD III); a western North American plant with showy flowers

Seneca grass 1814 (M) from the name of the people, from Dutch *Sennecaas,* probably of Mahican origin (AHD III); sweet grass, or holy grass

Senecan (geol.) - (etym. above); geologic time division

Seneca oil 1795 (OED) (etym. above); a crude petroleum formerly in medical use

Seneca root 1775 (Adair—see chap. 6) (etym. above); a North American milkwort or its dried root

senega 1738 (OED) variation of *Seneca* (which see under *Seneca grass*); *senega* or *Seneka snakeroot* (or *senega root,* or *senega snakeroot,* or *Seneka root*)

senega root ca. 1846 (W 10) (etym. above); Seneca root

senegin - named after *senega* (etym. above); saponin, or ingredient of soap, obtained from senega root

Seneka snakeroot 1728 (OED) (etym. above); see above, named for its use by the Senecas as a remedy against snakebite

Sequoia 1847 (M) from Cherokee leader *Sequoyah* (1760?–1843); redwood or giant sequoia

Sequoiadendron - (etym. above); a genus of coniferous trees

Sequoia pitch moth - (etym. above); a clearwing moth whose larvae are especially destructive to lodgepole pine and western yellow pine

sewan \SEE-wahn\ (or seawan or seawant) 1627 (M) Dutch (New Amsterdam) *sewan, zeewän,* or *zeewant,* of Algonquian origin, akin to Natick *seawan, sewan,* loose beads (W III); wampum

sewellel \suh-WEL-uhl\ 1806 (M) Chinook *šwalál* robe of sewellel skins (AHD III); a small rodent of the Pacific coast of North America also called *mountain beaver* shaganappi 1743 (Isham, 46) Swampy Cree *pi'sa'kana'piy* (RH II); a thread, cord, or thong of rawhide

shagbark hickory 1751 (M) Virginia Algonquian *pocohiquara,* drink made of pressed hickory nuts; a hickory with edible nuts and shaggy bark

Shalako \shuh-LAH-koh\ (or Shalako dancer) - Zuñi (W III); dancer impersonating a Zuñi mythical being, or the ceremony in which Shalakos play a central role

shallon 1806 (M) (see *salal*); salal or the fruit of the salal

Shasta cypress 1897 (OED) from Mt. *Shasta,* Calif., from tribal name of Hokan linguistic stock (Harder); MacNab cypress

Shasta daisy 1893 (M) (etym. above); a large-flowered garden daisy

Shasta red fir (or Shasta fir) 1897 (OED) (etym. above); an immense evergreen tree of the Pacific coast of North America

Shasta Sam - (etym. above); a card game

Shawanese salad (or Shawnee salad or Shawnee) 1780 (OED) Shawnee *shaawanooki,* "those of the south, Shawnee" (AHD III); Virginia waterleaf

Shawneewood 1909 (OED) (etym. above); western catalpa

shawny - (etym. above); Virginia waterleaf

shenango (or chenango) - from the *Chenango* River and *Chenango* Canal, N.Y., Onondaga "bull thistle" (Harder); a casually employed dock worker

shoepac (or shoepack) 1755 (M) alteration influenced by *shoe* of pidgin Delaware *seppock,* shoe, shoes from Unami Delaware *chípahko,* shoes (AHD III); a waterproof laced boot of rubber, leather, or canvas

Siberian chipmunk - *chitmunk,* apparently from Ojibwa; baronduki, a Siberian ground squirrel

Siberian husky 1930 (OED) probably from *Eskimo* from French *Esquimaux* from Montagnais *ayashkimew,* Micmac (AHD III); a breed of dogs developed in northeastern Siberia

sieva bean (also seewee bean or sewee bean) 1888 (OED) perhaps alteration of *seewee* or *sewee* bean, probably after the *Sewee,* an extinct Indian tribe of eastern South Carolina (RH II); any of several bush or weakly vining edible beans silver squeteague - of Algonquian origin (AHD III); a common weakfish of the Atlantic coast of North America

sipapu \SEE-pah-poo\ 1891 (OED) Hopi *síipaapu* (W III); a hole in the floor of a kiva symbolizing the place where the mythical ancestors first appeared from the underworld regions

siscowet 1837 (DC) short for Ojibwa *pēmitēwiskawēt: pimitēw* (oil) + *iskawē* (to have flesh of a specified type) (AHD III); a kind of lake trout found in the upper part of Lake Superior

Sitka alder - from *Sitka,* Alaska, from Tlingit name of Baranof Island; a shrub or small tree ranging from Alaska to California

Sitka crab - (etym. above); a small crustacean found from Alaska to California that resembles a crab

Sitka cypress 1884 (OED) (etym. above); yellow cedar

Sitka spruce 1879 (Muir, 187) (etym. above); a tall spruce of the northern Pacific coast

Sitka spruce beetle - (etym. above); a bark beetle the larva of which attacks the Sitka spruce

Sitka spruce weevil - (etym. above); a weevil that is very destructive to the Sitka spruce

Sitka willow - (etym. above); a willow ranging from Alaska to Oregon

Siwash (an Indian) 1847 (OED) Chinook Jargon from North American French *sauvage,* Indian (in French, "wild" or "savage") (RH II); in the Northwest, an Indian

Siwash (jargon) 1902 (OED) (etym. above); the jargon used by and in talking with Siwashes

Siwash (v.) 1904 (OED) (etym. above); to camp or travel with little or no equipment, rough it

Siwash (college) 1911 (RH II) (etym. above); from humorous novel *At Good Old Siwash;* a small college that is provincial in outlook

skookum 1838 (M) Chinook Jargon, powerful, evil spirit, from Chehalis *skukm* (W III); an evil spirit

skookum (adj.) 1847 (M) (etym. above); marked by strength or power, first-rate

skookum-house ca. 1873 (OED) (etym. above); jail

skunk (n.) 1634 (Wood—see chap. 4) Massachusett *squnck* (AHD I); the animal

skunk (v.) 1843 (W 10) (etym. above); shut out, defeat conclusively

skunk bear 1876 (M) (etym. above); wolverine

skunkbill - (etym. above); the surf scoter (duck)

skunk bird or skunk blackbird - (etym. above—so called because of the male's coloring); bobolink

skunkbrush (also skunkbush) - (etym. above); any of various shrubs having an offensive odor, such as bear brush or squawbush

skunk cabbage 1751 (M) (etym. above); a perennial herb of eastern North America with an offensive smelling spathe in early spring, or similar plant, or pitcher plant

skunk currant 1817 (OED) (etym. above); wild currant of the eastern United States that bears offensive-smelling fruit

skunkery 1890 (M) (etym. above); place where skunks are bred and raised

skunk grass - (etym. above); a grass so called because of its odor

skunk porpoise 1884 (OED) (etym. above); spectacled dolphin, so named because of its black-and-white stripes

skunk spruce 1894 (OED); a kind of white spruce

skunktail (or skunktail grass) - (etym. above); squirreltail, a kind of grass

skunk turtle - (etym. above); musk turtle

skunkweed 1738 (M) (etym. above); any of several offensive-smelling herbs

skunk works ca. 1974 (W 10) (etym. above); a usually small and often isolated department, as for engineering, within a company

skunky 1897 (OED) (etym. above); having the characteristics of a skunk

snapping terrapin - Virginia Algonquian *torope* (AHD I); snapping turtle

sockeye (or sockeye salmon) 1869 (W 10) by folk etymology from Salish (dialectal) *suk-kegh* (AHD I); a salmon of northern Pacific waters, also called *blueback salmon* or *red salmon* sofkee 1796 (M) Muskogean *safki* (W III); a thin mush of gruel made of cornmeal

Southern Senega - variation of *Seneca* (which see under *Seneca grass*); the dried root of a plant related to the senega found in the central and southern United States

spaghetti squash 1975 (W 10) Naragansett *askútasquash* (AHD III); a winter squash that has a spaghettilike texture when cooked

spotted terrapin - Virginia Algonquian *torope* (AHD I); spotted turtle or tortoise, a small American freshwater tortoise

squam \SKWAHM\ short for Indian-derived name of *Annisquam* in Massachusetts, where it was originally worn by fishermen (W III); sou'wester, a long oilskin coat or a hat with a wide slanting brim longer in back than in front

squanter-squash 1634 (Wood—see chap. 4) from *isquotersquash* from Narragansett *askútasquash* (AHD III); summer squash

squantum 1812 (M) probably from *Squantum,* former Indian village in Massachusetts, Algonquian name; New England clambake, a social gathering where food is prepared and eaten outdoors

squash 1643 (Williams—see chap. 4) Narragansett *askútasquash* (AHD III); the plant

squash beetle 1867 (M) (etym. above); small beetle often harmful to the leaves of the squash and cucumber, squash ladybird

squashberry 1937 (OED) (etym. above); the fruit of any of the plants of the genus *Viburnum* or the plant itself

squash blossom 1923 (OED) (etym. above); hair dressed in large loops over each ear in a style once peculiar to Hopi girls

squash borer (or vine borer) 1891 (M) (etym. above); a small clear-wing moth or its larva that bores in the squash vine

squash bug 1846 (M) (etym. above); a brownish-black American insect harmful to squash vines

squash flea beetle - (etym. above); potato flea beetle

squash ladybird (or ladybug) - (etym. above); a ladybird that feeds on the squash, pumpkin, melon, and cucumber

squash vine - (etym. above); a plant that bears squashes

squash yellow - (etym. above); a variable color averaging a brilliant yellow redder and deeper than butter yellow or average daffodil and redder and stronger than lemon chrome

squaw 1622 (Morton—see chap. 4), Massachusett *squà,* younger woman (AHD III); Indian woman, especially a wife

squawberry 1852 (OED) (etym. above); deerberry, partridgeberry, or any of several sumacs

squawbush 1832 (M) (etym. above); so called from the use of the berries among Indians to fix colors when dyeing; cranberry tree, a sumac of western North America, any of several shrubs of the genus *Cornus,* or dwarf cornel

squaw cabbage 1915 (M) (etym. above); Indian lettuce, or any of various plants of the family *Cruciferae* reputedly used as potherbs by the Indians

squaw carpet - (etym. above); mahala mat, mountain misery

squaw corn - (etym. above), so called from its widespread cultivation by the Indians; soft corn

squaw currant 1909 (M) (etym. above); a spineless shrub native to the central and western United States with a crimson berry

squaw dance 1864 (OED) (etym. above); a round dance of the Plains Indians and Navajo in which the girls choose partners

squaw-drops - (etym. above); cancerroot, or squawroot (herb that is parasitic on oak and hemlock)

squaw duck - (etym. above); eider

squawfish 1881 (M) (etym. above); any of several large cyprinid fish, or a common surf fish of the Pacific coast of North America

squawflower - (etym. above); purple trillium

squaw grass - (etym. above); a turkey beard of the mountains of the Pacific Northwest, also called *pine lily*

squaw hitch 1887 (OED) (etym. above); a knot used in tying a pack on an animal

squaw huckleberry 1857 (M) (etym. above); deerberry

squaw lettuce - (etym. above); a waterleaf of the southwestern United States squaw man 1866 (M) (etym. above); a white man married to an Indian woman, or a bardash (homosexual male)

squaw mint - (etym. above); pennyroyal

squawroot 1815 (M) (etym. above); an herb parasitic on oak and hemlock, or blue cohosh, or purple trillium, or yamp

squaw sachem 1622 (M) (Morton—see chap. 4) (etym. above) + Narragansett *sâchim,* chief (AHD I); a female sachem or the wife of a sachem

squaw side - (etym. above); the right side of a horse, so called because the squaws of some tribes customarily mounted a horse from that side

squaw vine 1850 (M) (etym. above); partridgeberry

squaw-weed (or squaw waterweed) 1828 (M); any of various herbs

squaw winter 1861 (OED) (etym. above); a brief period of wintry weather occurring in autumn

squaw wood 1914 (M) (etym. above) (so called because squaws could gather it since an ax was not needed); small dead branches low on a tree

squeteague \skwuh-TEEG\ (or squet or squiteague or squetee, etc.) 1803 (M) Algonquian; weakfish or any of several fishes related to the weakfish

Star of Texas from a Caddo word, meaning "friends" or "allies," that the Spanish and then the Americans adopted as *Tejas* or *Texas* (see chap. 10); an herb with yellow flower heads common in the prairie regions of the southern United States

stinking poke - Virginia Algonquian, see *poke* (pokeweed); skunk cabbage

stogie (or stogy) (shoe) 1847 (M) from Conestoga, Pa., (named after an Iroquoian tribe that became extinct in 1763); a stout coarse shoe or brogan

stogie (or stogy) (cigar) 1893 (M) (etym. above) perhaps from drivers of Conestoga wagons who smoked them; a cheap cigar

stone caribou - Micmac (AHD III) perhaps "shoveler of snow"; a large dark caribou widely distributed from central Alaska to the arctic slopes striped opossum - Virginia Algonquian *aposoum* (AHD I); any of several phalangers in Queensland and New Guinea

striped skunk - ca. 1882 (W 10) Massachusett *squnck* (AHD I); any of several skunks of the genus *Mephitis*

succotash 1643 (Williams—see chap. 4) Narragansett *msíckquatash,* boiled whole-kernel corn; a stew consisting of kernels of corn, lima beans, and sometimes tomatoes

sugar opossum - Virginia Algonquian *aposoum* (AHD I); a small widely distributed Australian opossum also called *sugar squirrel*

summer cohosh - Eastern Abenaki; a bugbane of the eastern North American woodlands

summer squash 1815 (M) [1745–55, RH II] Narragansett *askútasquash* (AHD III); any of several varieties of squash that are eaten shortly after being picked rather than stored

Sunapee trout 1900 (M) from *Sunapee* Lake, N.H., from Pennacook "rocky pond" (Harder); a brilliantly colored char of Sunapee and other lakes of New Hampshire and Maine

sunck (or suncke or sunk squaw) 1662 (M) Algonquian; a female American Indian chief

supawn \suh-PAWN\ (or suppawn) 1612 (Strachey—see chap. 2) Dutch *sappaen* of Algonquian origin (W III); hasty pudding: cornmeal mush usually served hot with milk and maple sugar or molasses

Susquehanna salmon 1871 (M) Iroquoian (Harder) from the *Susquehanna* River of New York, Pennsylvania, and Maryland; walleye or walleyed pike

Suwannee chicken - from *Suwannee* River in Georgia and Florida, perhaps Seminole (Harder); an edible Florida river terrapin

swago bass - alteration of *Oswego* (from the Iroquoian *Oswego* River of New York); bass, smallmouth black bass

swamp squawweed - Massachusett *squà,* younger woman (AHD III); golden ragwort

swamp tupelo - probably Creek *'topwila: íto* (tree) + *opílwa* (swamp) (AHD III); tupelo

taconic (geol.) 1849 (OED) from *Taconic* range in northeastern United States, Algonquian (Harder); geologic time division taconite 1892 (OED) (etym. above); a flintlike rock containing granules of iron oxide

Tahoe trout 1902 (M) from Lake *Tahoe* on the California-Nevada boundary, Washo "big water" (Harder); a large cutthroat trout found in Lake Tahoe and neighboring regions

Tahoka daisy - from *Tahoka,* Tex., believed to be Spanish-Indian (Harder); an aster of the southern United States and Mexico

tamarack 1805 (M) Canadian French *tamarac,* probably of Algonquian origin (AHD III); a North American larch tree

tamarack pine - (etym. above); lodgepole pine

Tammany - from *Tammany* Hall, headquarters of the *Tammany* Society, after *Tamanend* "the affable," seventeenth-century Delaware chief (AHD I); of an organization exercising or seeking municipal political control by methods often associated with corruption or bossism

Tammanyism - (etym. above); the political principles or practices associated with Tammany Hall

Tammanyite - (etym. above); one associated with Tammanyism

Tammanyize - (etym. above); to bring under Tammany rule or the domination of Tammanyism

Targhee \TAHR-gee\ - from *Targhee* Pass, Mont., from the name of a Shoshonean chief (Harder); an American breed of sheep

tautog \taw-TAWG\ (or tautaug) 1643 (Williams—see chap. 4) Narragansett *tautaûog;* a common food and sport fish

tawkee (or tawkin) 1725 (M) of Algonquian origin (W III); golden club (an aquatic plant) or an arrow arum

tegua \TAY-gwuh\ 1889 (M) perhaps Keresan; an ankle-high moccasin worn in parts of Mexico and the Southwest

Tennessee Walking Horse (or Tennessee Walker) 1938 (W 10) from the Cherokee town *Tenesi* on the Little Tennessee River; an American breed of large easy-gaited saddle horses

Tennessee warbler 1811 (M) (etym. above); small warbler of North America that nests in Canada and winters in northern South America

tepee (tipi or teepee) 1743 (Isham, 46) Dakota *ti-* (dwell) + *-pi* (third person plural) (AHD I); a cone-shaped tent terrapene - Virginia Algonquian *torope* (AHD I); a genus comprising the box tortoises

terrapin 1613 (Whitaker—see chap. 2) (etym. above); any of various North American aquatic turtles

terrapin scale - (etym. above); a small insect that is harmful to several cultivated trees

Texas (part of steamer) 1853 (OED) from a Caddo word, meaning "friends" or "allies," that the Spanish and then Americans adopted as *Tejas* or *Texas* (see chap. 10); a structure on a steamboat containing the officers' cabins

Texas adelia - (etym. above); swamp privet

Texas bedbug - (etym. above); conenose, a bloodsucking bug

Texas bluegrass 1882 (M) (etym. above); a vigorous forage grass of the southern United States

Texas brown-eyed Susan - (etym. above); a bristly annual herb of the southern United States

Texas buckeye (or Texan buckeye) - (etym. above); Spanish buckeye (shrub)

Texas buckthorn - (etym. above); lote (a low spiny shrub of Mexico and southern Texas)

Texas catclaw - (etym. above); a tall shrub or a tree in the southwestern United States that yields firewood

Texas (cattle) fever 1905 (W 10) (etym. above); an infectious disease of cattle transmitted by the cattle tick

Texas citrus mite - (12,000 Words) (etym. above); a red spider

Texas fever tick 1866 (W 10) (etym. above); a cattle tick

Texas fly - (etym. above); horn fly

Texas leaf-cutting ant - (etym. above); a leaf-cutting ant that is sometimes a destructive defoliator in Texas and Louisiana

Texas leaguer 1905 (W 10) (etym. above); a fly in baseball that drops between an infielder and an outfielder for a hit

Texas longhorn 1908 (OED) (etym. above); a breed of heavy beef cattle with low wide horns

Texas millet 1858 (OED) (etym. above); an annual weedy grass used for hay

Texas nettle - (etym. above); Texas thistle or buffalo bur

Texas nighthawk - (etym. above); a goatsucker of the southwestern United States and parts of Mexico

Texas palmetto - (etym. above); a tall palm of southern Texas and Mexico

Texas pea - (etym. above); a perennial bushy herb of the southwestern United States that yields forage

Texas plume - (etym. above); standing cypress

Texas Ranger 1846 (OED) (etym. above); a member of a mounted police force in Texas

Texas red oak (or Texas oak) - (etym. above); a usually small to medium-sized oak of dry Texas uplands

Texas root rot - (etym. above); cotton root rot

Texas sage - (etym. above); a perennial herb

Texas snakeroot - (etym. above); a birthwort of the southwestern United States that resembles the Virginia snakeroot in its medicinal properties

Texas sparrow 1909 (M) (etym. above); a finch of southern Texas and Mexico

Texas star 1909 (M) (etym. above); an annual Texan herb, or prairie sabbatia

Texas steer - (etym. above); a small side branded steer hide

Texas tender - (etym. above); a waiter in the Texas of a steamboat

Texas thistle - (etym. above); a basket flower or Texas nettle

Texas tower 1954 (OED) (etym. above); a radar-equipped platform in the ocean forming part of an offshore warning system against air attack

Texas umbrella tree 1903 (M) (etym. above); an ornamental tree that has a crowded often flattened crown

Tex-Mex 1949 (OED) (etym. above); a blend of Mexican and southwestern U.S. cultural elements

Tillamook cheese - from *Tillamook,* town and county in Oregon, from Chinook for "people of Nekelim" (Harder); a cheddar cheese of crumbly texture and sharp flavor

tillicum 1847 (OED) Chinook Jargon from Chinook *txlam,* people

(W III); person or friend, in the Northwest—people, especially the common people of a tribe as distinguished from the chiefs

Timiskaming \tuh-MIHS-ka-ming\ (geol.) from *Timiskaming,* lake and district of Ontario, Canada, from Indian (Harder); geologic time division

tiponi \TEE-puh-nee\ - Hopi *tíiponi,* idol or amulet seen only by owner (W III); a sacred badge of authority of the Hopi Indians worn or displayed by a chief, priest, or religious society

tiswin \tihz-WEEN\ (tizwin) 1877 (M) Apache perhaps ultimately Nahuatl (RH II); corn beer

titi \TIGH-TIGH\ 1827 (M) possibly Timucuan; any of several trees including one of the southern United States called the *buckwheat tree,* or *sourwood* (different word from the Aymara homonym)

toboggan (n.) ca. 1820 (W 10) Micmac *tophagan* (AHD III); a long narrow runnerless sled

toboggan (v.) 1846 (OED) (etym. above); to coast on a toboggan, or figuratively to decline suddenly and sharply

toboggan cap - (etym. above); stocking cap

toboggan chute 1913 (OED) (etym. above); toboggan slide

tobogganer (or tobogganist) 1878 (OED) (etym. above); one who toboggans

tobogganing 1849 (DC) (etym. above); act or sport of riding a toboggan

toboggan slide 1884 (OED) (etym. above); a slide for coasting on toboggans

tomahawk (n.) 1605 (Rosier—see chap. 2) Virginia Algonquian *tamahaac* (AHD III); a light ax, or similar implement or weapon

tomahawk (v.) ca. 1650 (W 10) (etym. above); to cut, strike, or kill with a tomahawk, to criticize or attack savagely

tomahawker - (etym. above); one who wields a tomahawk

Tonawanda pine - from *Tonawanda* Creek, New York, from the Iroquoian word for "swift water" (Harder); a white pine

totem 1609 (Lescarbot—see chap. 2) Ojibwa *nindoodem,* "my totem" (AHD III); an animal, plant, or natural object serving as the emblem of a clan or family, or a venerated emblem or symbol

totemic 1846 (W 10) (etym. above); of or pertaining to a totem

totemism 1768–82 (DC) (etym. above); a belief in totems or a social system based on affiliations to totems

totemist 1881 (OED) (etym. above); one who believes in totems or participates in a social system based on totems

totemistic 1873 (OED) (etym. above); of or about the belief in totems or the participation in a social system based on totems

totemite 1904 (OED) (etym. above); a totemist

totem pole 1879 (Muir—see chap. 10) (etym. above); a post carved and painted with a series of totemic symbols, a hierarchy

truckee pine - from *Truckee* River, Nevada, from the name of an Indian guide (Harder); Jeffrey pine

Truckee trout - (etym. above); Tahoe trout

tuckahoe 1612 (Smith—see chap. 2) Virginia Algonquian *tockwhogh, tockawhoughe, taccaho,* arrow arum root (used for bread) (RH II); either of two plants having rootstocks used as food: arrow gum, golden club; the edible rootstock of a tuckahoe; edible part of a subterranean fungus also called Indian bread

tucket 1856 (M) probably Algonquian akin to *tuckahoe* (W III) (see above); a green ear of corn

tulapai \too-LAH-pie\ - Apache, a fermented beverage made by Apache Indians of sprouted fermented corn often with various roots or herbs

tullibee 1789 (OED) Canadian French *toulibi* from Ojibwa (AHD III); a large thick-backed cisco of the Great Lakes

tump or tumpline 1796 (M) alteration of *mattump* of southern New England Algonquian origin (AHD III); strap around chest or forehead for help in carrying a pack on the back

tupelo 1731 (Catesby—see chap. 6) (M) probably Creek *'topilwa: íto* (tree) + *opílwa* (swamp) (AHD III); any of several trees of the southeastern United States having soft light wood

tupelo gum 1885 (OED) (etym. above); a swamp tree occurring especially in the southeastern United States and having softer wood than the related black gums

turban squash 1909 (M) Narragansett *askútasquash* (AHD III); any
of various winter squashes having hard-shelled fruit shaped
somewhat like a turban

tuxedo 1889 (OED) from *Tuxedo* Park, N.Y., Algonquian, probably "round-foot-he-has": wolf (Stewart); a man's jacket worn
for formal or semiformal occasions

tuxedo jacket - (etym. above); see above

tuxedo sofa - (etym. above); an upholstered sofa with slightly
curved arms that are the same height as the back

tweeg 1825 (M) Delaware *twi'kw* (RH II); hellbender, a large
salamander

tyee \TIGH-ee\ 1792 (OED) Chinook Jargon from Nootka *ta'yi'*,
elder brother, senior (W III); chief, boss, leader

tyee salmon 1863 (M) (etym. above); a king or Chinook salmon
especially when of large size

uintaite (or uintahite) 1888 (OED) from *Uinta* Mountains of Utah
from name of a subtribe of the Utes of Shoshonean linguistic
stock (Harder); a black lustrous asphalt occurring especially in
Utah that is useful in the arts

uintathere - *Uinta* County, Wyo. (etym. above); a mammal of the
genus *Uintatherium*

uintatherium - (etym. above); a genus of extinct large herbivorous
ungulate mammals resembling elephants in size and the shape
of their limbs

umbrella catalpa - Creek *katalpa* from *ka*-(head) + *talpa* (wing)
(from the shape of their flowers, "head with wings") (AHD
III); a horticultural catalpa with an umbrella-shaped head
formed of numerous leaf-bearing branches

unakite \YOON-uh-kight\ 1874 (W 10) from *Unaka* Mountains
in North Carolina and Tennessee from Cherokee "white" for
the color of the rocks (Harder); an altered igneous rock with
green, black, pink, and white flecks used as a gemstone

upland hickory - Virginia Algonquian *pocohiquara,* drink made of
pressed hickory nuts; shagbark hickory

upland moccasin 1853 (OED) Algonquian, compare Natick *moh-*

kussin (AHD I); a snake of the southern United States that is probably a dark variety of the copperhead

uppówoc \uh-POH-wahk\ (archaic) 1588 (Harriot—see chap. 1) Carolina Indian *uppówoc;* tobacco

uta \YOOD-uh\ - from *Ute* Indian from American Spanish *Yuta* (AHD III) perhaps from Navajo; a large genus of iguanid lizards found from New Mexico to Lower California, any lizard of *Uta* or a related genus

Utah juniper - from *Utah* State (etym. above); a small juniper of the midwestern and Rocky Mountain regions of the United States

utahlite - (etym. above); the mineral variscite

Uto-Aztecan 1891 (OED) from *Ute* (for etym., see *uta* above); a language phylum that includes Ute, Hopi, Nahuatl, and Shoshone

Virginia opossum - Virginia Algonquian *aposoum* (AHD I); the common opossum of North America

Virginia poke 1887 (M) Virginia Algonquian akin to *puccoon* (AHD III); a pokeweed or American hellebore

vulpine opossum 1789 (OED) Virginia Algonquian *aposoum* (AHD I); vulpine phalanger, a common Australian opossum

wabeno ca. 1804 (DC) Ojibwa *wabanow,* literally, "I am a sorcerer" (W III); an Ojibwa shaman

wahoo (Dakota) 1857 (M) Dakota *wáhu* from *wá* (arrow) + *hu* (wood) (W 10); a shrub or small tree also called *burning bush,* also strawberry bush

wahoo (not Dakota) 1770 (OED) possibly Indian, an elm tree of the southeastern United States or any of several similar trees

wakan \wah-KAHN\ (or wakanda or wakon or wakonda) 1776 (DC) Siouan (W III); a supernatural force believed by the Sioux to pervade animate and inanimate objects

wampee \wahm-PEE\ 1802 (M) Algonquian (W III); South: pickerel weed or arrow arum

wampum 1636 (Winthrop—see chap. 4) short for Massachusett *wampompeag* for *wampan* (white) + *api* (string) + *-ag* (pl. suffix) (W 10); beads made from polished shell and fashioned into strings or belts wampum belt 1676 (M) (etym. above); a belt of varicolored wampum used as a mnemonic device or ceremonially

wampumpeag 1627 (Bradford—see chap. 4) (etym. above); wampum made of white shell beads

wampum snake 1736 (M) (etym. above); any of several brightly marked American snakes

wanigan \WAH-nuh-guhn\ (or wannigan or wangan or wangun) 1848 (OED) Ojibwa *waanikaan,* storage pit (AHD III); a boat or small chest equipped with supplies for a lumber camp, provisions for a camp or cabin, a small house or shed mounted on skids and towed behind a tractor train as eating and sleeping quarters, or an addition built onto a trailer house

wankapin \WAHNK-uh-pin\ 1832 (M) Ojibwa *wankipin,* literally "crooked root" (W III); water chinquapin

wapatoo \WAHP-uh-too\ (or wapata or wapato or wappato) 1805 (M) Chinook Jargon *wapatoo* from Cree *wāpatowa,* white mushroom (W III); either of two aquatic plants with edible tubers

wapiti \WAHP-uh-tee\ 1806 (M) Shawnee *waapiti* (AHD III), white rump; a large light brown or grayish-brown North American deer with long branching antlers, also called *American elk* or *elk*

Washita (geol.) - from Fort *Washita,* Tex., alternative spelling of *Wichita* from tribal name (Stewart); geologic time division

washita stone - from *Washita* River, Ark. *(Ouachita);* a porous variety of novaculite used especially for sharpening woodworking tools

Washoe process 1876 (M) *Washoe* County, Nev., from Indian tribe in Nevada and adjacent parts of California; a process of treating silver ores

watap \wa-TAHP\ (or watape or wattape) 1761 (DC) Ojibwa *wadab* (AHD III); a stringy thread made from the roots of various conifers and used by certain Indian peoples in sewing and weaving

water chinquapin 1836 (M) Virginia Algonquian *chechinkamin,* chestnut (AHD III); an American lotus or its edible nutlike seed that has the flavor of chinquapin water hickory 1810 (M) Virginia Algonquian *pocohiquara,* drink made of pressed hickory nuts; a hickory of the southern United States

water moccasin 1821 (M) Algonquian, compare Natick *mohkussin* (AHD I); a semiaquatic pit viper of the southern United States also called *cottonmouth*

water opossum 1846 (OED) Virginia Algonquian *aposoum* (AHD I); the yapock, an aquatic opossum of South America

water tupelo 1731 (M) probably Creek *'topilwa: íto* (tree) + *opilwa* (swamp) (AHD III); tupelo gum tree

Waucobian (geol.) - from *Waucoba* Mountains, California, from Paiute for "pine" (Stewart); geologic time division

Waukegan juniper - Indian word meaning "sheltering place" (Harder); a creeping juniper having long branches and blue-green leaves that turn purplish in the winter

wavey (or wavy) 1743 (DC) Eastern Abenaki *we'hwe'w* (RH II) probably onomatopoetic, snow goose

wawaskeesh \wuh-WAH-skeesh\ 1754 (DC) probably Ojibwa *wâ-wâshkeshi,* deer (W III); wapiti

wejack 1743 (DC) (M) Cree *oček* (AHD III); the marten, a carnivorous mammal of North America

werowance 1585 (Lane—see chap. 1) perhaps Carolina Algonquian; a North American Indian chief, especially in Virginia

western catalpa - Creek *katalpa* from *ka-*(head) + *talpa* (wing) (from the shape of its flowers, "head with wings") (AHD III); a large often cultivated tree, sometimes called *cigar tree* or *hardy catalpa*

western tamarack - Canadian French *tamarac,* probably of Algonquian origin (AHD III); western larch

whisky jack 1743 (DC) alteration of *whisky-john* by folk etymology from Cree dialectal *wiiskachaan* (AHD III); gray jay, also called *Canada jay* or *moosebird*

white camas - Chinook Jargon *kamass;* a camas chiefly of the eastern United States having a creamy white flower suffused with green, bronze, or purple

white cohosh - Eastern Abenaki (AHD III); white baneberry

white hickory 1750 (M) Virginia Algonquian *pocohiquara,* drink made of pressed hickory nuts; any of several hickories (as the shagbark or mockernut)

white puccoon - Virginia Algonquian *poughkone* (RH II); bloodroot

white titi - possibly Timucuan; any of several trees of the genus *Cyrilla*

wickape - variation of *wicopy* (which see)

wickawe - variation of *wicopy* (which see)

wickawee - Algonquian (W III); an Indian paintbrush

wickiup 1852 (M) Fox *wiikiyaapi,* wigwam (AHD III); a frame hut covered with matting, as of bark or brush, used by nomadic Indians

wicopy (wickape or wickup) 1612 (Strachey—see chap. 2) Eastern Abenaki *wikəpi,* inner bark used for cordage; leatherwood, or basswood, or willow herb

wigwam 1628 (Levett—see chap. 4) Eastern Abenaki *wikəwam* (AHD I); an originally Indian dwelling with an arched or conical framework overlaid with bark or hides

windigo (or wendigo) 1714 (OED) Ojibwa *wi'ntiko* (RH II); cannibalistic creature of Algonquian mythology

winninish (winnonish) 1883 (OED) Montagnais *wananish* diminutive of *wanans,* salmon (W III); *ouananiche* (a salmon), of which the name is a variation

winter squash 1775 (M) [1740–50, RH II] Narragansett *askútasquash* (AHD III); any of several thick-rinded varieties of squash that can be stored for long periods

Wisconsin (geol.) 1894 (OED) probably from Ojibwa *Wees-kon-san,* "the gathering of the waters" (Harder); geologic time division

Wisconsin weeping willow - (etym. above); a hybrid willow derived from the weeping willow and the crack willow

Wisconsin white pine - (etym. above); a common white pine

wokas 1878 (M) Klamath *wókas,* seed of the wokas (W III); a western American spatterdock or the dried and roasted seeds of the wokas used as food by the Klamaths

wokowi \woh-KOH-wee\ - Comanche (W III); mescal

woodchuck 1674 (M) presumably a reshaping by folk etymology of a word in a Southern New England Algonquian language; cf. Narragansett *ockqutchaun,* woodchuck (RH II); the animal

woodland caribou 1853 (DC) Micmac (AHD III); any of several rather large caribou of wooded regions

wood terrapin - Virginia Algonquian *torope* (AHD I); a wood tortoise or wood turtle the shell of which is marked with strong grooves and ridges like sculptured figures

woolly opossum - Virginia Algonquian *aposoum* (AHD I); an opossum having no well-developed pouch and carrying its young on the mother's back

Wyandot(te) 1884 (M) from *Wyandot,* Iroquoian tribal name (AHD III); a breed of chicken developed in North America for its eggs and meat

xat \ KHAHT \ - Haida (W III); a carved pole erected as a memorial to the dead by some Indians of western North America

Yakutat bear - from *Yakutat* Bay, Alaska, from name of Tlingit subtribe (Harder); a large brown bear from Yakutat Bay area related to the Kodiak bear

Yakutat hut - (etym. above); a square demountable temporary structure built of prefabricated wood panels

yamp 1845 (M) Shoshonean; either of two western North American plants with fleshy edible roots, also called *squawroot*

yaupon \ YAW-pahn\ (or yapon or yapa or youpon) 1709 (Lawson—see chap. 6) Catawba *yopún* diminutive of *yop,* tree, shrub (W III); a holly of the southern United States used as a tea especially in the black drink of the Indians also called *cassina*

yeibichai \ YAY-buh-chigh\ - Navajo *ye'ibeshichai;* a Navajo supernatural represented by a masked dancer, or the ceremony performed by yeibichai dancers

yellow-bellied terrapin - Virginia Algonquian *torope* (AHD I); a terrapin of the southeastern United States having a carapace marked with yellow lines and the plastron yellow or brownish

yellow moccasin flower (or yellow noah's ark) - Algonquian, compare Natick *mohkussin* (AHD I); a yellow lady's slipper yockernut (or yockeynut) - irregular from *wankapin* (which see) + *nut;* water chinquapin

yoncopin (or yonkapin or yankapin) - modification of *wankapin* (which see) (W III); water chinquapin

yukonite - from *Yukon,* territory in Canada, from Indian for "the river" or "big river" (Harder); arseniosiderite, the mineral

Yukon time (or Yukon standard time) 1950 (W 9) (etym. above); Alaska standard time

Yuma point 1932 (OED), from *Yuma* County, Colo., from *Yuma* people from Spanish from Papago *yuumi;* a kind of ancient stone projectile point first found in northeastern Colorado

zebra opossum 1855 (OED) Virginia Algonquian *aposoum* (AHD I); Tasmanian wolf or zebra wolf

zuisin \ZAW-iz-uhn\ - perhaps Algonquian (W III); baldpate or a white-crowned widgeon that breeds in northwestern North America and winters along both coasts of the United States and in Mexico

Zuñi brown - from a people living in New Mexico, from Spanish, from Keres (W III); auburn

Zunyite 1885 (OED) (etym. above), from *Zuñi* Mine, Colorado; a mineral

GLOSSARY 2

English Loanwords from the Eskimo and Aleut Languages

THE FOLLOWING ESKIMO AND ALEUT LOANWORDS and loan terms come from *Webster's Third New International Dictionary* (1971) and its supplements, *6,000 Words* (1976) and *12,000 Words* (1986). See the introduction to glossary 1 for an explanation of the presentation.

agpaite - from *Agpa* in southern Greenland, "a land of rock"; a group of feldspathoid rocks from Greenland

alaska 1902 (OED) Aleut *Alaeksu, Alaschschak, Alaschka,* or *Alaxa,* "mainland" (Harder); a storm rubber overshoe having a rubberized cloth vamp

Alaska blackfish - (etym. above); a blackfish

Alaska cedar 1880 (Muir—see chap. 9) (etym. above); yellow cedar

Alaska cod - (etym. above); a cod

Alaska cypress 1897 (M) (etym. above); yellow cedar

Alaska goose - (etym. above); lesser snow goose

Alaska grayling 1890 (DAE) (etym. above); a northern arctic grayling

Alaska longspur (etym. above); a longspur of northwestern North America

Alaskan malamute 1938 (W 10) (etym. above) + Eskimo *malamute,* which see; a breed of dogs developed from native Alaskan sled dogs

Alaska pine 1897 (M) (etym. above); a valuable timber hemlock of northwestern North America

Alaska pollack - (etym. above); walleye pollack

Alaska time 1945 (W 10) (etym. above); Alaska standard time

alaskite 1889 (M) (etym. above); a kind of granite

angakok (or angekok) 1745 (Egede—see chap. 9) Eskimo *angeqok* (RH II); Eskimo shaman

anorak 1922 (OED) Greenlandic Eskimo *annoraaq,* formerly spelled *anorâk* (AHD III); a heavy jacket with a hood, a parka

Atka mackerel (or Atka fish) 1886 (Elliott—see chap. 9); a greenling of Alaska and nearby waters valued as a food fish

baked Alaska 1909 (M) (etym. above); cake topped with ice cream covered with meringue, which is then quickly browned in an oven

igloo (or iglu) 1662 (Olearius—see chap. 9) Canadian Eskimo *iglu* house (AHD III); an Eskimo dwelling built of blocks of packed snow or of other material, a dome-shaped structure

Inugsuck \EEN-ug-sook\ - Eskimo; of a stage of Eskimo culture in western Greenland (A.D. 1200–1400) resulting from contact with Norse cultures

Ipiutak 1948 (RH II) from *Ipiutak,* locality in Alaska where remains of the culture were discovered; of an Eskimo culture in western Alaska of about A.D. 100–600

Kachemak Bay - from *Kachemak* Bay, Alaska, from Eskimo for "water-cliff-big" (Stewart); of or relating to a Pacific Eskimo and Aleutian culture of about A.D. 100–1700

kakortokite \kuh-KAWRD-uh-kight\ - from *Kakortok,* Greenland Eskimo name for the settlement of Julianehaab; a rock of variable composition occurring in Greenland in green, black, white, and red sheets

kamik \KAH-mik\ 1744 (DC) Eskimo (W III); an Eskimo sealskin boot or mukluk

kamleika \kam-LIGH-kuh\ (or kamelaika) 1740 (Coxe—see chap. 9) Eskimo *kamleika* (W III); a waterproof pullover shirt made of dried animal intestines and worn in the Aleutians

kayak (or kyak, etc.) (n.) 1662 (Olearius—see chap. 9) Canadian and Greenlandic Eskimo *qajaq* (AHD III); a watertight Eskimo canoe or similar canoe

kayak (v.) 1875 (OED) (etym. above); to travel by kayak

Kodiak (also Kadiak) bear 1899 (OED) from *Kodiak* Island, Alaska, perhaps from Eskimo for "island"; a brown bear inhabiting islands and coastal areas of Alaska

komatic 1824 (OED) Eskimo *qamutik* (RH II); an Eskimo sledge with wooden runners and crossbars lashed with rawhide

kooletah 1882 (DC) Eskimo (Greenland dialect) (W III); Eskimo coat made of caribou skin

makluk - Eskimo *makliok, muklok* (W III); a large seal, specifically bearded seal

malamute (or malemute) 1898 (OED) short for *malamute* dog from *Malemute,* an Alaskan Eskimo people, from Inupiaq *malimiut* (AHD III); a breed of powerful dog developed in Alaska as a sled dog and having a thick coat

manak - Eskimo *manaq* (RH II); wooden ball with sharp hooks thrown on a long line to secure and recover a seal slain at a distance

maupok method - Eskimo *maupok,* literally "he waits" (W III); method of hunting seals by watching at breathing holes in the ice in order to spear them

mukluk (or muckluc or mucluc) 1898 (DC) Yupik Eskimo *maklak,* bearded seal (AHD III); a soft Eskimo boot made of reindeer skin or sealskin, or a slipper resembling this boot

muktuk 1835 (OED) Eskimo (W III); whale skin used as food

nunatak 1877 (OED) Eskimo (West Greenlandic) *nunataq* (RH II); a hill or mountain that has been completely encircled by a glacier

Okvik - from *Okvik,* site on Punuk Island in the Bering Sea; an early phase of the Old Bering Sea culture in northern Alaska and northeastern Siberia

parka 1780 (Coxe—see chap. 9) Aleut or Yupik from dial. Russian *párka* from Komi from Nenets (a Uralic language) (RH II); a coat or jacket with a hood and a warm lining for cold-weather wear piblokto (or piblockto) 1898 (OED) *pibloktoq* (RH II); a hysteria among Eskimos characterized by excitement and sometimes mania usually followed by depression

pingo 1928 (OED) Inupiaq or Inuit *pinguq* (AHD III); an arctic mound or conical hill with an outer layer of soil covering a core of solid ice

Punuk - from *Punuk,* group of islets in the Bering Sea; an Eskimo culture of about A.D. 500–1000

qiviut SKEE-vee-uht\ - Eskimo *(6,000 Words);* soft wool of the undercoat of the musk-ox

tupik \TOO-pik\ (or tupek) 1836 (DC) Eskimo (W III); an Eskimo summer dwelling, specifically a sealskin tent

ulu \OO-loo\ (or ulo) 1824 (DC) Eskimo (RH II); knife with nearly semicircular blade used by women

umiak \OO-mee-ak\ (or oomiak, etc.) 1743 (DC) Canadian and Greenlandic Eskimo *umiaq* (AHD III); a large open Eskimo boat made of skins stretched on a wooden frame, usually propelled by paddles

APPENDIX

English Loanwords from the Latin American Indian Languages

THE FOLLOWING LISTS COMPRISE WORDS GLEANED from *Webster's Third New International Dictionary* (1971) and its supplements, 6,000 *words* (1976) and *12,000 words* (1986). Most English loanwords from the Latin American Indian languages in these sources are listed here, but the lists are not exhaustive. (Note that not all of the etymologies have been updated in the light of recent research. A question mark after a word indicates uncertainty about its etymology.)

ARAWAKAN

Chapter 5 does not distinguish among the members of the Arawakan family of languages. Words from Taino, the bulk of those in the Arawakan group, appear in the Taino list that follows this list.

acana - timber tree
anole - lizard
anolis - genus of lizards
bay-bay - shrub
Brazilian guava
cacique
caciquism
camoodi - snake

cannibal
canoa (from Carib)
canoe (from Carib)
canoe birch, cedar, tilting
canoewood - tulip tree
Caribbean pine
caribe - fish
Carib grass

cattley guava
ceiba (prob.) - genus of trees
ceibo (prob.) - kapok
cocobol - timber tree
coco plum
cohoba - narcotic snuff
corial (or Carib) - dugout
courbaril - tree
courbaril copal
dalli (prob.) - tree
guana - iguana
guano - iguana
guava - fruit
guayaba or guayabo - guava
horned iguana
houtou - bird
icaco - coco plum
iguana
iguanadon
iguanid
iguanidae
iguanodontoidea
iguanoid
ita or eta palm
Jamaica

Jamaica apple, banana, bayberry, bloodwood, buckthorn, bullace plum, cherry, cucumber, dogwood, ginger, honeysuckle, ironwood, mignonette, pepper, plum, quassia, rum, sarsaparilla, seal, senna, tree, sorrel, thistle, vervain, walnut
juvia - Brazil nut
labba - paca
latania (prob.) - genus of palms
latania scale (prob.)
latanier (prob.) - fan palm
manicole - assai
marine iguana
native guava
pejibaye (perh.) - palm
pineapple guava
silver balli - tree
siruballi - silver balli
strawberry guava
wallaba - tree
wamara - tree

TAINO

Included here are most of the Arawakan words cited in the text.

aguaji (prob.) - marine fish
aji - plant

annona - genus of trees
annonaceae - family of trees

anon - sweetsop

anoncillo - fiber

areito - dance

barbecue (prob.)

barbecue pit, sauce

batata - sweet potato

batatas - ipomoea

batatilla - plant family

bejuco - vine, rattan

bixa - genus of trees

bixaceae

bixin - acid ester

black mangrove

bright maize

cabuya - fiber

caimitillo - tree

caimito - star apple

caoba - mahogany

caretta - genus of turtles

carey - turtle

cassava

cebu maguey

cigua - lancewood

ciguatera (prob.) - kind of
  poisoning

copei - pitch apple

copey oak

cucujo - a beetle

cupay - pitch apple

emajagua - tree

guacacoa - tree

guacimo - tree

guaiac - tree

guaiacol resin, wood

guaiacum - tree

guaican - remora

guaiol - kind of alcohol

guama - plant

guanabana - soursop

guano - balsa

guao - tree

guapena - fish

guaraguao - tree

guavina - fish

guayacan - tree

guazuma - tree

guiro (prob.) - percussion
  instrument

gum guaiacum

hammock

hammock batten, clew,
  cloth, hickory, netting or
  berthing

henequen - fiber

hicatee or hicotee (prob.) -
  tortoise

huasina, var. guacimo

hurricane

hurricane bird, deck or
  roof, globe or glass or
  shade, lamp or lantern

hurricane-proof
hurricano
hutia or jutia - rodent
Indian maize
Indian potato
Indian tobacco (prob.)
Irish potato
jacana (prob.) - tree
jagua - genipap
jaguëy - tree
jobo - plant
jocum - tree
ladies' tobacco (prob.)
macana - weapon
maguey - agave
maguey worm
mahoe or maho - tree
maize
maize billbug
maizebird
maize dance, mildew, oil
maizer - bird
maize smut
majagua or mahagua - tree
mammee - tree
mammee apple - tree
mangle - tree
mangrove
mangrove crab, cuckoo,
  cutch, family, fish,
mullet, oyster, skipper,
  snapper, swamp
mani - peanut
manila maguey
native potato
nigua - chigoe
olive mangrove
pitahaya - cactus
pod maize
pomato - potato + tomato
potato
potato alcohol, aphid, apple, ball, bean, beetle or
  bug, blight or disease or
  mildew or mold or mur-
  rain, cake, canker, chip,
  crisp, family, fern, flea
  beetle, flour or starch,
  fork, fungus, grub, hook,
  leafhopper, masher, mo-
  saic, moth or tuber
  moth, mottle or virus X
  or X virus, onion,
  psyllid, race, ring, root
  eelworm or root nema-
  tode, rot nematode, scab,
  set, sick, slump, stalk
  borer, tree, tuberoom,
  vine, wart, weevil, wilt,
  worm
potato-digger
potato-leaved tomato

prairie potato

prickly potato

rabbit tobacco (prob.)

red tobacco (prob.)

river tobacco (prob.)

savanna or savannah or
    sabana

savanna blackbird, flower,
    woodland

savannah grass, sparrow

small potato

swamp potato

swan potato

sweet cassava

sweet maize

sweet-potato beetle, flea
    beetle, hornworm or
    sphinx, scurf, weevil or
    borer, worm

tabanuco or tabonuco
    (prob.) - candlewood

tobacco (prob.)

tobacco barn or shed, bee-
    tle, box or tobacco-box
    skate, brown, brush,
    budworm, bug, cloth,
    dove, etch, flea beetle,
    hatchet or spud, hawk-
    moth, heart, hornworm,
    juice, leaf miner, mil-

dew, mosaic, moth, road,
    splitworm, stick or lath,
    stopper, thrips, tongs,
    water or liquor, wilt,
    worm

tobaccoroot

tobacco-sick

tobaccoweed

tobacco-wood

topato - pomato

topinambour - Jerusalem
    artichoke

tuna - prickly pear

Uruguay potato

vijao - herb

waxy maize

white potato

wild potato

wild sweet potato

yaba bark (prob.) - angelim

yacca - evergreen tree

yacca gum

yagua - a palm

yaguaza (prob.) - tree duck

yautia - tuber

yellow guayacan

yuca or juca - cassava

zemi - spirit or fetish

zemism

CARIBAN (Including Galibi)

acuyari palm (prob.)

acuyari wood

alouatta - genus of monkeys

alouatte - howler monkey

annatto - red dyestuff

annatto tree

apa - tree

araguato - ursine howler

balata - tree

bebeerine - alkaloid

bebeeru - evergreen

black caiman (prob.) - reptile

bully tree or bullet tree

cabassou (prob. Galibi) - armadillo

caiman or cayman (prob.)

calabia - tree

canoa

canoe

canoe birch, cedar, tilting, canoe-wood

caraibe - brown sugar

carape (Galibi) - tree

cassiri (fr. Tupi) - fermented drink

chigoe (Galibi) - flea

copaiyé family (Macusi) - trees

copaiyé wood

corial (or Arawakan) - dugout

couratari (Galibi) - tree

courlan (Galibi) - bird

curare

curariform

curarine

curarization

curarize

curiara - dugout

cusparia bark - angostura bark

cusparine

divi-divi - palm

grugru - palm

grugru grub, worm

hura (prob.) - tree

jigua - tree

loro (prob.) - parrot fish

manatee (prob.)

manatee grass (prob.)

manatus (prob.) - genus of mammals

mico - marmoset

mombin - tree

oorali or urali - curare

ourouparia (Galibi) - vine

parinari (Galibi) - tree

parinaric acid

parinarium - genus of
shrubs

peai (Galibi) - medicine
man

pecari - genus of wild
swine

peccary

periagua - piragua

pettiauger - piragua

pipa (Galibi) - toad

pirogue or piroque -
dugout

sika - chigoe

simarouba (Galibi) - genus
of trees

simaroubaceae

souari (Galibi) - tree

souari nut

souari nut family

tamanoir - ant bear

tamarin (Galibi) - marmoset

tibourbou (Galibi) - tree

tinamidae (Galibi) - bird
family

tinamiformes (Galibi) -
order of birds

tinamine

tinamou (Galibi) - bird

tomalley - liver of lobster

viajaca - fish

vochysia (Galibi) - genus of
trees

vochysiaceae

vouacapoua (Galibi) - tree

white-lipped peccary

yarke or yarkee - monkey

yaw - lesion of yaws

yaws

yaws fly

yawshrub

yawweed

yaya - tree

yellow mombin - plum

zaman - tree

NAHUATL

achiote - pigment

aguacate - avocado

ahuatle - water-insect eggs

ahuehuete - tree

alligator cacao

amate - tree

amole - plant

anacahuita - tree

anaqua - tree

atlatl

atole - cornmeal mush
avocado
axolotl - salamander
ayacahuite - tree
Aztec lily, marigold,
 maroon
bisnaga or biznaga - cactus
black sapote - persimmon
cacao
cacao brown, butter, moth,
 nib, thrips
cacaxte - crate
cacomistle - animal
calmecac - Aztec school
calpulli - Aztec clan
camachile - tree
camote - sweet potato
camote de raton - herb
campeachy hat (?)
campeachy wood (?) -
 logwood
canacuas (?) - wedding
 dance
capulin - tree
cascalote - tree
chacate - shrub
chachalaca - bird
chalchihuitl or chalchuite -
 turquoise
chayote or chinchayote -
 vine

chia - plant
chicalote - poppy
chichipate - tree
chicle
chicle bleeder - chiclero
chiclero - chicle gatherer
chiclero ulcer
chico - greasewood
chico - sapodilla
chico mamey - fruit
chicozapote - sapodilla
chilacayote or chilicojote -
 gourd
chile con carne
chili, chile, or chilli
chili dog
chilipepper - fish
chili pepper, powder, sauce,
 vinegar
chinampa - artificial garden
chinin - avocado
chocolate
chocolate-box
chocolate brown, cream,
 flower, house, maroon,
 moth, prune, soldier,
 spot, tree
chocolaty
cochil sapota - tree
cocoa
cocoa bean, brown, butter,

plant, powder, red,
  sedge, shells
cocoyam - taro
colin - bobwhite
comal - griddle
conacaste or guanacaste -
  tree
conepate - skunk
conepatus - animal genus
copal - resin
copalcocote - tree
copaliferous
copalite - resinous
  substance
copalm - a balsam
copal tree
coydog
coyol - palm
coyote
coyote blast, brush, dance,
  getter, hole, willow
coyotillo - shrub
cracked cocoa
crème de cacao
cuaguayote - tree
cuapinole - tree
curly mesquite
elotillo - squawroot
enchilada
estafiata - plant
false mesquite

guacamole
guachipilin - tree
guan - bird
guapinol - tree
guayule or huayule - shrub
hackmatack - tree (different
  word from the Algon-
  quian homonym)
hoatzin or hoactzin - bird
honey mesquite
huajillo - plant
huamuchil or guamuchil or
  cuamuchil - tree
huehuetl - drum
huipil - garment
huisache - tree
huiscoyol - palm
ilama - tree
istle or ixtle - fiber
izote or isote - plant
jacal - hut
jalap - purgative
jicama - vine or its edible
  root
jicara - calabash
jocote - shrub
jocote de mico - tree
knackaway - tree
malinche - figure in dance
mazama - genus of deer
mecate - rope

mescal or mezcal - cactus or beverage

mescal bean, button, maguey

mescaline

mescalism

mesquital - area where mesquite grows

mesquite, mezquit, or mezquite

mesquite bean, grass, gum

metate - grinding stone

Mexican asphalt, bamboo, bean beetle, blue oak, breadfruit, broomroot, buckeye, cedar, chicken bug, clover, cypress, devil-weed, dollar, eagle, elm, fever, fiber, fire plant, fruit fly, hairless, hog, jumping bean, onyx, orange, persimmon, piñon, poppy, red, rose, rubber, scammony, sisal, skipjack, snapper, Spanish, standoff, star or star-of-Bethlehem, stud, sunflower, tea, tiger, tulip poppy, weed, whisk, white pine

milk chocolate

milpa - field

mitote - dance

mole - sauce

Montezuma cypress

nagual - guardian spirit

nagualism

nance - tree

new cocoa

New Mexican locust, piñon

nixtamal - prepared corn

nopal - prickly pear

nopalea - genus of cacti

nopalry - nopal plantation

ocelot

ocote - pine

ocotillo - shrub

ololiuqui - vine

otate - grass

paixtle - dance

patolli - board game

pellotine - narcotic alkaloid

petate - mat

peyote, peyotl, payote, pellote

peyote cult, dance

peyotism, peyotist

pinacate bug - beetle

pinole - flour

pisote - coati, a mammal

pochote - tree

pomato - potato + tomato

popotillo - Mormon tea

posol - soup

pulque (prob.) - fermented drink

pulqueria

quamoclit - vine

quelite - greens

quetzal - bird

quetzal dance

sacahuiste (akin to Nah. word) - grass

sacaton - grass

sapodilla, sapotilla, or sapotilha - tree

sapodilla family

sapota - sapodilla

sapotaceae

sapota gum

sapote - marmalade tree

singkamas or sincamas - yam bean

sotol - plant

strawberry tomato

tacamahac or tacamahaca or tacamahack or takamaka - tree

talaje - tick

tallote - chayote

talpatate or talpetate - rock

tamale

tecoma - genus of shrubs

teguexin - lizard

telpuchcalli - Aztec school

temalacatl - stone used in sacrificial rites

temescal or temascal - sweathouse

teocalli - temple

teonanacatl - hallucinogenic mushroom

teopan - temple precincts

teosinte - grass

tepache - drink

tepetate - caliche

teponaxtle - drum

tequila

tequila sunrise - cocktail

tiger cocoa - tree

tilma - cloak

tlachtli - ball game

tlaco - coin

tocalote - herb

tolguacha - plant genus

tomatillo - plant

tomatine - alkaloid

tomato

tomato black rot, blight, canker, eggplant, fruitworm, gall, hornworm, mite or russet mite, pinworm, psyllid, sphinx, streak, wilt, worm

tonalamatl - divinatory book

tonalpohualli - Aztec calendar period

topato - pomato

topepo - tomato + pepper

toxcatl - Aztec festival

tree tomato

tule - bulrush

tule bettle, fog, goose, mint, potato, root

ule or hule - tree

vine mesquite

white sapota - tree

wild tomato

yellow tacamahac - tree

zacate - herbage

zacaton - grass

TUPIAN

Words from the entire Tupian language family are included here, except for Guarani. See next list for words from that language.

acajou - cashew or mahogany

acapu - timber

acara - fish

agua (prob.) - toad

ai - a sloth

ajari - tree

ambay - tree

ameiva - genus of lizards

American ipecac

American white ipecac

anda - tree

andira - tree genus

andiroba - crabwood

anhima - genus of birds

anhimidae - family of birds

anhinga - snakebirds

ani - bird

aniba - genus of trees

animé - resin

apa - wallaba

apar - armadillo

aperea - cavy

ara (prob.) - genus of macaws

araba (prob.) - monkey

araça - tree

aracanga - macaw

aracari - toucan

arapaima - fish

arariba - tree

araroba - goa powder

assacu - tree

assai - palm

assai palm
ayapana - shrub
bacaba - palm
bacury - tree
bakupari - tree
balsam copaiba
barbatimao - tree
bastard ipecac
bayacura root
becuiba - tree
biacuru - herb
biriba - tree
black ipecac
blue acara
Brazilian ipecac
buccan - frame for cooking meat
buccaneer
burgao - shell
bussu - palm
caapi - vine
caatinga - forest
caboclo - half-breed
cabreuva - tree
cacajao - genus of ouakaris
cahinca root
caiarara - monkey
camara - tree
camara nutmeg
candiru - catfish

capybara - rodent
caracara - hawk
caraguata - plant
caraipi - tree
carajura - plant
cariama - bird
carioca - samba
caroa - plant
caroba - leaflet
Carolina ipecac
carpincho - capybara
Cartagena ipecac
cashew
cashew apple, family, lake, nut, nutshell liquid
cavia - genus incl. guinea pigs
caviary - place for raising guinea pigs
caviidae - family of rodents
caviuna wood - Brazilian rosewood
cavy - rodent
cayenne
cayenne cherry, linaloe oil, pepper
chiquichiqui palm
coaita - monkey
coati, coatimundi - mammal

coendou - genus of porcupines
coerebidae - songbird family
copaene - chemical
copaiba - tree
copaiba balsam oil, resin
copaifera or copaira - genus of trees
cotinga - bird
cotinga purple
cotingidae - family of birds
cougar
couma - tree
coumara (cumara) nut
coumarin - chemical
coumarone
coumarone-indene resin
coumarou - tree
couxia - monkey
crested cariama
cumay - tree
curiboca - Brazilian of mixed blood
curuba - calabash
curucucu - snake
dicoumarol - chemical compound
embira - fiber
eyra - wildcat
false ipecac

false paca
farinaceous ipecacuanha
genipap - tree
giboia - boa constrictor
gravata - fiber
Guadalupe caracara - hawk
guara - bird
guarabu - tree
guarana - drink
guariba - monkey
guatambu - tree
guaxima - fiber
hairy saki - monkey
humiria - tree
humiriaceae
icica - tree
imbauba - trumpet
imbe - cordage
imbirussú - tree
inaja - tree
inga - tree
ipecac
ipecac spurge
ipecacuanha
ipecacuanhic - of ipecac
itauba - tree
jabiru - bird
jaborandi or jamborandi - dried leaves of shrub
jaboticaba - shrub

jacamar - bird

jacamaralcyon - genus of
jacamars

jacameropine

jacamerops - genus of birds

jacana - bird

jacanidae

jacaranda - tree

jacare - caiman

jacitara palm

jacu - bird

jacutinga - iron ore

jaguar

jaguarundi - wildcat

jaragua - grass

jararaca - snake

jararacussu - snake

jatoba - tree

jequitiba - tree

jiboa - snake

jupati - palm

jurara - turtle

karatas - plant

licury - a palm

licury wax

long-tailed paca

macacahuba - tree

macaranduba - tree

macaw (prob.)

macawood

macaw palm

macuca - bird

maguari - bird

mameluco - mestizo

manaca - medicine

mangabeira - vine

mangabeira rubber

manicoba rubber - tree

manihot - genus of shrubs

manioc - cassava

maraca (prob.) - musical
instrument

maracan - macaw

margay - kind of cat

maringouin - blackfly

marupa - tree

massaranduba - tree

matamata - turtle or tree

military macaw (prob.)

milk ipecac

miriti palm

moco - rodent

mora - tree

moriche - palm

mountain paca

mucuna - genus of herbs
and vines

muirapiranga - tree

munguba - tree

muriti palm

murumuru - palm
murumuru fat or oil
musk cavy
mussurana - snake
nana - pineapple
nandu or nandow - bird
nicuri - palm
oiticica - tree
oiticica oil
orabassu - monkey
ouakari or uakari - monkey
ouricury or ourucuri - palm
ouricury oil, wax
paca - rodent
pacarana - false paca
pacoury - tree
Panama (prob.) balata, bark
    or wood, disease, gum,
    hat plant or hat palm,
    ipecac, orange, redwood,
    tree
parica - snuff
Patagonian cavy
patauá oil
paxiuba - palm
pearl tapioca
peba - armadillo
peroba - tree
petunia
petunia violet
pheasant-tailed jacana

pian - yaws
piassava - fiber
pichurim - flavoring agent
piquia - tree
piranha
pirarucu - fish
pitanga - cherry
pitangua - genus of
    flycatchers
pupunha - palm
querimana (prob.) - fish
quica - opossum
red coati
roucou or rocou - annatto
sabia - bird
sagoin - marmoset
sajou - monkey
saki - monkey
sambaqui - midden
sapajou - monkey
sapucaia - tree
sapucaia nut
sapucaia-nut family
sapucainha - tree
sauba or sauva ant
seriema - bird
soco - heron
sucupira - bird
sucuri - snake
surucucu - bushmaster

tabebuia - genus of trees

tamandua - anteater

tanager

tanagra - genus of tanagers

tanagridae

tapeti or tapiti - rabbit

tapioca

tapioca fish

tapioca plant

tapir

tapirid

tapiridae

tapiridian

tapirine

tapiroid

tapiroidea

tapirus

tataupa - bird

tatou or tatu - armadillo

tatou peba - armadillo

tatu or tatuasu - armadillo

tatusia - genus of armadillos

tayassu - genus of swine

tayra or taira - mammal

teiid, teiidae, tejidae - family of lizards

teju - lizard

tiburon (prob.) - shark

timbo - vine

tipiti - cylinder to press juice

toco - toucan

tonka bean (prob.)

toucan

toucanet

tucandera or tucondera - ant

tucum

tucunaré - fish

tunga - genus of fleas

uca - genus of crabs

ucuuba - tree

ucuuba butter, tallow, or oil

umbra tree

umbu-rana - tree

umiri or umiry - balsam

unau - sloth

urubu - vulture

urucú - annatto

urucu-rana - tree

urucuri iba - palm

urutu - snake

uva grass

water cavy

white ipecac

wild ipecac

yakamik - bird

ynambu - tree

GUARANI

Included here are words from the Guarani member of the Tupian family.

agouara or aguara or guara - wild dog

agouti or agouty - rodent

ananas - plant genus

carandá - palm

caranday - palm

chaja (prob.) - bird

chibigouazou - ocelot

cipo - liana

cuica - musical instrument

curupay - tree

genip or ginep - plant

genipa - plant genus

guayabi - tree

guazuti - deer

jabiru - bird

jacana - bird

jacanidae

jaguarundi or jaguarondi - wildcat

jararacussu - snake

mitu or mitua - bird

nana - pineapple

nandu - bird

nandubay - tree

nanduti - lace

ombu - tree

pindo palm

piriigua - bird

pororoca - tidal bore

poyou - armadillo

saimiri - monkey

tatouay - armadillo

terutero - bird

urunday - tree

QUECHUA

achira - plant

aini - assistance

airampo - cactus

alco - dog

amauta - wise man

Andes berry (poss. Aymara) - a bramble

andesine - kind of feldspar

andesinite - rock related to andesine

andesite - a volcanic rock

antara - panpipe

anu - herb

apple of Peru - herb

arracacha - herb
ayahuasco - vine
ayllu - clan
balsam of Peru or Peru balsam
biguanide - drug
cancha - jai alai court
cantua - genus of shrubs
cantuta or kantuta - shrub
caoutchouc
caoutchouc tree
carancha - hawk
caucho - wild rubber
chacra - small farm
chaguar (prob.) - plant
chalaco - fish
charqui or charque or xarque - jerky
cherimoya or chirimoya (prob.) - tree
china (prob.) - cinchona
chinchilla (prob.) - rodent
chino - person of mixed blood
chiripa - garment
chonta - palm
Chuncho - jungle people
chuño or chuñu - potato foodstuff
coca
cocaine
cocaine family, plant
cocainism, cocainization, cocainize
coke
condor
condurangin - poisonous glucoside
condurango - dried bark of a vine
coto - bark used as medicine
cuca - coca
cuichunchilli - root of a shrub
curaca - member of Inca nobility
cusco or cuzco bark - cinchona
cuscohygrine
cusconine
fique (prob.) - hemp
Florida quinine
gaucho (prob.)
guanaco or huanaco - mammal
guanaquito - pelt of guanaco
guanay (prob.) - cormorant
guanidine - chemical
guanidino
guanidoacetic acid

guaniferous
guanine - chemical
guano
guanophore - chemical
guanosine
guanyl - chemical
guanylic acid - chemical
guaso - Chilean laborer
huaca or guaca - object inhabited by a god
huaco - relic
huanuco coca - dried coca leaves
ichu or hichu - grass
Inca bone, dove
jerk - to dry beef
jerky - dried beef
lagniappe
llama
llautu - cord for head
lucuma - eggfruit
marvel-of-Peru - flower
maté or matté - beverage
mita - forced labor
mitimae - resettled people
molle - pepper tree
mountain vizcacha
nitroguanidine
oca or oka - wood sorrel
pacay - plant

paco - alpaca
paco - ore
palla - princess
palta - avocado
pampa
pampas cat, deer, fox, grass, hare
pampero
papa - potato
Peruvian balsam, bark, coca, cotton, cypress, daffodil, lily, mastic tree, nutmeg, rhatany, saltpeter, yellow
pique - tick
pirca - masonry wall
plains vizcacha
pongo - canyon
Pucara - an Andean culture
puma
puna or puno - bleak region
quena or cuena - reed flute
quinacrine
quinamine
quinaphthol
quinate
quinazoline
quinic acid
quinicine
quinidine

quinine

quinine bush, cherry, flower, tree, water

quininic acid

quinoa or quinua - pigweed

quinoline blue, dye, yellow

quinolinic acid

quinolinol

quinolinyl

quinologist

quinology

quinone

quinone diimine, imine, oxime

quinonization

quinonize

quinonoid

quinonyl

quinophan

quinotannic acid

quinovic acid

quinovin

quinovose

quinoxaline

quinquina

quinuclidine

quipu - string record

quirquincho - armadillo

rhatany - a dried root

soroche - mountain sickness

tambo - wayside tavern

tara - plant

totora - cattail

ullucu or olluco - plant

vicuña or vicuna or vicugna

vigogne yarn

vinchuca - bug

vizcacha or viscacha or biscacha - rodent

vizcachera - vizcacha burrows

vizcachon - plains vizcacha

wild quinine

yana cona - serf

yareta or llareta - herb

yunga - wooded valley

MISCELLANEOUS

acouchi or acuchi (name in Guyana) - resin

alpaca (Aymara) - animal

Araucana (Araucan) - chicken

Araucaria (Araucan) - genus of trees

Araucariaceae - family of plants

araucarioxylon (Araucan) - fossil wood

arrau (Maipure) - turtle

babracot (prob. S. Am.) - genus of herbs

bacopa (prob. name in Guianas) - genus of herbs

Bahama duck, grass, pintail, sisal

balche (Mayan) - fermented drink

banak (prob. native word in Honduras) - tree

boco (name in Guiana) - crab

bocor or bokor (Haitian Creole) - witch doctor

boldo (Araucan) - shrub

boldu (Araucan) - shrub

cahoun palm (Miskito)

cajun (Mayan) - plant

calisaya bark (?) - cinchona bark

canchalagua (Araucan) - herb

caranna (prob. native name in Venezuela) - medicinal gum

Ceará rubber (?) (state in Brazil) - wild rubber

cenote (Mayan) - deep sinkhole

chacmool or chacmol (Mayan) - reclining figure

chagual gum (?) - gum from Chile

chechem (prob. W. Ind.) - tree

chicha or chica (Cuna) - beer

chihuahua (?) (state of Mexico)

chihuahua pine

Chile-bells

Chile bonito, hazel, mill, nettle, niter, pine, saltpeter

Chilean bellflower, guava, jasmine, laurel, nitrate, nut, strawberry

chinchilla (prob. Aymara or Quechua)

chinchilla rat

chinchillidae - family of rodents

chinchillon - vizcacha

chullpa or chulpa (Aymara) - stone tower

cigar (perh. Mayan)

cigar-box cedar

cigar casebearer

cigaresque

cigarette

cigarette beetle, drain,
   flower, girl, paper, plant,
   spot, store, tree
cigarillo
cigarless
cigarro
cigar-store Indian
cohune or cohune palm
   (Mosquito) - palm
cohune-nut oil
cohune oil, fat
coigue or coihue (Araucan)
   - evergreen
colpeo (Araucan) - dog
copaiyé family (Macusi) -
   genus of trees
copaiyé wood
courida (native name in
   Guyana) - black
   mangrove
coyo (Mayan) - avocado
coypu or coypou (Araucan)
   - rodent
Cuba bark or bast, grass,
   libre
cubalaya - fowl
Cuban - a tobacco
Cuban bast, blindfish,
   cedar, crocodile, ebony,
   eight, heel, lily, macaw,
   oysterwood, pine, sand,
   spinach, vanilla

cubanite
cucubano (?) (Puerto Rico)
   - beetle
culpeo (Araucan) - mammal
curaçao (?) - liqueur
curaçao orange (?) - sour
   orange
curassow (?) - bird
curoro (Araucan) - rodent
determa (native name in
   Guiana) - tree
dory (Mosquito)
doryman
dory trawler
douroucouli or dourocouli
   or durukuli (native name
   in S. Am.) - monkey
fotui (native name in
   Guyana) - tree
gobbe (native name in Ca-
   ribbean) - groundnut
guemal (Araucan) - deer
Guiana plum, tree
hackia (native name in
   Guyana) - tree
haiari (native name in
   Guyana) - plant
hevea (Amer. Ind.) - tree
hikuli (Huichol lang.) -
   peyote
huapango (?) - dance

iguape (?) (from Braz. port) - candlenut

jalapeño (?) (MexSp) - pepper

jalapin (?)

jalpaite (?) (Mex. town) - mineral

jipijapa (?) (town in Ecuador) - plant

jiqui or jique (?) (AmerSp) - tree

jocu (?) (AmerSp) - fish

jojoba or jajoba (?) (MexSp) - shrub

juamave (?) - fiber

juey (?) (AmerSp) - crab

kakaralli or kakarali or kakeralli (?) (native name in Guyana) - nut

kanaima (?) (native name in Guyana) - evil spirit

katun (Mayan) - time period

keratto or karatto (?) (prob. native name in W. Ind.) - agave

kex (Mayan) - rite

kodkod (?) (perh. native name in Chile or Argentina) - wildcat

labaria or labarri or labarria or labarea (?) - snake

lapacho (Amer. Ind.) - tree

lapachol (Amer. Ind.) - coloring matter

lingue (Araucan) - tree

loxa or loja bark (from prov. in Ecuador) - cinchona bark

mabi (?) (AmerSp) - tree

machancha (?) (AmerSp) - snake

machi (Araucan) - shaman

madia (Araucan) - herb

madia oil (Araucan)

maloca (Araucan) - dwelling

mamaloi (Haitian Creole) - voodoo priestess

mambo (prob. from Haitian Creole) - dance

mamoncillo (?) (prob. native name in Venez.) - genip

maniu (?) (AmerSp) - tree

maqui (Mapuche) - shrub

mara (perh. Araucan) - rodent

Maracaibo (?) (city in Venez.) bark, boxwood, coffee, lignum vitae

mataco (?) (AmerSp) - armadillo

Maya - color

Maya arch

mayten (Araucan) - evergreen

maytenus (Araucan) - genus of trees

mechoacan (?) (from a state in Mex.) - a jalap

Medellin (?) (city in Colombia) - coffee

merengue (Haitian Creole) - dance

miriki (native name in Brazil) - monkey

morabukea or morabucquea (native name in Guyana) - tree

mountain curassow (?) - bird

muermo (Araucan) - tree

nantokite (?) (village in Chile) - chemical

nayarit or nayarita (Amer. Ind.) - plant

ocotea (?) (native name in Guyana) - genus of trees

Orinoco crocodile (?) (Orinoco River, Venez.)

oronoco or oronoko (?) (perh. from Orinoco River) - variety of tobacco

oroya fever (?) (from town in Peru)

paiche (prob. Amer. Ind.) - tortoise

papaiinase

papain

papaloi (Haitian Creole) - male voodoo priest

papaw or pawpaw or poppaw or papa (Amer. Ind.) - tree

papaya (Amer. Ind.) - tree

papayaceae

papayotin

Pará grass, nut, piassava, rhatany, rubber, rubber tree, sarsaparilla (?) (from city in Brazil)

Paraguay bur, tea (?)

Paraná pine (?) (from river and state in Brazil)

patashte (Mayan) - tree

Pernambuco cotton, jaborandi, rubber, wood (?) (from city in Brazil)

peumus (Mapuche) - evergreen

pichi (Araucan) - shrub

pictun (Mayan) - time period

pilori or pilori rat (?) (perh.

Arawakan or Cariban) - rodent

pinguin (?) (native name in W. Ind.) - plant

pisco (?) (fr. Pisco, Peru) - brandy

pisco sour (?)

poncho (Araucan)

potarite (river in Guyana) - mineral

pudu (Mapuche) - deer

quila (Araucan) - grass

quillai (Mapuche) - soapbark

quillaic acid

quillaja (Mapuche) - genus of trees

rat chinchilla

rutuburi (Tarahumara) - dance

samohu (native name in S. Am.) - tree

seegar or segar (perh. Mayan) - cigar

sicana (native name in Peru) - genus of vines

sicu or siku (native name in Bolivia) - panpipe

simaba (native name in Guyana) - genus of trees

sincosite (?) (from Sincos, Peru) - mineral

sisal (?) (from Sisal, Yucatan) - fiber

sisalana - sisal

Surinam cabbage tree, cherry, cockroach, disease, quassia, toad (?) (country in S. Am.)

Tabasco (?) (fr. state in Mex.) - sauce

Tabasco mahogany (?)

tagua (Araucan) - palm

tala (Quiche) - tree

talpacoti (Amer. Ind.) - dove

tamarugite (?) (Chilean place-name) - mineral

tampico fiber, hemp, jalap (?) (Mex. place-name)

tania or tanier or tannia or tannier or tanya or tanyah (Amer. Ind.) - taro

tarapacaite (?) (from Tarapacá, Chile) - mineral

tecali (?) (from Tecali, Mex.) - alabaster

Tehuantepecer (?) (from Gulf of Tehuantepec, Mex.) - violent wind

tepa (native name in Chile) - tree

tibouchina (native name in Guyana) - genus of shrubs

titi (Aymara) - monkey

tobosa grass (Amer. Ind.)

tola (Aymara) - plant

tsantsa (Jivaro) shrunken head

tun (Mayan) - period of 360 days

tuno (prob. Miskito) - tree

tzolkin (Mayan) - period of 260 days

tzut or tzute (Amer. Ind.) - cloth square

uinal (Mayan) - twenty-day period

ulmo (Araucan) - tree

uma (Amara) - genus of lizards

uta (native name in Peru) - disease

warree (Miskito) - peccary

wourali (Macushi) - curare

yapock or yapok or oyapock (?) (river in S. Am.) - aquatic opossum

yariyari (native name in Guyana) - tree

yaruru (native name in Guyana) - certain woods

yaxche (Mayan) - tree

yeni (Amer. Ind.) - tanager

yetapa (prob. Amer. Ind.) - bird

yucatan (?) (from Yucatan, Mex.) - French yellow

Linguist William Bright additionally notes that *shark* may be from Yucatec Mayan *xooc*, pronounced "sho-ok." The English word first appeared in 1589, introduced by English sailors returning from the Gulf of Mexico (personal communication, September 18, 1992).

Notes

CHAPTER 1

This chapter is indebted to John W. Shirley's definitive *Thomas Harriot: A Biography* and to David Beers Quinn's *The Roanoke Voyages, 1584–1590,* which includes Harriot's *A Briefe and True Report.*

1. Shirley, *Thomas Harriot,* 82–83.
2. "Colony Site."
3. Quinn, *Roanoke,* 847–48.
4. Ibid., 381.
5. Ibid., 358, 356, 366.
6. Burrage, *Early English,* 247.
7. Quinn, *Roanoke,* 899.
8. Ibid., 376.
9. Ibid., 892.
10. Hakluyt, *Voyages,* 307, III.
11. von Baeyer, "Picture This," 48.
12. Shirley, *Thomas Harriot,* 236.
13. Shirley, *Thomas Harriot,* 147.
14. Ibid., 474.

Words introduced or possibly introduced by Thomas Harriot (quoted in Quinn, *Roanoke Voyages,* vol. 1)
cushaw, 349
macock, 340, 342
manitou, 372
tsinaw, 348, 349
uppówoc, 344, 345
werowance, 233, 370, 374, 377, 378

CHAPTER 2

1. Burrage, *Early English,* 378.
2. Ibid., 394.

3. Barbour, *Three Worlds*, Gorges quoted on 92.
4. Burrage, *Early English*, 358.
5. Quoted in Culliford, *William Strachey*, 5; Campion, *Works*, 269.
6. Strachey, *Historie of Travell*, xv.
7. Harris, "Spoonbread."
8. Lescarbot, *Nova Francia*, x.
9. Vaughan, *American Genesis*, 45.

Words introduced by James Rosier (quoted in Purchas, *Purchas his Pilgrimage*, vol. 18)
caribou, 358
moose, 358
pone, 359
tomahawk, 359

Words introduced by James Rosier (quoted in Burrage, *Early English*)
powwow, 374
sagamore, 392

Words introduced by John Smith (in *Complete Works*, ed. Barbour)
assapan—*Assapanick*, 1:154
chinquapin—*Chechinquamins*, 1:152
cockarouse—*Caw-cawwassoughes*, 1:146
hickory—*Pawcohiscora*, 1:152 (for *Pawcohiccora*)
hominy—*Ustathamen*, 1:158
maracock—1:153, 158
matchcoat—*Matchcores*, 1:136
muskrat or musquash—*Mussacus*, 1:155
netop—*Netoppew*, 1:137
persimmon—*Putchamins*, 1:152
puccoon—*Pocones*, 1:154, 168, 170, 171, 172; *Pocone*, 1:161
raccoon—*Rahaughcums*, 1:53; *Raugroughcuns*, 1:61
roanoke—*Rawranoke*, 2:168; *Rawrenoke*, 2:249
tuckahoe—*Tockawhoughe*, 1:153; *Tocknough* (berries), 1:162

Words introduced by William Strachey
cantico, 190
pecan, 205
supawn, 174
wicopy, 187

Words introduced by Marc Lescarbot
moccasin, 189
totem, 178

Word introduced in A true declaration (quoted in Mathews, *Dictionary*)
opossum, 1164

Words introduced by Alexander Whitaker
possum, 41
terrapin, 42

CHAPTER 3

1. Driver, *Indians,* 25.
2. Smithsonian, *American Indian Languages.*
3. Barringer, "Tongues That Dance."
4. Smithsonian, *Linguistic Interpretation.*
5. Harrington, "Great Invention."
6. Terrell, *Almanac,* 336.
7. Sebeok, *Native Languages,* 516.
8. Sapir, *Language,* 228.
9. Ibid., 71.
10. Northern Cheyenne Language, *Dictionary.*
11. Whitman, *Poems,* 21.
12. Williams, *Key,* 174.
13. Northern Cheyenne Language, *Dictionary.*
14. Rhodes, *Dictionary.*
15. Rand, *Dictionary.*
16. Wood, *New England's Prospect,* 92.
17. Washburn, *Indian-White Relations,* 16.
18. McLuhan, *Touch the Earth,* 35, 110.
19. Armstrong, Virginia Irving, *I Have Spoken,* 115.
20. McLuhan, *Touch the Earth,* 128.
21. Thomas, "American Indian Culture," 53.
22. Leap, "Indian Language Renewal"; U.S. Senate Bill 1781, "Native American Languages Act."
23. Barringer, "Tongues That Dance."

CHAPTER 4

1. Bradford, *Of Plimoth Plantation,* 32.
2. Ibid., 95.
3. Arber, *Story,* 591.
4. Bradford, *Of Plimoth Plantation,* 273.
5. Date from *OED.*
6. Winthrop, *Journal,* 185.
7. Mathews, *Dictionary,* 1502.

8. Mathews, *Dictionary,* 49.
9. *OED.*
10. Wood, *New England's Prospect,* title page.
11. Lechford, *Plain Dealing,* 117.
12. Williams, *Key,* 210, 174.
13. Berkhofer, *White Man's Indian,* 22; Rogow, *Thomas Hobbes,* 74–77.
14. Mathews, *Dictionary,* 1483.
15. *OED.*
16. Mathews, *Dictionary,* 1888.

Words introduced by George Morton (quoted in Cheever, *Journal of the Pilgrims*)
sachem, 72
squaw, 90

Words introduced by William Levett (quoted in Winship, *Sailors' Narratives*)
wigwam, 264
sannup, 284

Words introduced by William Wood (quoted in *OED*)
nocake
papoose
skunk
squanter-squash

Words introduced by Roger Williams
menhaden
mummichog
nasaump
quahog
samp
scuppaug
squash
succotash
tautog

CHAPTER 5

1. Columbus, *Log,* 167, 154, 138, 115, 101.
2. Serjeantson, *Foreign Words,* 251.
3. Arber, *First,* 30.
4. Ibid., 216, 67.
5. Ibid., 72, 66, 93, 76, 131, 230, 230, 67, 85, 175, 67, 131, 212, 228, 67.
6. Ibid., 76.

7. Ibid., 342.
8. Galvin, "Sybaritic to Some"; Sass, "Sweet Magic"; Young, "Chocolate."
9. Weil, *Brazil,* 102.
10. Durning, "Violence"; "Insects Come Out."
11. Edward Tuttle quoted in Chiappelli, *First Images,* 604.

CHAPTER 6

1. Swift, *Journal,* 419.
2. Daniel Defoe quoted in Bond, *American Kings,* 77.
3. *OED.*
4. Beverley, *State of Virginia,* 9.
5. Lawson, *New Voyage,* 1.
6. Ibid., 235.
7. Ibid., 197, 198, 47.
8. Ibid., 162, 221.
9. Mathews, *Dictionary,* 162, 1779.
10. Isham, *Observations,* 156.
11. Hamilton, *Letters to Washington* 1:99.
12. Adams, *Diary* 1:238.
13. Mathews, *Dictionary,* 1103.
14. Belknap, *New Hampshire* 3:33.
15. *OED.*
16. Ibid.
17. Leach, *Northern Colonial Frontier,* 145.

CHAPTER 7

1. Burrage, *Early English,* 236.
2. Stewart, *American Place-Names,* 407.
3. Whitman, p. 21; George, "I Was Born," 20.
4. Quoted in Stewart, *Names on the Land,* 52–53.
5. Ibid., 59.
6. Quoted in Krapp, *The English Language,* 175.
7. Gray, "Elusive Mystery of Its Name."
8. Bunnell, *Discovery,* 57–63; also cited in Stewart, *Names on the Land.*
9. Rasky, "What's in a Name?"
10. Ibid.

11. Burns, "For Faraway Places."
12. Orth, "Field Procedures."

CHAPTER 8

1. Jefferson, *Writings,* 1295–96.
2. Ibid., 1083.
3. Ibid., 1128.
4. Ibid., 1389.
5. Mathews, *Dictionary,* 249, 1445, 1829.
6. Ibid., 1702.
7. Ibid., 1829.
8. Irving, *History, Tales, and Sketches,* 1011.
9. Simpson, *American English,* 210.
10. Fitzgerald, "Rewriting American History," 48 (March 5, 1979).
11. Safire, *New Language,* 405.
12. Allen Walker Read in Heller, *Names;* Mencken, "Podunk Mystery," 80.
13. Kron, "For a Perfect Host."
14. Kemble, *Records,* 281.

CHAPTER 9

1. Oswalt, *Eskimos and Explorers,* 27.
2. Nelson, *Hunters,* 398–403.
3. Hakluyt, *Discourse,* 88.
4. Entry for "Eskimo" in AHD III.
5. Burch, *The Eskimos,* 13–14.
6. Oswalt, *Eskimos and Explorers,* 70.
7. *OED.*
8. Ibid.
9. Lobdell, "High Arctic Adventure," 42.
10. *Dictionary of Canadianisms.*
11. Coxe, *Russian Discoveries,* 211.
12. Stewart, *American Place-Names;* Harder, *Dictionary.*
13. American Heritage, *Cookbook,* 577; Cannon and Brooks, *Presidents' Cookbook,* 289.
14. Muir, *Travels in Alaska,* 237.
15. Mathews, *Dictionary.*
16. Latter two dates from W 10.

17. *OED.*
18. Ibid.
19. Elliott, *Our Arctic Province,* 182.
20. *OED.*
21. *Dictionary of Canadianisms.*
22. *OED.*
23. Grossmann, "Quiet," 84.

CHAPTER 10

1. Longfellow quoted in Keiser, *The Indian,* 192.
2. Longfellow, *Song of Hiawatha,* 111–12.
3. Thoreau, *Annals* 8:126.
4. Utley, *Indian Frontier,* xiii–xiv.
5. Mathews, *Dictionary,* 315.
6. Ibid.
7. Muir, *Travels in Alaska,* 72.
8. Wilkinson, "The Uncommitted Crime," 67–68.
9. Mathews, *Dictionary,* 826.
10. *OED.*
11. Terrell, *Almanac,* 404.
12. *OED.*
13. Mathews, *Dictionary,* 936.
14. Dockstader, *The Kachina,* 9, 77–78.
15. Weber, *The Spanish Frontier,* 153.
16. Gibson, *Kickapoos,* ix.
17. Ibid., 10, Terrell, *Almanac,* 240.
18. Robbins, "Kickapoo Indian Medicine Company," 4.
19. Thoreau, *Walden,* 482.
20. American Heritage, *Cookbook,* 528.
21. *American Heritage Dictionary,* first ed.
22. Heckewelder, *History, Manners,* 300–301; Mushkat, *Tammany,* 8–12.
23. *New York Times,* "Chautauqua, 1980."
24. Stewart, *American Place-Names,* 500.
25. *OED.*
26. Harder, *Dictionary,* 501.
27. Thoreau, *Maine,* 125.
28. Utley, *Indian Wars,* 289–90.
29. Prucha, *American Indian Policy,* 284.
30. Ibid., 287.

31. Twain, *Tom Sawyer Abroad,* 396.
32. Utley, *Indian Frontier,* 261.

CHAPTER 11

1. Dixon, *Vanishing Race,* 189 (italics added).
2. Ibid., (italics added).
3. Mathews, *Dictionary,* 873.
4. Sewall, *New England,* 121.
5. H. E. Smith, *Colonial Days* (1900), 49, in Mathews, *Dictionary.*
6. Washington, *Writings* 1:27.
7. Hutchinson, *History of Mass.,* 1:469, in Mathews, *Dictionary.*
8. Adair, *History,* 436–37.
9. *N.C. Col. Rec.,* 1:813, in Mathews, *Dictionary.*
10. Adair, *History,* 159, 389.
11. Crèvecoeur, *Sk. 18th Cent. Amer.* (1925), 41, in Mathews, *Dictionary.*
12. Mathews, *Dictionary.* 879.
13. Catlin, *Life among the Indians,* 83–84.
14. Mathews, *Dictionary.* 1041.
15. Ibid., 1041.
16. Schoolcraft, *Mo. Lead Mines,* 176, in Mathews, *Dictionary.*
17. Bradbury, *Travels,* 25.
18. Frémont, *Exped.,* 134, in Mathews, *Dictionary.*
19. G. A. McCall's *Letters from Frontiers* (1868) in *OED.*
20. *OED.*
21. Irving, *Journals* 3:180; Twain, quoted in Flanigan, "American Indian English," 135.
22. Mary Rita Miller, "Attestations," 142.
23. Bradbury, *Travels,* 95; Flanigan, "American Indian English," 156.
24. Thoreau, *Maine,* 304.
25. Heckewelder, *History, Manners,* 293.
26. Benedict, "The Vision," 142.
27. *Newsweek,* July 3, 1989, 8.
Mathews, *Dictionary,* is the main source for dates of first use given in this chapter.

Other sources, when not listed in the text, are *OED* (Great Father, Indian chickweed, Indian cup, Indian paint, Indian rice, Indian sign, Indian tobacco, moon, war song), W 10—(half-breed, red man), and *DC* (calumet, firewater, Great father, medicine lodge, moon, parfleche, pipestone).

CHAPTER 12

1. Hoxie, *Final Promise*, 93.
2. Dixon, *Vanishing Race*, 208, 209, 211.
3. Marsden and Nachbar in Washburn, *History*, 609.
4. *OED.*
5. Ibid.
6. Ibid.
7. Davies, *Skyline Trail*, 49.
8. Kipling, *Verse* 3:115.
9. *OED.*
10. Meyer, "Flower Power."
11. Marckwardt, *American English*, 37.
12. Lockhart, *Nahuas and Spaniards*, 15–16.
13. Lockhart, *Nahuas after the Conquest*, 261.
14. David Barnhart, quoted in Bernstein, "He Prowls."
15. Personal communication, April 16, 1991.
16. Ibid., April 22, 1991.
17. Ibid., April 9, 1991.
18. Ibid., January 28, 1991.
19. *New York Times,* September 17, 1989, May 22, 1990; Heth, *American Indian Dance.*
20. Personal communication, April 16, 1991.
21. Simson, "Native American Fiction."
22. Personal communication, April 24, 1991.
23. Thoreau, *Maine*, 185; Sayre, *Thoreau*, 214.

Bibliography

Adair, James. *History of the American Indians.* New York: Johnson Reprint Corp., 1968 (1775).

Adams, John. *Diary and Autobiography of John Adams.* Ed. L. H. Butterfield. 4 vols. Cambridge: Harvard University Press, 1961.

American Heritage Cookbook. New York: American Heritage Publishing Co., 1964.

The American Heritage Dictionary of the English Language. Boston: Houghton Mifflin Co., 1969.

The American Heritage Dictionary of the English Language. 3d ed. Boston: Houghton Mifflin Co., 1992.

Anderson, Marilyn J. "The Best of Two Worlds: The Pocahontas Legend as Treated in Early American Drama." *Indian Historian* 12 (Summer 1979).

Annals of America. Chicago: Encyclopaedia Britannica, 1976.

Arber, Edward. *The Story of the Pilgrim Fathers.* London: Ward and Downey, 1897.

———, ed. *The First Three English Books on America. . . . Being chiefly translations, compilations, &c., by Richard Eden. . . .* Edinburgh: Turnbull & Spears, 1885.

Armstrong, G. H. *Origin and Meaning of Place Names in Canada.* Toronto: Macmillan Company of Canada, 1930.

Armstrong, Virginia Irving. *I Have Spoken.* Chicago: Swallow Press, 1971.

Asimov, Isaac. *Words on the Map.* Boston: Houghton Mifflin Co., 1962.

Axtell, James. *After Columbus: Essays in the Ethnohistory of Colonial North America.* New York: Oxford University Press, 1990.

———. *Beyond 1492: Encounters in Colonial North America.* New York: Oxford University Press, 1992.

―――. *The Invasion Within: The Contest of Cultures in Colonial North America.* New York: Oxford University Press, 1986.

Back, George. *Narrative of the Arctic Land Expedition.* London: John Murray, 1836.

Barbour, Philip L. "The Earliest Reconnaissance of the Chesapeake Bay Area." *Virginia Magazine of History and Biography.* 80 (1972):21–51.

―――. *Pocahontas and Her World.* Boston: Houghton Mifflin Co., 1970.

―――. *The Three Worlds of Captain John Smith.* Boston: Houghton Mifflin Co., 1964.

Bareiro Saguier, Rubén. "The Indian Languages of Latin America." *UNESCO Courier,* July 1983, 12–14.

Barnett, Lincoln. *The Treasure of Our Tongue.* New York: Alfred A. Knopf, 1964.

Barnett, Louise K. *The Ignoble Savage.* Westport, Conn.: Greenwood Publishing Group, 1975.

Barringer, Felicity. "Tongues That Dance with Wolves. . . ." *New York Times,* January 8, 1991.

Bartram, William. *The Travels of William Bartram.* New York: Barnes & Noble, 1940 (1791).

Basso, Keith H. "'Speaking with Names': Language and Landscape among the Western Apache." *Cultural Anthropology* 3, (May 1988): 99–130.

Beer, David F. "Anti-Indian Sentiment in Early Colonial Literature." *Indian Historian,* Spring 1969.

Belknap, Jeremy. *The History of New Hampshire,* vol. 3. 3 vols. Boston: Belknap and Young, 1792.

Benedict, Ruth Fulton. "The Vision in Plains Culture." *American Anthropologist* 24 (January-March 1922): 1–23.

Benes, Peter, ed. *New England Prospect: Maps, Place Names, and the Historical Landscape.* Boston: Boston University, 1980.

Berkhofer, Robert F., Jr. *The White Man's Indian.* New York: Alfred A. Knopf, 1978.

Bernstein, Richard. "He Prowls English, Stalking New Words." *New York Times,* April 3, 1989.

Beverley, Robert. *The History and Present State of Virginia.* Ed.

Louis B. Wright. Chapel Hill: University of North Carolina Press, 1947.

Bishop, Morris. "Four Indian Kings in London." *American Heritage* 23 (December 1971).

Bolt, Christine. *American Indian Policy and American Reform.* London: Allen & Unwin, 1987.

Bond, Richmond P. *Queen Anne's American Kings.* Oxford: Clarendon Press, 1952.

Brackenridge, Hugh Henry. *Modern Chivalry.* New York: American Book Co., 1937 (1792).

Bradbury, John. *Travels in the Interior of America.* Liverpool: Sherwood, Neely, and Jones, 1817.

Bradford, William. *Bradford's History "Of Plimoth Plantation."* Boston: Wright & Potter Printing Co., 1898.

Brandon, William. *The Last Americans.* New York: McGraw-Hill, 1974.

Briceland, Alan Vance. *Westward from Virginia.* Charlottesville: University Press of Virginia, 1987.

Bright, William O. *American Indian Linguistics and Literature,* Hawthorne, N.Y.: Mouton de Gruyter, 1984.

———. "North American Indian Languages." *Encyclopaedia Britannica Macropaedia,* 15th ed. Vol. 13 (1974):208–13.

Brown, Douglas Summers. *The Catawba Indians.* Columbia: University of South Carolina Press, 1966.

Bunnell, Lafayette Houghton. *Discovery of the Yosemite and the Indian War of 1851.* Chicago: F. H. Revell, 1880.

Burch, Ernest S., Jr. *The Eskimos.* Norman: University of Oklahoma Press, 1988.

Burns, John F. "Accord to Give the Eskimos Control of a Fifth of Canada." *New York Times,* December 17, 1991.

———. "For Faraway Places, Strange-Sounding Names." *New York Times,* October 3, 1987.

———. "They Map the Arctic to a Finer Scale." *New York Times,* July 25, 1987.

Burrage, Henry S. *Early English and French Voyages.* New York: Barnes & Noble, 1959.

Byrd, William. *William Byrd's Histories of the Dividing Line betwixt*

Virginia and North Carolina. Ed. William K. Boyd. Raleigh: North Carolina Historical Commission, 1929.

Campbell, Hannah. *Why Did They Name It . . . ?* New York: Ace Books, 1964.

Campbell, Lyle, and Marianne Mithun, eds. *The Languages of Native America: Historical and Comparative Assessment.* Austin: University of Texas Press, 1979.

Campion, Thomas S. *The Works of Thomas Campion.* Ed. Percival Vivian. Oxford: Oxford University Press, 1969.

Cannon, Garland, and Beatrice Mendez Egle. "New Borrowings in English." *American Speech* 54 (Spring 1979):23–27.

Cannon, Poppy, and Patricia Brooks. *The Presidents' Cookbook.* New York: Funk and Wagnalls, 1968.

Carroll, Peter N. *Puritanism and the Wilderness.* New York: Columbia University Press, 1969.

Cassidy, Frederic G., ed. *Dictionary of American Regional English,* vols. 1, 2. Cambridge, Mass., and London: Belknap Press, 1985, 1991.

Catesby, Mark. *The Natural History of Carolina, Florida, and the Bahama Islands.* Savannah, Ga.: Beehive Press, 1974 (1731).

Catlin, George. *Life among the Indians.* Edinburgh: Gall and Inglis, 1867.

Ceci, Lynn. "Squanto and the Pilgrims." *Society,* May/June 1990.

"Chautauqua, 1980." *New York Times,* June 30, 1980.

Cheever, George B. *The Journal of the Pilgrims at Plymouth.* New York: John Wiley, 1848.

Chiappelli, Fredi. *First Images of America.* Berkeley: University of California Press, 1976.

Claiborne, William. "Canada, Eskimos to Create Vast Arctic Territory." *Washington Post,* December 17, 1991.

Clark, Robert, ed. *James Fenimore Cooper: New Critical Essays.* Totowa, N.J.: Barnes & Noble, 1985.

Clifton, James A. *The Invented Indian.* New Brunswick, N.J.: Transaction Publishers, 1990.

Clines, Francis X. "About Chautauqua." *New York Times,* August 2, 1979.

Cole, Douglas. "Underground Potlatch." *Natural History,* October 1991, 50–53.

"Colony Site Yields Relics of Science." *New York Times,* February 4, 1992.

Columbus, Christopher. *The Log of Christopher Columbus.* Trans. Robert H. Fuson. Camden, Maine: International Marine Publishing Co., 1987.

Cornell, Stephen. *The Return of the Native.* New York: Oxford University Press, 1988.

Cowen, Ron. "The Sacred Turnip." *Science News* 139 (May 18, 1991):316–17.

Coxe, William. *Account of the Russian Discoveries between Asia and America.* London: T. Cadell, 1787.

Craigie, William A., and James R. Hulbert, eds. *Dictionary of American English on Historical Principles.* 4 vols. Chicago: University of Chicago Press, 1938–44.

Crantz, David. *The History of Greenland.* London: Brethren's Society for the Furtherance of the Gospel among the Heathen, 1767.

Crawford, James M. *Studies in Southeastern Indian Languages.* Athens: University of Georgia Press, 1975.

Cronk, Lee. "Strings Attached." *Sciences,* May/June 1989, 2–4.

Cronon, William. *Changes in the Land.* New York: Hill and Wang, 1983.

Culliford, S. G. *William Strachey, 1572–1621.* Charlottesville: University Press of Virginia, 1965.

Cunliffe, Marcus. *The Nation Takes Shape: 1789–1837.* Chicago. University of Chicago Press, 1959.

Cutler, Charles L. "The Battle the Indian Won." *American History Illustrated,* January 1972, 20–27.

Cutright, Paul Russell. *Lewis and Clark: Pioneering Naturalists.* Urbana, Ill.: University of Illinois Press, 1969.

Damas, David, ed. *Arctic: Handbook of North American Indians,* vol. 5. Washington, D.C.: Smithsonian Books, 1984.

Davies, Mary Carolyn. *The Skyline Trail.* Indianapolis: Bobbs-Merrill Co., 1924.

Davis, Dave D. "Rumor of Cannibals." *Archaeology,* January/February 1992, 49–50.

Deane, Charles. "On the Origin of the Names of Towns in Massachusetts," *Proceedings of the Massachusetts Historical Society* 1823 (1871–73).

Debo, Angie. *A History of the Indians of the United States.* Norman: University of Oklahoma Press, 1970.

Delaney, Ted. "Confronting Hopelessness at Wind River Reservation." *Utne Reader,* January/February 1990, 61–63.

Dictionary of Canadianisms on Historical Principles. Toronto: W. J. Gage, 1967.

Dippie, Brian W. *The Vanishing American.* Middletown, Conn.: Wesleyan University Press, 1982.

Dixon, Joseph K. *The Vanishing Race.* Garden City: Doubleday, Page & Co., 1913.

Dockstader, Frederick J. *The Kachina and the White Man.* Albuquerque: University of New Mexico Press, 1985.

Dohan, Mary Helen. *Our Own Words.* New York: Alfred A. Knopf, 1975.

Dowdey, Clifford. *The Great Plantation.* Charles City, Va.: Berkeley Plantation, 1976.

Drinnon, Richard. *Facing West: The Metaphysics of Indian-Hating and Empire-Building.* Minneapolis: University of Minnesota Press, 1980.

Driver, Harold E. *Indians of North America,* 2d ed. Chicago: University of Chicago Press, 1969.

Durning, Alan B. "Violence in the Brazilian Jungle—a Global Concern." *Christian Science Monitor,* August 23, 1988.

Dykeman, Wilma. "Honoring a Cherokee." *New York Times,* August 2, 1987.

Elliott, Henry W. *Our Arctic Province.* New York: Charles Scribner's Sons, 1897.

Ewan, Joseph, and Nesta Ewan. *John Banister and His Natural History of Virginia, 1678–92.* Urbana: University of Illinois Press, 1970.

Fabricant, Florence. "Corn, the Omnipresent Staple." *New York Times.* November 14, 1990.

Farb, Peter. *Man's Rise to Civilization.* New York: E. P. Dutton, 1968.

Fiedler, Leslie A. *Return of the Vanishing Indian.* New York: Stein and Day, 1968.

Fitzgerald, Frances. "Rewriting American History." *New Yorker* 55 (February 26, March 5, March 12, 1979).

Flanigan, Beverly Olson. "American Indian English in History and Literature." Ph.D. diss., University of Indiana, Bloomington, 1981.

Forbes, Jack D. "Frontiers in American History and the Role of the Frontier Historian." *Ethnohistory* 15 (Spring 1968).

Foreman, Grant. *Sequoyah.* Norman: University of Oklahoma Press, 1938.

Galvin, Ruth Mehrtens. "Sybaritic to Some, Sinful to Others, but How Sweet It is!" *Smithsonian Magazine,* February 1986, 54–65.

George, Dan. "I Was Born 1,000 Years Ago. . . ." *UNESCO Courier,* January 1975, 20.

Gibson, Arrell M. *The Chickasaws.* Norman: University of Oklahoma Press, 1971.

———. *The Kickapoos.* Norman: University of Oklahoma Press, 1963.

Gray, Christopher. "The Elusive Mystery of Its Name." *New York Times.* August 15, 1993.

Greenberg, Joseph H. *Language in the Americas.* Stanford: Stanford University Press, 1987.

Grossmann, John. "Quiet." *Health,* February 1990, 58–61, 84.

Gruening, Ernest. *The State of Alaska.* New York: Random House, 1954.

Hagan, William T. *American Indians.* Chicago: University of Chicago Press, 1961.

———. *The Sac and Fox Indians.* Norman: University of Oklahoma Press, 1958.

Hakluyt, Richard. *Discourse on Western Planting* (1584) in *Documentary History of the State of Maine,* vol. 2. Cambridge, Mass.: Press of John Wilson and Son, 1877.

———. *The Principal Navigations Voyages Traffiques and Discoveries of the English Nation.* 12 vols. Glasgow: Maclehose, 1904.

———. *Voyages, Navigations, Traffiques, and Discoveries of the English Nation,* 3 vols. London: G. Bishop, R. Newberie and R. Barker, 1600.

Hall, Charles Francis. *Arctic Researches.* New York: Harper & Brothers, 1864.

Hallowell, A. Irving. "The Backwash of the Frontier." *Annual Report of the Board of Regents of the Smithsonian Institution.* Washington, D.C., 1958.

Hamilton, Stanislaus Murray. *Letters to Washington and Accompanying Papers.* 5 vols. Cambridge, Mass.: Houghton, Mifflin Co., 1898.

Harder, Kelsie B. *Illustrated Dictionary of Place Names.* New York: Van Nostrand Reinhold, 1976.

Harrington, John P. "The American Indian's Great Invention." *Christian Science Monitor,* n.d.

Harris, Ann Pringle. "Spoonbread, Virginia's Choice." *New York Times.* July 31, 1988.

Hatcher, Harlan. *The Great Lakes.* New York: Oxford University Press, 1944.

Havighurst, Walter. "Three Flags at Mackinac." *American Heritage,* August/September 1978, 50–59.

Hays, H. R. *Children of the Raven.* New York: McGraw-Hill, 1975.

Heckewelder, John. *History, Manners, and Customs of the Indian Nations.* Philadelphia: Historical Society of Pennsylvania, 1876 (1819).

Heller, Murray, ed. *Names, Northeast Adirondack Names.* Saranac Lake, N.Y.: North Country Community College Press, 1980.

Hendrickson, Robert. *The Facts on File Encyclopedia of Word and Phrase Origins.* New York: Facts on File, 1987.

Henry, Alexander. *Travels and Adventures in Canada.* New York: Riley, 1809.

Hertzberg, Hazel W. *The Search for an American Identity.* Syracuse: Syracuse University Press, 1971.

Heth, Charlotte. *American Indian Dance Theater* (program). New York, n.d.

Higginson, Francis. *New England's Plantation.* Ed. Alden T. Vaughan. Amherst: University of Massachusetts Press, 1977.

Holmer, Nils M. *Indian Place Names in North America.* Upsala, Sweden: American Institute in the University of Upsala, 1948.

Horsman, Reginald. *Expansion and American Indian Policy, 1783–1812.* East Lansing, Mich.: Michigan State University Press, 1967.

Hoxie, Frederick E. *A Final Promise: The Campaign to Assimilate Indians, 1880–1920.* Lincoln: University of Nebraska Press, 1984.

Huden, John C. *Indian Place Names of New England.* New York: Museum of the American Indian Heye Foundation, 1962.

Hughes, Geoffrey. *Words in Time.* Cambridge, Mass.: Blackwell Publications, 1988.

Hulton, Paul. *America 1585: The Complete Drawings of John White.* Chapel Hill: University of North Carolina Press, 1984.

Hume, Ivor Noël. "Digging Up Jamestown." *American Heritage,* April 1963.

Humins, John H. "Squanto and Massasoit: A Struggle for Power." *New England Quarterly,* March 1984.

Hunt, William R. *Alaska: A Bicentennial History.* New York: W. W. Norton & Co., 1976.

Hyde, Anne Farrar. *An American Vision.* New York: New York University Press, 1990.

"Insects Come Out of the Woodwork." *Washington Post,* March 22, 1985.

Irving, Washington. *Biographies and Miscellaneous Works.* London: Bell, 1867.

———. *History, Tales, and Sketches.* New York: Library of America, 1983.

———. *Journals.* 3 vols. Boston: Bibliophile Society, 1919.

Isham, James. *James Isham's Observations on Hudsons Bay, 1743.* London: The Champlain Society, 1949.

Jacobs, Wilbur R. *Dispossessing the American Indian.* New York: Charles Scribner's Sons, 1972.

James, James Alton. *The First Scientific Exploration of Russian America.* Evanston, Ill.: Northwestern University, 1942.

Jane, Cecil, ed. *Select Documents Illustrating the Four Voyages of Columbus,* vols. 1, 2. London, 1930, 1933. (Hakluyt Society, Series 2, vols. 65, 70).

Jefferson, Thomas. *Thomas Jefferson: Writings.* New York: Library of America, 1984.

Johnson, Edward. *Good News from New England.* Delmar, N.Y.: School Facsimiles, 1974 (1648).

———. *Wonder-Working Providence of Sion's Saviour in New England.* Delmar, N.Y.: Scholar's Facsimiles & Reprints, 1974 (1654).

Jordan, David Starr, and Barton Warren Evermann. *American Food and Game Fishes.* Garden City, N.Y.: Doubleday, Page & Co., 1920.

Josephy, Alvin M., Jr. *The Indian Heritage of America.* New York: Alfred A. Knopf, 1968.

——, ed. *America in 1492.* New York: Alfred A. Knopf, 1992.

Josselyn, John. "An Account of Two Voyages to New England." *Massachusetts Historical Society Transactions and Collections,* 3d ser., vol. 3 (1833). Cambridge: E. W. Metcalf and Co., 1833.

Kastner, Joseph. "The Conundrum of Corn." *American Heritage* 31 (August/September 1980): 14–17, 26–29.

Keiser, Albert. *The Indian in American Literature.* New York: Oxford University Press, 1933.

Kemble, Frances Ann. *Records of Later Life.* New York: H. Holt, 1882.

Kipling, Rudyard. *Rudyard Kipling's Verse.* London: Hodder and Stoughton, 1919.

Krapp, George Philip. *The English Language in America.* 2 Vols. New York: Century Co., 1925.

Kratochvil, Antonin. "Destroyer and Healer." *In Health,* September/October 1990, 66–76.

Krauss, Michael. "The World's Languages in Crisis." *Language* 68 (1992): 4–10.

Krim, Arthur J. "Acculturation of the New England Landscape." In Peter Benes and Jane Montague Benes, eds., *New England Prospect: Maps, Place Names, and the Historical Landscape.* Boston: Boston University, 1980.

Kron, Joan. "For a Perfect Host, *Everything* Goes." *New York Times,* October 18, 1991.

Laird, Charlton. *Language in America.* New York: World Publishing Co., 1970.

Lambert, Eloise, and Mario Pei. *The Book of Place-Names.* New York: Lothrop, Lee and Shepard, 1959.

Lawson, John. *A New Voyage to Carolina.* Chapel Hill: University of North Carolina Press, 1966 (1709).

Leach, Douglas Edward. *The Northern Colonial Frontier, 1607–1763.* New York: Holt, Rinehart and Winston, 1966.

Leap, William L. "American Indian Language Maintenance." *Annual Review of Anthropology* 10 (1981): 209–36.

———. "Indian Language Renewal." *Human Organization* 47 (1988).

Lechford, Thomas. *Plain Dealing; or, Newes from New-England.* Boston: J. K. Wiggin & W. P. Hunt, 1867 (1642).

Lefler, Hugh T., and William S. Powell. *Colonial North Carolina.* New York: Scribner, 1973.

Lescarbot, Marc. *Nova Francia, a description of Acadia.* New York: Harper & Brothers, 1928 (Written in 1606, trans. by P. Erondelle in 1609).

Levine, Stuart, and Nancy Oestreich Lurie. *The American Indian Today.* Baltimore: Penguin Books, 1968.

Lobdell, John E. "High Arctic Adventure." *Archaeology,* May/June 1988, 38–43, 65.

Lockhart, James. *The Nahuas after the Conquest.* Stanford: Stanford University Press, 1992.

———. *Nahuas and Spaniards.* Stanford: Stanford University Press, 1991.

Longfellow, Henry Wadsworth. *The Song of Hiawatha.* Boston: Ticknor and Fields, 1856.

Lupe, Ronnie. "The White Mountain Apache." *National Geographic,* February 1980, 260–90.

McDonnell, Janet A. *The Dispossession of the American Indian: 1887–1934.* Bloomington: Indiana University Press, 1991.

McFee, William. *The Life of Sir Martin Frobisher.* New York: Harper & Brothers, 1928.

Mackenzie, Alexander. *Voyages from Montreal.* New York: Allerton Book Co., 1922.

McLuhan, T. C. *Touch the Earth.* New York: E. P. Dutton, 1971.

Marckwardt, Albert H. *American English,* 2d ed. New York: Oxford University Press, 1980.

Mardock, Robert Winston. *The Reformers and the American Indian.* Columbia: University of Missouri Press, 1971.

Martin, Laura. "Eskimo Words for Snow." *American Anthropologist* 88 (June 1986): 418–23.

Mathews, Mitford M. *A Dictionary of Americanisms.* Chicago: University of Chicago Press, 1951.

Matthiessen, Peter. *Indian Country.* New York: Penguin, 1984.

Maxwell, James A., ed. *America's Fascinating Indian Heritage.* Pleasantville, N.Y.: Reader's Digest Association, 1978.

Mencken, H. L. *The American Language,* supplement I. New York: Alfred A. Knopf, 1952.

———. "The Podunk Mystery." *New Yorker* 14 (September 25, 1948).

Mereness, Newton D. *Travels in the American Colonies.* New York: Macmillan Co., 1916.

Merriam-Webster's Collegiate Dictionary, 10th ed. Springfield, Mass.: Merriam-Webster Inc., 1993.

Meyer, Eugene L. "Flower Power Flourishes at Arboretum." *Washington Post,* August 21, 1987.

Miller, John C. *This New Man, the American.* New York: McGraw-Hill Book Co., 1974.

Miller, Mary Rita. "Attestations of American Indian Pidgin English in Fiction and Non fiction." *American Speech* 42 (1967): 142–47.

Mitchell, Lee Clark. *Witnesses to a Vanishing America.* Princeton: Princeton University Press, 1981.

Morison, Samuel Eliot. *The European Discovery of America.* New York: Oxford University Press, 1971.

Muir, John. *Travels in Alaska.* Boston: Houghton Mifflin Co., 1915.

Mushkat, Jerome. *Tammany: Evolution of a Political Machine.* Syracuse: Syracuse University Press, 1971.

Nelson, Richard K. *Hunters of the Northern Ice.* Chicago: University of Chicago Press, 1969.

Newsweek, July 3, 1989, 8.

Northern Cheyenne Language and Culture Center. *English-Cheyenne Student Dictionary.* Lame Deer, Mont.: Language Research Department of the Northern Cheyenne Title VII ESEA Bilingual Education Program, 1976.

Orth, Donald J. "Field Procedures for the Investigation of Native American Placenames." Reston, Va., 1989.

Oswalt, Wendell H. *Alaskan Eskimos.* San Francisco: Chandler Publishing Co., 1967.

———. *Eskimos and Explorers.* Novato, Calif.: Chandler & Sharp Publishers, 1979.

Oxford English Dictionary, 2d ed. *(OED)* Oxford: Clarendon Press, 1989.

Paramore, Thomas C. "With Tuscarora Jack on the Back Path to Bath." *North Carolina Historical Review* 64 (April 1987).

Pearce, Roy Harvey. *Savagism and Civilization.* Berkeley: University of California Press, 1988.

Poe, Edgar Allan. *Marginalia.* Charlottesville: University Press of Virginia, 1981.

Porter, H. C. *The Inconstant Savage.* London: Duckworth, 1979.

Prucha, Francis Paul. *American Indian Policy in Crisis.* Norman: University of Oklahoma Press, 1964.

———. *Americanizing the American Indians.* Cambridge: Harvard University Press, 1973.

———. *A Bibliographical Guide to the History of Indian-White Relations in the United States.* Chicago: University of Chicago Press, 1977.

———. *The Indians in American Society.* Berkeley: University of California Press, 1985.

———, ed. *The Indian in American History.* New York: Holt, Rinehart and Winston, 1971.

Pullum, Geoffrey K. *The Great Eskimo Vocabulary Hoax.* Chicago: University of Chicago Press, 1991.

Purchas, Samuel. *Purchas his Pilgrimage.* 20 vols. Glasgow: James Maclehose and sons, 1906 (1613).

Quinn, David Beers. *England and the Discovery of America: 1481–1620.* New York: Alfred A. Knopf, 1974.

———. *Set Fair for Roanoke.* Chapel Hill: University of North Carolina Press, 1955.

———, ed. *The Roanoke Voyages, 1584–1590.* London: Hakluyt Society, 1955.

Rand, Silas Tertius. *Dictionary of the Language of the Micmac Indians.* New York: Johnson Reprint Corp., 1972.

Random House Dictionary of the English Language: Second Edition—Unabridged. New York: Random House, 1987.

Rasky, Susan B. "What's in a Name? For Indians, Cultural Survival." *New York Times,* August 4, 1988.

Read, Allen Walker. "An Updating of Research on the Name 'PODUNK.'" In *Names,* ed. Heller.

Reese, Richard Trevor. *Colonial Georgia.* Athens: University of Georgia Press, 1963.

Rhodes, Richard A. *Eastern Ojibwa-Chippewa-Ottawa Dictionary.* Berlin and New York: Mouton, 1985.

Ringle, Ken. "Indecipherable Heroism." *Washington Post,* September 18, 1992.

Robbins, Peggy. "The Kickapoo Indian Medicine Company." *American History Illustrated,* May 1980, 4.

Robinson, W. Stitt. *The Southern Colonial Frontier, 1607–1763.* Albuquerque: University of New Mexico Press, 1979.

Rogow, Arnold A. *Thomas Hobbes.* New York: W. W. Norton, 1986.

Rountree, Helen C. *The Powhatan Indians of Virginia.* Norman: University of Oklahoma Press, 1989.

Rowse, A. L. *The Elizabethans and America.* New York: Harper, 1959.

Ruby, Robert H., and John A. Brown. *The Chinook Indians.* Norman: University of Oklahoma Press, 1976.

Ruhlen, Merritt. *A Guide to the World's Languages.* Vol. 1, *Classification.* Stanford: Stanford University Press, 1987.

———. "Voices from the Past." *Natural History,* March 1987, 6–10.

Sabine, David B. "Corn: The All-American Grain." *American History Illustrated,* April 1967, 12–17.

Safire, William. *The New Language of Politics.* New York: Collier Books, 1972.

Sapir, Edward. *Language: An Introduction to the Study of Speech.* New York: Harcourt, Brace & World, 1921.

Sass, Lorna J. "Sweet Magic." *Americas,* May/June 1985, 8–12.

Sayre, Robert F. *Thoreau and the American Indians.* Princeton: Princeton University Press, 1977.

Scidmore, Eliza Ruhamah. *Alaska: Its Southern Coast and the Sitkan Archipelago.* Boston: D. Lothrop and Co., 1885.

Sebeok, Thomas A. *Native Languages of the Americas.* 2 vols. New York: Plenum Press, 1976.

Serjeantson, Mary S. *A History of Foreign Words in English.* London: K. Paul, Trench, Trubner & Co., 1935.

Sewall, Samuel. *New England Historical and Genealogical Register* 24 (1870): 121.

Shaffer, Paul. "A Tree Grows in Montana." *Utne Reader,* January/February 1990.

Shirley, John W. *Thomas Harriot: A Biography.* Oxford: Oxford University Press, 1983.

————, ed. *Thomas Harriot: Renaissance Scientist.* Oxford: Clarendon Press, 1974.

Simpson, David. *The Politics of American English, 1776–1850.* New York: Oxford University Press, 1986.

Simson, Maria. "Native American Fiction, Memoirs Blossom into Print." *Publishers Weekly,* June 7, 1991, 22–24.

6,000 Words: A Supplement to Webster's Third New International Dictionary. Springfield, Mass.: G. & C. Merriam Co., 1976.

Smith, Bradford. *Captain John Smith.* Philadelphia and New York: Lippincott, 1953.

Smith, Henry Nash. *Virgin Land.* Cambridge, Mass.: Harvard University Press, 1950.

Smith, John. *The Complete Works of Captain John Smith (1580–1631).* Ed. Philip L. Barbour. 3 vols. Chapel Hill: University of North Carolina Press, 1986.

————. *Travels and Works of Captain John Smith.* Ed. Edward Arber and A. G. Bradley. 2 vols. Edinburgh: A. G. Bradley, 1910.

Smithsonian Institution, Department of Anthropology. *American Indian Languages.* Washington, D.C., n.d.

————. *Linguistic Interpretation of North American Indian Words.* Washington, D.C., 1980.

Snell, Tee Loftin. *The Wild Shores: America's Beginnings.* Washington, D.C.: National Geographic Society, 1974.

Stanley, David, and Deke Castleman. *Alaska-Yukon Handbook.* Chico, Calif.: Moon Publications, 1988.

Stedman, Raymond William. *Shadows of the Indian.* Norman: University of Oklahoma Press, 1982.

Stevenson, Alexander. "The Development of the North." *UNESCO Courier,* January 1975, 12–13, 30–31.

Steward, Julian H., and Louis C. Faron. *Native Peoples of South America.* New York: McGraw-Hill, 1959.

Stewart, George R. *American Place-Names.* New York: Oxford University Press, 1970.

————. *Names on the Globe.* New York: Oxford University Press, 1975.

————. *Names on the Land.* New York: Random House, 1945.

————. "The Source of the Name 'Oregon.'" *Names: Journal of the American Name Society* 15 (September 1967).

Strachey, William. *The Historie of Travell into Virginia Britania.* Ed. Louis B. Wright and Virginia Freund. Nendeln/Liechtenstein: Kraus Reprint, 1967.

Swagerty, W. R. *Scholars and the Indian Experience.* Bloomington: Indiana University Press, 1984.

Swift, Jonathan. *The Journal to Stella.* Ed. George A. Aitken. New York: G. P. Putnam's Sons, 1901.

Ten Kate, Herman F. C. "The Indian in Literature." *Indian Historian,* Summer 1970.

Terrell, John Upton. *American Indian Almanac.* New York: World Publishing Co. 1971.

Thomas, Robert. "American Indian Culture at Risk." *Futurist,* March–April 1990, 53–54.

Thoreau, Henry David. *The Maine Woods.* Cambridge, Mass.: Riverside Press, 1894.

———. *Walden.* Cambridge, Mass.: Riverside Press, 1894.

Twain, Mark. *Tom Sawyer Abroad.* New York: Harper & Brothers, 1899 (1878).

12,000 Words: A Supplement to Webster's Third New International Dictionary. Springfield, Mass.: Merriam-Webster Inc., 1986.

Tyler, Lyon Gardiner. *Narratives of Early Virginia.* New York: Barnes & Noble, 1966.

Tyrrell, J. B., ed. *Journals of Samuel Hearne and Philip Turnor.* Toronto: Champlain Society, 1934.

Utley, Robert M. *The Indian Frontier of the American West, 1846–1890.* Albuquerque: University of New Mexico Press, 1984.

Utley, Robert M., and Wilcomb E. Washburn. *Indian Wars.* Boston: Houghton Mifflin, 1977.

Vanderwerth, W. C. *Indian Oratory.* Norman: University of Oklahoma Press, 1971.

Van Dusen, Albert E. *Connecticut.* New York: Random House, 1961.

Vaughan, Alden T. *American Genesis.* Boston and Toronto: Little, Brown and Co. 1975.

———. *New England Frontier.* Boston: Little Brown and Co., 1965.

Vaughan, Alden T., and Daniel K. Richter. *Crossing the Cultural Divide.* Worcester, Mass.: American Antiquarian Society, 1980.

Viola, Herman J. *Exploring the West.* Washington, D.C.: Smithsonian Institution, 1987.

Vogel, Virgil J. *American Indian Medicine*. Norman: University of Oklahoma Press, 1970.

———. *This Country Was Ours*. New York: Harper & Row, 1972.

Vogt, Evon Z. "The Acculturation of American Indians." *Annals of the American Academy of Political and Social Science* 311 (May 1957): 137–46.

von Baeyer, Hans Christian. "Picture This." *Sciences,* January/February 1991.

Walker, Deward E., Jr. *The Emergent Native Americans*. Boston: Little, Brown and Co., 1972.

Washburn, Wilcomb E. *History of Indian-White Relations*. Vol. 4 of *Handbook of North American Indians*. Washington, D.C.,: Smithsonian Institution, 1988.

———. *The Indian in America*. New York: Harper & Row, 1975.

Washington, George. *Writings*. 14 vols. New York: G. P. Putnam's Sons, 1889.

Weatherford, Jack. *Indian Givers*. New York: Crown Publishers, 1988.

———. *Native Roots: How the Indians Enriched America*. New York: Crown Publishing Group, 1991.

Weber, David J. *The Spanish Frontier in North America*. New Haven, Conn.: Yale University Press, 1992.

Webster's Ninth New Collegiate Dictionary. Springfield, Mass.: Merriam-Webster, 1988.

Webster's Third New International Dictionary. Springfield, Mass.: G. & C. Merriam Co., 1971.

Weil, Thomas, et al. *Area Handbook for Brazil*. Washington, D.C.: U.S. Government Printing Office, 1971.

Whipple, Chandler. *The Indian and the White Man in New England*. Stockbridge, Mass.: Berkshire Traveller Press, 1972.

Whitaker, Alexander. *Good Newes from Virginia*. New York, 1936 (1613).

Whitman, Walt. *Collected Poems*. Garden City, N.Y.: Blue Ribbon Books, 1942.

Whorf, Benjamin. *Language, Thought, and Reality*. Cambridge, Mass.: M.I.T. Press, 1956.

Wilkinson, Alex. "The Uncommitted Crime." *New Yorker,* November 26, 1990, 61–118.

Willard, Caroline McCoy. *Life in Alaska.* Philadelphia: Presbyterian Board of Education, 1884.

Williams, Roger. *A Key into the Language of America.* Ed. John J. Teunissen and Evelyn J. Hinz. Detroit: Wayne State University Press, 1973 (1643).

Winship, George Parker, ed. *Sailors' Narratives of Voyages along the New England Coast.* New York: Burt Franklin, 1905.

Winslow, Edward. *Good News from New England* (1624). (*See* Arber, *The Story of the Pilgrim Fathers.*)

Winthrop, John. *Winthrop's Journal, "History of New England,"* *1630–49.* Ed. James Kendall Hosmer. New York: Barnes & Noble, 1959.

Wood, William. *New England's Prospect.* Ed. Alden T. Vaughan. Amherst: University of Massachusetts, 1977 (1634).

World Almanac and Book of Facts. New York: Pharos Books, 1993.

Yinger, J. Milton, and George Eaton Simpson. "The Integration of Americans of Indian Descent." *Annals of the American Academy of Political and Social Science* 436 (March 1978): 137–51.

Young, Gordon. "Chocolate: Food of the Gods." *National Geographic,* November 1984, 664–87.

Zepeda, Ofelia, and Jane H. Hill. "The Condition of Native American Languages in the United States." *Diogenes,* Spring 1991, 45–65.

Ziff, Larzer. *Puritanism in America.* New York: Viking Press, 1973.

Index

Note: Indianisms, loanwords and loan terms, and place-names of Indian origin are entered in *italic* type.

Abalone, 108–109, 119
Acorn squash, 150
Adair, James, 127, 128
Adams, John, 60
Adams, Samuel, 60
Adirondack chair, 139, 150
Adirondack Mountains, 69, 139
Ainus, 136
Alabama, state of, 72
Alabamine, 150
Alaska (overshoe), 99, 100
Alaska, state of, 75, 97–101
Alaska blackfish, 98
Alaska cedar, 98
Alaska cod, 98
Alaska cypress, 98
Alaska goose, 98
Alaska grayling, 98
Alaska longspur, 98
Alaskan malamute, 97, 98, 100
Alaska pine, 98
Alaska pollack, 98
Alaska time, 98, 100
Alaskite, 99
Alcoholism, Indians and, 143
Aleut (lang.), 24, 75, 97, 98, 100. *See also* Eskaleut; Eskimo-Aleut
Aleutian Islands, 93. *See also* Atka
Aleuts, 93
Algebra, as Harriot interest, 10, 12
Algonkian (geol.), 122. *See also* Algonquian (lang.)
Algonquian (lang.), 5, 23, 24, 26–29, 40n, 62; Penn on, 70; Pilgrims and, 33–35; range of, 26–27; Smith and, 19. *See also* Cheyenne; Fox; Macro-Algonquian; Micmac; Narragansett; Ojibwa; Proto-Algonquian
Allegheny Mountains, 69
Allegheny spurge, 150
Allegheny vine, 119
All-hallown summer. See *Indian summer*
Allocochick, 119
Alphabet, Algonquian phonetic, 5
Amazon River, 49, 51
American Indian Dance Theatre, 146
American Revolution, 60–61, 72, 128. *See also* Sons of Tammany
Amerind (lang. group), 24
Andes Mountains, 51
Angakok, 96, 141
Anne, queen of Great Britain and Ireland, 54
Anorak, 100
Antelope, 123
Apache (helicopter gunship), 140
Apache (ruffian), 140, 148
Apache dance, 140, 149
Apache Indians, 24, 29, 105. *See also* White Mountain Apaches
Apalachee crape myrtle, 141
Aphrodisiac, chocolate as, 48

Apishamore, 88
Appalachian dulcimer, 151
Appalachian Mountains, 69
Appalachian tea, 120
Appaloosa, 140, 149
Arapaho Indians, 136
Arawak (lang.), 44–47
Arawak Indians, 47, 49
Arcticon (Harriot), 4
Arizona, state of, 75, 110
Arizona pine, 111, 122
Arizona ruby, 111, 122
Arizonite, 111, 149
Arkansas, state of, 72, 111
Arkansas goldfinch, 111, 119
Arkansas kingbird, 111, 120
Arkansas River, 68
Arkansas stone, 111, 120
Arkansas toothpick, 82, 90, 111
Arrow arum. See *Tuckahoe*
Arrowroot. See *Wapatoo*
Artifacts, 152; from Harriot explorations, 6; Lewis and Clark–collected, 129; at Louisiana Purchase Exposition, 136; naming, 145
Assapan, 19, 20, 249n.9
Assiniboine Indians, 58
Astronomy, Harriot achievements in, 10–11
Atamasco lily, 37
Atchafalaya River, 68
At Good Old Siwash (Fitch), 140
Athabaskan (lang.), 24
Atka, 99
Atka mackerel, 99
Atkins, J. D. C., 117

Avocado, 48
Aztec Indians, 48, 51, 52, 124, 142. *See also* Nahuatl
Aztec-Tanoan (lang. group), 24

Babiche, 88
Baffin Island, 92, 93
Baggataway, 65
Baked Alaska, 98
Ballistics, Harriot interest in, 10
Balsam hickory, 66
Bands, wampum, 35
Bannerstone, 134
Barbecue, 47
Barlowe, Arthur, 5, 67
Barren ground caribou, 89
Barter, Indians and, 26, 35. *See also* Fur trade
Barton, B. S., 80–81
Bass, Lake Champlain, 61. See also *Bayou bass; Oswego bass*
Basso, Keith H., 76
Bath, N. C., 55
Bayou, 60, 62, 65
Bayou bass, 148
Beads, wampum, 35
Beaver, Pilgrim focus on, 35
Beef, dried. See *Jerky*
Benedict, Ruth, 134
Beshow, 121
Beverley, Robert, 55–57
Big chief, 134
Bigfoot. See *Sasquatch*
Big knife, 134
Bilingual Education Act, 31
Black cohosh, 89
Blackfish. See *Alaska blackfish; Tautog*
Blackfoot Indians, 129
Black hickory, 66
Blaine, James, 84
Blanket Indian, 134
Blueback. See *Sockeye salmon*
Blue cohosh, 89
Bogan, 122
Bogue, 89
Boyle, Robert, 57
Boy Scouts of America, 138
Braddock, Edward, 59
Bradford, William, 33–35
Braves (warriors), 131; Tammany Society, 114
Brazil, 49

Breech cloth, 134
Brewster, William, 32–33
Briefe and True Report, A (Harriot), 8, 12, 13
Bright, William, 145
British North American Act, 73
Broom hickory, 89
Buccaneer, 49
Buck(skin) (dollar), 133
Buffalo, 116, 123. See also *Medicine buffalo; Medicine dance*
Buffalo dance. See *Medicine dance*
Buffalo wallow, 123
Bunnell, Lafayette H., 74–75
Burden strap, 134
Busk, 62, 65
Buttercup squash, 150
Butternut squash, 150

Cacao, 48. See also *Chocolate*
Cachina. See *Kachina*
Cacique, 44, 46
Cacti. See *Mescal; Saguaro; Tuna*
Caiman, 47
"Caliban" (*The Tempest*), 45
California, state of: loanwords from, 108–109
Calumet, 114, 126
Camas(s), 80, 88. See also *Death camass*
Camas rat, 91
Campion, Thomas, 20
Campoody, 119
Canada, 73, 82, 115; Harrison victories in, 81; loanwords of, 115–16; place-names of, 72–73, 77–78; vs. potlatch, 86
Canada Act of 1791, 73
Canada anemone, 148
Canada balsam, 82, 88
Canada blueberry, 115, 119
Canada bluegrass, 148
Canada goose, 43. See also *Canadian goose*
Canada jay, 63, 65
Canada lily, 149
Canada lyme grass, 116, 122
Canada lynx, 82, 90
Canada mayflower, 150
Canada moonseed, 63, 66

Canada pea, 122
Canada plum, 82, 91
Canada porcupine, 63, 66
Canada root, 82, 89
Canada snakeroot, 82, 89
Canada thistle, 63, 66
Canada violet, 82, 89
Canada warbler, 82, 90
Canader, 122
Canadian bacon, 150
Canadian football, 150
Canadian goldenrod, 82, 90
Canadian goose, 82, 88. See also *Canada goose*
Canadian hemlock, 116, 122
Canadian hemp, 148
Canadian holly, 63, 66
Canadianism, 120
Canadianize, 89
Cannibal, 44–46
Cannibalism, among Indians, 45, 131
Canoe, 8, 44, 46, 47, 85. See also *Canader; Pirogue*
Canola, 151
Canola oil, 151
Cantico, 20, 249n.9
Caoutchouc, 50
Carcajou, 54, 64
Carey (turtle), 47
Cariban (lang.), 47
Caribbean Sea, 45
Caribe, 45
Carib Indians, 45, 47, 49. *See also* Cariban (lang.); Island Carib
Caribou, 16, 249n.9. See also *Barren ground caribou; Mountain caribou; Woodland caribou*
Caribou moss, 119
Carolinas, English exploration of, 55, 67. *See also* Raleigh, Walter; Roanoke Island
Carson, Kit, 110
Cartier, Jacques, 73
Cashew, 49
Cassava, 8, 44, 46
Cassina, 10. See also *Yaupon*
Cassioberry, 63, 65
Catalpa, 57, 62, 64
Catalpa worm, 149
Catawba (grape), 119
Catawba (lang.), 63
Catawba (wine), 90

Catawba rhododendron, 89
Catawba tree, 89
Catesby, Mark, 57
Catlin, George, 130
Cattle, Indian slaughter of settler, 42
Caucas Clubb, 60
Caucus, 60, 65, 141
Cawquaw, 66
Cayman. See *Caiman*
Cayuse, 82, 90
Champlain, Lake, 61
Char. See *Sunapee trout*
Charles, prince of Wales, 69
Charles River, 69
Charqui. See *Jerky*
Chautauqua, 114, 120
Chautauqua Institution, 114
Chautauqua Lake, 114
Chautauqua Literary and Scientific Circle, 114
Chautauqua muskellunge, 114–15
Chebacco boat, 89
Chebog, 122
Cheechako, 107, 122
Cherokee (lang.), 87
Cherokee Indians, 57, 81, 87, 105
Cherokee rose, 81, 89
Chesapeake Bay retriever, 120
Chewing gum. See *Chicle*
Cheyenne (lang.), 28, 29
Chicago (card game), 150
Chickasaw plum, 62, 65
Chicle, 48
Chief Joseph, 30, 105
Chili, 48
China (word), 10
Chinook (lang.), 86. See also *Chinook Jargon*
Chinook (wind), 106, 120
Chinook Indians, 85, 105, 106
Chinook Jargon, 26, 63, 80, 85, 86, 90, 106, 107, 132, 139, 141
Chinook licorice, 106, 122
Chinook salmon, 106, 119
Chinquapin, 19, 20, 249n.9. See also *Giant chinquapin; Water chinquapin*
Chinquapin oak, 66. See also *Dwarf chinquapin oak*
Chinquapin perch, 121
Chipmunk, 83, 89

Chippewa crape myrtle, 141
Chippewa Indians, 111
Chittamwood, 90
Chocolate, 48
Choctaw (gibberish), 82, 90
Choctaw (lang.), 82
Choctaw (skating), 122
Chogset, 90
Choupique, 62, 65
Christianity, Indians and, 135
Chuck (inlet), 120
Chuckwalla, 109, 120
Chumpa, 119
Chum salmon, 139, 148, 149
Chunkey, 63, 64
Cibolero, 90
Cisco, 91
Clams, edible. See *Geoduck; Mananosay; Pismo clam; Quahog*
Clark, Edward, 71–72
Clark, William, 79. *See also* Lewis and Clark Expedition
Clemens, Samuel L. (pseud. Mark Twain), 118, 132
Cleveland, Grover, 84
Coca, 50
Cocaine, 50
Cocash, 89
Cocashweed, 120
Cochise, 105
Cockarouse, 19, 249n.9. See also *Caucus*
Cocoa, 48
Cody, William S., 118
Coho, 120
Cohosh, 66. See also *Black cohosh; Blue cohosh*
College, American Indians in, 147
Colonel Cobb, 30
Columbus, Christopher, 44–46, 125
Comanche (lang.), 26
Comanchean (geol.), 149
Comanche crape myrtle, 141
Condor, 50
Conestoga (brogan), 122
Conestoga, Pa., 58
Conestoga Indians, 58
Conestoga wagon, 59, 64
Connecticut, state of, 71; place-names of, 70
Connecticut River, 71

Connecticut warbler, 89
Coon, 65, 90
Coon cat, 148
Coon cheese, 151
Coon dog, 90
Coon grape, 149
Coonhound, 149
Coon oyster, 120
Coonroot, 122
Coon's age, 90
Coon shouter, 149
Coonskin, 89
Coon song, 90
Coontail, 149
Coontie, 62, 66
Coony, 149
Cooper, James Fenimore, 84, 131, 132
Corn, 124; centrality of, 124–25; as chocolate ingredient, 48; history of, 124; as Jamestown staple, 18; and lima beans (see Succotash). *See also* Cornmeal; *Hominy; Indian harvest; Nasaump; Nocake; Pone; Sagamité; Samp;* Spoon bread; *Succotash; Supawn*
Corn bread. See *Indian bread; Pone*
Cornmeal, 21, 37, 125. See also *Indian meal; Indian pudding; Nocake*
Corn mush. See *Supawn*
Corn pone. See *Pone*
Cortés, Hernán, 48
Costanoan Indians, 108
Cottonmouth moccasin, 121
Cougar, 49. See also *Puma*
Council, 134. *See also* North American Indians, "Last Great Council" of
Council fires, 123, 124, 126
Coup, 134
Coupstick, 134
Cous, 88
Cowish. See *Cous*
Coxe, William, 96
Coyote, 48
Crafts, Indian, 146
Crape myrtles, 141
Cree Indians, 58
Creek Indians, 81
Cree potato, 148
Cross-staff, 4

Croton bug, 90
Cui-ui, 120
Cultus, 91
Cunner fish. See Tautog
Curare, 47
Currency, wampum as
  Dutch, 35
Cushaw, 8, 248n.14
Custer, George A., 124. See
  also White Chief of the
  Long Hair
Cutthroat trout. See Tahoe
  trout
Cuttyhunk (isl.), 139
Cuttyhunk, 139, 149

Dakota (apt. bldg.), 72
Dakota (geol.), 120
Dances, Indian, 146
Dances with Wolves (film),
  147
Davies, M. C., 140
Dawes, Henry L., 143. See
  also Indian Allotment Act
Dawes Act. See Indian
  Allotment Act
Death camas, 121
Deerskins, Indian trade in,
  57, 133
Defoe, Daniel, 54
Deh Cho (Mackenzie River),
  77
Denali (Mt. McKinley), 76
Denali National Park, 69,
  76
Déné Nation, 77
Denmark, Eskimo captives
  in, 95
Deseret, 72
Diamondback terrapin, 121
Dictionaries, American
  Indian, 24
Dil Hil I (river), 76
Diseases, white man's, 57, 86,
  106, 108. See also Plague
Dockmackie, 89
Dog salmon. See Chum
  salmon
Donne, John, 20
Dowitcher, 90
Drake, Francis, 7
Dwarf chinquapin oak, 149
Dzil Ligai (mountain), 76

East, American: loanwords
  from, 112–16
Eden, Richard, 45–48

Egolf, Don R., 141
Elizabeth I, queen of En-
  gland and Ireland, 93
Elk, American. See Wapiti
Enchilada, 48
Erian (geol.), 120
Erie, Lake, 68
Eskaleut (lang.), 93–101
Eskimo (lang.), 24, 72, 94,
  98, 100. See also Eskaleut;
  Yupik
Eskimo-Aleut (lang. group),
  24. See also Eskaleut
Eskimo curlew, 89
Eskimo dog, 63, 65. See also
  Husky
Eskimoid, 149
Eskimo Pie, 140, 150
Eskimo potato, 150
Eskimos, 92–101; as London
  curiosity, 92, 95; range
  of, 93. See also Inuits
Eulachon, 88

Fairy lily. See Atamasco lily
Firewater, 134
Fish, of Pacific Northwest,
  105
Fitch, George H., 140
Fitzgerald, Frances, 84
Flanigan, Beverly O., 132, 133
Florida, state of, 10, 59, 81
Forked tongue, 127
Fort Clatsop, 79
Fort Mackenzie, 82
Fox (lang.), 28
Fox Indians, 111
Franklin, state of, 71. See
  also Tennessee, state of
Freeman, Randolph, 77
Frémont, John Charles, 131
French (lang.), 60
Frobisher, Martin, 77, 92–
  93, 95
Frobisher Bay, 77, 92
Fur trade, North American,
  57–59, 105

Gans, Joachim, 6
Garnet. See Arizona ruby
Geechee, 150
Geoduck, 108, 121
George, Dan, 68
George II, king of Great
  Britain and Ireland, 57
George III, king of Great
  Britain and Ireland, 60

Geronimo, 105, 116
Ghost Dance, 117, 135
Giant chinquapin, 149
Giant sequoia, 87, 150
Gifts, Indians and, 127. See
  also Potlatch
Gila Indians, 110
Gila monster, 110, 121
Gila River, 110
Gila trout, 110, 119
Gila woodpecker, 110, 119
Gilbert, Humphrey, 4
Glotov, Stepan, 96–97
Glottal stop, 28n, 83
Gold: Alaskan, 97, 100;
  Baffin Island, 93; Califor-
  nia, 103
Gorges, Ferdinando, 15, 36
Graffenried, Christopher de,
  56, 128
Grammars, American In-
  dian, 24
Grand Sachem, Tammany,
  114
Great Father, 135. See also
  Great White Father
Great Spirit, 135
Great White Father, 123, 135
Greenberg, Joseph H., 24
Greenland, place-names of,
  77
Groundhog. See Woodchuck
Guacamole, 48
Guaiacol, 44
Guaiacum, 8, 44, 45
Guaican, 46
Guano, 50
Guarani (lang.), 49
Guava, 46
Gunpowder plot, Harriot
  and, 11

Hackmatack, 61, 66
Haddo, 121
Hakluyt, Richard, 94–95
Half-breed, 128
Hammock, 44, 46
Happy hunting ground, 132
Hard-bark hickory, 122
Harriot, Thomas, 3–14, 16,
  22, 23, 44, 144, 248n.14;
  accomplishments of, 10–
  13; death of, 12
Harrison, William Henry,
  81
Hasty pudding. See Supawn

Hawaii, state of, 75
Heap (plenty), 132
Heckewelder, John, 133
Hempton, Gordon, 101
Henequen, 46
Hiawatha, 102. See also *Song of Hiawatha, The*
Hickory, 19, 20, 141, 142, 249n.9. See also *Balsam hickory; Black hickory; Broom hickory; Hard-bark hickory; King nut hickory; Mockernut hickory; Nutmeg hickory; Pignut hickory; Shagbark hickory; Water hickory; White hickory*
Hickory elm, 121
Hickory horned devil, 89
Hickory nut, 88
Hickory oak, 122
Hickory pine, 121
Hickory poplar, 122
Hickory shad, 88
Hickory shirt, 90
High-muck-a-muck, 106, 119
Hobbes, Thomas, 41
Hogan, 110, 120
Hog and hominy, 65
Hog-nosed skunk, 149
Hohokam, 121
Hokan (lang. group), 24
Holly. See *Canadian holly; Cassina; Yaupon*
Hollywood, Indians per, 138, 147
Hominy, 19, 249n.9. See also *Hog and hominy; Lye hominy; Nasaump; Samp*
Hominy grits, 121
"*Honest Injun*," 135
Honk(ing), 113, 119
Hooch(inoo), 107, 121, 122
Hootsnoowoos Indians, 107
Hopi crape myrtle, 141
Hopi Indians, 109. See also *Squash blossom*
How (salutation), 89, 132–33
Hoxie, Frederick E., 136–37
Hubbard squash, 120
Hunkpapa Sioux, 105
Huron Indians, 54
Hurricane, 46
Huskanaw, 43
Husky (dog), 97, 119. See also *Siberian husky*

Ice, Eskimo language on, 94
Idaho (potato), 150
Idaho, state of, 72
Igloo, 95–96
Iguana, 46
Ilex vomitoria, 10
Illinium, 150
Illinoian (geol.), 122
Illinois, state of, 72
Illinois Indians, 111
Illinois nut, 65
Illite, 150
Inca Indians, 50–52
Indian (word), 127, 148. See also Indians (people)
Indiana, state of, 72
Indian Allotment Act, 143–44
Indian bread, 125
Indian corn. See Corn
Indian doctor, 126
Indian gift, 127
Indian harvest, 125
Indianisms, 123–35, 144; defined, 124
Indian maize, 125. See also Corn
Indian meal, 125
Indian moccasin, 90
Indian Peace Commission, 117
Indian poke, 66
Indian pudding, 125
Indians (people): North American (*see* North American Indians); South American, 44–52
"Indians," cigar-store, 118
Indians (aircraft), 134
Indian summer, 128–29. See also *Squaw summer*
Inouye, Daniel K., 31
Insects, of Amazon rain forest, 51
Intermarriage: Indian/fur trader, 57; Spanish/Indian, 52
Inuit (lang.), 24, 72
Inuits, 78, 95
Inuktitut (lang.), 78
Iowa, state of, 72
Iowan (geol.), 122
Ipecac, 49
Iqaluit, NW Terr., 77
Iron horse, 123

Iroquois Indians, 53
Iroquois League, 61
Irving, Washington, 83, 132
Isham, James, 58
Island Carib (lang.), 47
Jackson, Andrew, 71, 81
Jaguar, 49
Jamestown, Va., 17–21, 124
Jefferson, Thomas, 79, 81, 129. See also Lewis and Clark Expedition; United States, westward expansion of
Jerky, 50
Jesuits, Brazil-based, 49
Jonson, Ben, 20
Kachina, 109, 120, 145
Kachina dolls, 109
Kalevala, 102
Kalmia glauca, 115
Kamleika, 97
Kamloops, Br. Col., 108
Kamloops trout, 108, 122
Kansan (geol.), 122
Kansas, state of, 72
Kayak, 92, 95
Keekwilee-house, 149
Keewatin, 121
Kemble, Fanny, 86
Kentucky, commonwealth of, 71
Kentucky bluegrass, 82, 91
Kentucky coffee tree, 66
Kentucky jean, 90
Kentucky rifle, 82, 89
Kentucky warbler, 89
Kepler, Johannes, 10–11
Keweenawan, 120
Kiccowtan, Va., 70
Kickapoo, 111–12
Kickapoo Indian Medicine Company, 112, 118
Kickapoo Indians, 112
Killifish. See *Mummichog*
King Hancock, 56
King nut hickory, 122
King Philip, 41–42, 126
King Philip's War, 126
King salmon. See *Chinook salmon*
Kinkajou, 66
Kinnikinni(c)k, 62, 66
Kiowa (scout helicopter), 140
Kipling, Rudyard, 141

Kiva, 109, 120
Klamath River, 139
Klamath weed, 139, 149
Klondike (card game), 148
Klondike (source of wealth), 122
Klootchman, 90
Kodiak bear, 99
Kokanee, 106, 120
Komatic, 97
Koshare, 122

Labrador tea, 115
Lady's slipper (plant). See *Moccasin flower*
Lahontan, Louis-Armand de, 54
Lakota (lang.), 23, 147
Lane, Ralph, 9
Languages, Indian: North American (*see* North American Indians, languages of); South American, 52 (*see also* Arawakan; Cariban; Nahuatl; Quechua; Tupi[an])
Larch. See *Hackmatack; Tamarack*
Last of the Mohicans, The (Cooper), 84, 131
Latin America, loanwords from, 44–52. *See also* West Indies, loanwords from
Laudonnière, René Goulaine de, 10
Lawrence, D. H., 141
Lawson, John, 55–57
Leap, William, 31, 144, 147
Leatherwood. See *Wicopy*
Lescarbot, Marc, 21–22, 249n.9
Levett, William, 36, 251n.16
Lewis, Meriwether, 79, 80
Lewis and Clark Expedition, 79–80, 85, 87, 129–30
Light, Harriot study of, 10
Lignum vitae. *See Guaiacum*
Lilies. See *Atamasco lily; Camas; Sego lily;* Water lily
Lima beans, corn and. See *Succotash*
Llama, 50
Loanwords, Indian, 8, 143, 152–53; Algonquian

dominance of North American, 26–28; compound, 142; English-to-Indian, 40–41; Eskimo-Aleut, 92–101, 134; Latin American, 44–52; North American, 13, 22, 26–28, 63–64 & n, 143 (*see also* Indianisms; Place-names, U.S. Indian-origin); Spanish, 142–43
Lockhart, James, 142–43
Lodge pole, 123
Logan, 121
Lok, Michael, 93
Longe. See Lunge
Longfellow, Henry W., 102–103
Longhouse, 126
Long knife(-ives), 123, 124, 135
Louisiana Purchase, 136
Louisiana Purchase Exposition, 136–37
Louisiana Territory, 60
Lucayo (lang.), 47
Lunge, 119
Lupe, Ronnie, 76–77
Lye hominy, 89

McAllester, David P., 146
Macaulay, Thomas B., 87
Macaw, 49
Macbeth (Shakespeare), 54
McGee, W. J., 136
Mackenzie, Alexander, 77
Mackenzie River, 77
Mackinac Island, 83
Mackinaw, 82–83, 89. See also *Mackinaw coat*
Mackinaw boat, 83, 89
Mackinaw City, Mich., 82
Mackinaw coat, 83, 148
Mackinaw trout, 83, 90
McKinley, Mount, 75–76
McKinley, William, 75
Macock, 9, 248n.14
Macro-Algonquian (lang. group), 24
Macro-Siouan (lang. group), 24
Maguey, 46
Mahala, 119
Maine, state of, 14, 36
Maine coon, 150

Maize, 8, 46, 125. *See also* Corn
Makluk, 99
Malamute, 99. See also *Alaskan malamute*
Malibu, Calif., 139
Malibu board, 139, 151
Malimiut, 99
Mananosay, 56, 64
Manatee, 47
Mandan Indians, 129
Mangas Coloradas, 105
Mangrove, 47
Manhattan (cocktail), 115, 122
Manhattan (NYC borough), 115
Manhattan clam chowder, 150
Manhattan Indians, 115
Manioc, 49
Manitoba, province of, 73
Manitoba maple, 121
Manitou, 9, 248n.14
Manteo, 5, 7, 10
Maracock, 19, 20, 249n.9
Marckwardt, Albert, 141–42
Marrow squash, 120
Martyr, Peter, 45–46, 48
Maryland, state of, 36
Maskinonge, 103
Massachuset River, 69
Massachusetts, commonwealth of, 69, 71; colonization of (*see* Pilgrims)
Massachusetts ballot, 122
Massachusetts Bay, 71
Massachusetts Bay Colony, 33, 36, 38–39, 70
Massasauga, 119
Massasoit, 34, 41, 42
Matchcoat, 19, 20, 249n.9
Mathemeg, 66
Mattowacca, 121
Maudlin, Stanislaus, 145
Mayflower (ship), 33, 34
Maypop, 119
Medicine (magical power), 123, 124, 129–31
Medicine bag, 130
Medicine Bow, Wyo., 131
Medicine buffalo, 131
Medicine dance, 130
Medicine dog, 131
Medicine iron, 131
Medicine Lake, Mont., 131
Medicine line, 131

Medicine lodge, 130
Medicine Lodge, Kans., 131
Medicine man, 130. See also
    Indian doctor
Medicine Mound, Tex., 131
Medicine Park, Okla., 131
Medicine River, 130
Medicines (curatives), 130
Medicine shows. *See* Kick-
    apoo Indian Medicine
    Company
Medicine woman, 130
Menhaden, 40, 251n.16
Menominee Indians, 111
Menominee whitefish, 111, 121
Mescal, 48. See also *Peyote*
Metacom. *See* King Philip
Metasequoia, 150
Mexico: Kickapoo exiles in,
    112; Spain and, 48; U.S.
    vs., 103
Michigan (card game), 150
Michigan, Lake, 68
Michigan, state of, 72
Michigan bankroll, 150
Michigan grayling, 121
Micmac (lang.), 29
Mico, 62, 64
Midewiwin, 120
Midges. See *No-see-ums*
Midwest, American: loan-
    words of, 111–12
"*Minnehaha*" (*The Song of
    Hiawatha*), 103
Minnesota, state of, 72
Missey-moosey, 122
Mississippi, state of, 72
Mississippian (geol.), 120
Mississippi kite, 89
Mississippi River, 68, 77
Missouri, state of, 72
Missouri currant, 119
Missouri River, 68
Missouri skylark, 119
Miwok Indians, 75
Mobile River, 68
Moccasin, 21, 249n.9. See
    also *Shoepac; Upland moc-
    casin; Water moccasin*
Moccasin flower, 43
Moccasin telegraph, 138, 149
Mockernut hickory, 89
Mocock, 65
Moctezuma II, 48
Mohawk (aircraft), 53
Mohawk (skating), 121

Mohawk haircut, 53
Mohawk Indians, 53–54,
    126
Mohawk weed, 149
Mohegan Indians, 39
Mohock, 53, 54, 64
Monadnock, 115, 122
Monadnock, Mount, 115
Monomoy, Mass., 70
Monongahela (whiskey), 88
Montagnais (lang.), 94
Moon (time period), 135
Moors, Iberians and, 52
Moose, 16, 21, 148, 249n.9
Mooseberry, 66
Moosebird, 89
Moosebush, 66
Moosecall, 122
Moose elm, 89
Mooseflower, 119
Moose fly, 90
Moose maple, 90
Moosemise, 120
Moose tick, 120
Moosewood, 65
Mormons, 72
Morton, George, 34, 251n.16
Mossbunker. See *Menhaden*
Mother-of-pearl, from aba-
    lones, 109
Mountain caribou, 149
Mountain Chief, 137
Muckamuck, 90, 141, 149.
    See also *High-muck-
    a-muck*
*Mugwump(-ery; -ian; -ish;
    -ism)*, 84–85, 89, 121,
    141, 142, 149
Muir, John, 98, 107
Mukluk, 99–100
Muktuk, 97
Mulligan, Mary, 147
Mummichog, 40, 251n.16
Murine opossum, 66
Mush (command), 97
Mush, corn. See *Supawn*
Music, Indian, 147
Musical instruments, In-
    dian, 146
Muskeg, 65
Muskellunge, 61, 66. See also
    Chautauqua muskellunge
Muskie(-ky), 122
Muskogean (lang.), 62–63
Muskrat, 19 & n, 20,
    249n.9

Muskrat weed, 122
Musquash. See *Muskrat*
Musquash root, 88
Musquashweed, 65
Musquaw, 120
Myrtle. *See* Crape myrtles
Mystic, Conn., 38

Na-Dene (lang. group), 24
Nahuatl (lang.), 48, 50, 52,
    142–43
Nakai, R. Carlos, 147
Namaycush, 65
Narragansett (lang.), 29,
    39–41
Narragansett Indians, 34,
    38–41
Narragansett pacer, 65
Nasaump, 40, 251n.16
Natchez crape myrtle, 141
National Arboretum, U.S.,
    141
Navaho blanket, 82, 90
Navajo (lang.), 24, 28n
Navajo Code Talkers, 28n
Navajo Indians, 24, 29, 110
Nebraska, state of, 72
Nebraskan (geol.), 149
Nelson, Richard K., 94
Netop, 19, 20, 249n.9
New England: Indian/white
    confrontation in, 38–39,
    41–43 (*see also* Pilgrims);
    loanwords from, 115;
    naming of, 69. *See also*
    Connecticut; Maine; Mas-
    sachusetts; Massachusetts
    Bay Colony; Pilgrims;
    Plymouth Colony
Newfoundland (isl.), 4
Newfoundland, province of,
    73
New Mexico, state of, 75
New York, N.Y., 71–72
Nez Percé Indians, 105, 129,
    140
Niagara, 87, 90
Niagara Falls, 69
Niagara green, 148
Nocake, 37, 251n.16
Nootka cypress, 108, 122
Nootka Indians, 108
North America, renaming
    of, 67–78. *See also* Can-
    ada; United States
North American Indians: of

Alaska, 98; as British curiosities, 5, 14–16, 53–54, 57, 93; and British paternalism, 53–54, 57, 60; Christian, 135; "civilizing" of, 30, 61, 116–19, 144; cruelty of, 56; culture of, 51, 87, 146–48, 152–53; derogation of (see *Half-breed;* "Indians," cigar-store; *Red man; Redskin*); as doomed, 83; as Exposition displays, 136, 137; and French/English conflict, 59; and fur trade, 57; Harriot and, 6–10, 23; languages of, 23–31, 52, 79, 105, 108, 114, 117 (*see also* Algonquian; Aztec-Tanoan; Catawba; Chinook Jargon; Comanche; Eskimo-Aleut; Glottal stop; Hokan; Lakota; Macro-Algonquian; Macro-Siouan; Muskogean; Na-Dene; Navajo Code Talkers; Penutian; Pidgin English; Sign language; Siouan; Timucuan); "Last Great Council" of, 137; Pilgrims and, 33–35; and puberty (see *Huskanaw*); Raleigh crew and, 5, 6–7, 10; resistance to whites by, 32, 38, 41–42, 72, 104, 127–28, 131 (*see also* King Philip's war; North American Indians, warlike); schools for, 57; Smith among, 17–19, 22, 23, 32; stereotypes, 118 (*see also* Hollywood, Indians per; North American Indians, as Exposition displays); taciturnity of, 29–30; today, 143, 146–48; warlike, 104, 111, 112, 126, 128, 131 (see also *Braves; Coup*); white persecution of, 81, 83, 104–105, 108, 110, 112, 116–18, 123, 143–44 (*see also* North American Indians, "civilizing" of; Reservations, Indian; United

States, westward expansion of); white sympathy for, 87, 105. See also *Blanket Indian; Braves; Sachem; Squaw; and individual tribes by name*
North *Dakota*, state of, 72
Northumberland, earl of. *See* Percy, Henry
Northwest Ordinance, 61
Northwest Passage, Frobisher search for, 92
Northwest Territories, Can.: place-names of, 77–78
Norwalk, Conn., 70
No-see-ums, 133
Nouns, verbalized, 141–42
Nunavut (Inuit territory), 78
Nutmeg hickory, 90

Ocelot, 48
Of Plimoth Plantation (Bradford), 33, 35
Oglala Sioux, 105
Ohio, state of, 72
Ohio buckeye, 89
Ohio River, 68
Oil, Alaska, 100
Ojibwa (lang.), 29, 107
Ojibwa Indians, 102
Oka, 150
Okeechobee, Lake, 69
Okie, 150
Oklabar, 150
Oklahoma (card game), 150
Oklahoma, state of, 75
Old-squaw, 90
Old Wives' summer. See *Indian summer*
Olearius, Adam, 95
Oneida Indians, 136
Onomatopoeia, as Indian language element, 28–29
Ontario, Lake, 68
Ontario, province of, 73, 81
Opechancanough, 41
Opelousa Indians, 140
Opossum, 22, 249n.9. See also *Murine opossum; Possum; Vulpine opossum; Water opossum; Zebra opossum*
Opossum mouse, 90
Opossum shrimp, 90
Oquassa, 121
Oregon, state of, 72, 108
Oregon alder, 108, 120

Oregon ash, 108, 120
Oregon cedar, 108, 120
Oregon crab apple, 108, 121
Oregon grape, 108, 119
Oregon jay, 149
Oregon lily, 151
Oregon myrtle, 150
Oregon pine, 90
Oregon robin, 108, 120
Orenda, 149
Organic Act of 1884, 97
Osage crape myrtle, 141
Osage orange, 81, 89
Oswego bass, 65
Oswego tea, 65
Ouananiche, 88
Oxford English Dictionary (OED), Indian words in, 147–48

Pac, 120. See also *Shoepac*
Pacific Northwest, loanwords of, 105–108
Pahaska, 123
Paho, 121
Painted terrapin, 120
Paleface, 132
Palouse River, 140
Pampas, Patagonian, 51
Papoose, 37, 251n.16
Papoose board, 119
Papooseroot, 89
Paraguay, 49
Parfleche, 135
Parka, 96
Passionflower. See *Maracock*
Patagonia, 51, 136
Pattypan squash, 148
Patuxet Indians, 33
Peace belt, 135
Peace pipe, 135
Peag. See *Wampum*
Pecan, 20, 60, 64, 249n.9. See also *Illinois nut*
Peccary, 47
Pecos crape myrtle, 141
Pekan, 65
Pembina, 65
Pemmican, 58, 63, 65, 103
Penn, William, 135
Penutian (lang. group), 24
Pequot Indians, 38–39
Pequot War, 38–39
Percy, George, 19n
Percy, Henry, 11
Persian Gulf War, 140

Persimmon, 19, 20, 145, 249n.9
Peru, 49–50
Peyote, 48
Philadelphia Centennial
    Exposition, 137
Phlip (beverage), 60
Pidgin English, 132–33
Pignut hickory, 64
Pike. See *Maskinonge*
Piki, 119
Pilgrims, 32–35, 125
Pima (lang.), 48
Pima cotton, 149
Pingo, 100
Pipestone, 135
Pipsissewa, 62, 66
Piranha, 49. See also *Caribe*
Pirogue, 47
Piskun, 88
Pismo Beach, Calif., 139
Pismo clam, 139, 149
Pizarro, Francisco, 49
Place-names, U.S. Indian-
    origin, 67–78
Plague, Indians devastated
    by, 33–34
Plains Indians, 26, 116. See
    also *Ghost Dance;* Sign
    language; Sioux Indians;
    Sun Dance
Plenty Coups, 123–24, 126,
    137
Plymouth Colony, 33–36,
    39, 70
Pocahontas, 18, 84
Pocan, 119
Pocosin, 37
Podunk, 85, 90
Pogamoggan, 66, 103
Pogonip, 120
Pogy, 90
Poke (pokeweed), 64. See
    also *Indian poke; Virginia
    poke*
Poke (tobacco), 37
Pokeberry, 65
Pokelogan, 89
Poke milkweed, 122
Pokeroot, 43
Poke salad, 121
Pokeweed, 65. See also *Poke*
    (pokeweed); *Puccoon*
Polysynthesis, as Algon-
    quian element, 27–28
Pone (corn bread), 16, 119,
    249n.9

Pone (lump), 122
Popham, John, 11, 16
Porridge, corn. See *Sagamité*
Portuguese (lang.), 49
Possum, 22, 89, 250n.9(ch.
    2). See also *Opossum*
Possum belly, 150
Possum grape, 150
Possum haw, 120
Possum oak, 121
Potato, 46. See also *Eskimo
    potato;* Idaho (potato)
Potato chips. See *Saratoga
    chips*
Potlatch, 86, 90, 106, 120
Poverty, of Indians, 143, 144
Powhatan, 17–18, 124
Powhatan Indians, 41
Powwows, 15, 39, 141,
    249n.9; present-day, 146
Praying Indian, 135
Prefixes, 142
Prickly pear. See *Tuna*
Pride of Ohio, 120
Proto-Algonquian (lang.),
    27
Providence, R.I., 39
Puccoon, 19, 20, 37, 249n.9
Pukeweed, 91
Puma, 50. See also *Cougar*
Pumpkins, 8–9. See also
    Macock
Pung, 89
Punkie(-ky), 65, 120
Punkwood, 121
Punky, 120
Pygmies, 136

Quahog, 40, 149, 251n.16
Quahogger, 150
Quapaw Sioux, 111
Quebec, 151
Quebec, province of, 73
Quechua (lang.), 49–50, 52
Quinine, 50
Quinnat salmon, 89
Quisutsch, 108, 121
Quoddy, 121
Quonset hut, 150

Raccoon, 18, 20, 142,
    249n.9. See also *Coon*
Raccoonberry, 120
Raccoon dog, 120
Raccoon fox, 119
Raccoon grape, 90
Raccoon oyster, 90

Railroads, U.S., 104. See
    also *Iron horse*
Rainbow, Harriot research
    on, 11
Rain forests, Latin Ameri-
    can, 51
Raleigh, Walter, 3–9, 11,
    16, 67
Rattlesnakes, white lawyers
    as, 127
Rawhide. See *Parfleche*
Red-bellied terrapin, 120
Red Cloud, 105
Red man, 128
Red salmon. See *Sockeye
    salmon*
Redskin, 126
Redwoods, 87
Religion, North American
    Indian, 9, 29–30, 109,
    117. See also Christianity,
    Indians and; *Ghost Dance;
    Great Spirit; Happy hunt-
    ing ground; Kachina; Man-
    itou; Medicine; Praying
    Indian; Vision quest;
    Wampum*
Remora. See *Guaican*
Reservation, 135
Reservations, Indian, 116,
    119, 143–44
Roanoke, 19, 67, 249n.9
Roanoke Indians, 7
Roanoke Island, 5–7, 14, 67.
    See also Raleigh, Walter;
    White, John
Rolfe, John, 18
Roosevelt, Theodore, 114
Rosier, James, 14–16,
    249n.9
Ross, John, 105
Rubber, natural. See
    Caoutchouc
Rum, 57, 112

Sacalait, 121
Sachem(s), 34, 121, 251n.16;
    Tammany Society, 114
Sagamité, 42
Sagamore, 15–16, 249n.9
Sagamore Indians, 36
Saguaro, 110, 119
Sagwa ("medicine"), 112
Sahuaro. See *Saguaro*
Saint John's-wort. See
    Klamath weed

Saint Louis, Mo., 136–37
Saint Martin's Day. See
    Indian summer
Salal, 80, 88
Salish (lang. family), 106
Salish Indians, 139
Salmon, 97, 106. See also
    Chinook salmon; Chum
    salmon; Quisutsch; Sebago
    salmon; Sockeye salmon; Sus-
    quehanna salmon; Tyee
    salmon
Salt-marsh terrapin, 120
Salway, Harold D., 23
Samoset, 33
Samp, 40, 251n.16
Sannup, 36, 251n.16
Sapodilla, 48
Saratoga chips, 113, 120
Saratoga Springs, N.Y., 113
Saratoga trunk, 113, 119
Saskatchewan, province of, 73
Saskatoon, 88
Sasquatch, 139, 150
Savannah, 46
Scalp dance, 135
Scalping, 128
Scalplock, 131
Scalp yell, 135
Scituate, Mass., 70
Scoke, 65
Scup, 91
Scuppaug, 40, 251n.16
Scuppernong (grape; wine),
    81, 89
Seapoose, 42
Seawan. See Sewan
Sebago Lake, 115
Sebago salmon, 115, 121
Sego lily, 90
Seminole Indians, 81
Seneca grass, 89
Seneca Indians, 63
Seneca oil, 63, 66
Seneca root, 63, 65
Senega, 63, 64, 90
Seneka snakeroot, 63, 64
Sequoia, 90. See also Giant
    sequoia
Sequoia National Park, 69,
    87
Sequoyah, 87
Seuketat, 101
Sewan, 35. See also Wampum
Seward, William, 97
Sewellel, 88

Shaganappi, 65
Shagbark hickory, 65
Shakespeare, William, 20,
    45
Shallon, 88
Shasta, Mount, 109
Shasta cypress, 122
Shasta daisy, 109, 122
Shasta Indians, 109
Shasta red fir, 122
Shawnee Indians, 81
Shawnee (Shawanese) salad,
    65
Shawneewood, 149
Shenandoah National Park,
    69
Shoepac, 59, 65
Shoshone (lang.), 48
Shoshone crape myrtle, 141
Shoshone Indians, 129
Siberian husky, 150
Sieva bean, 121
Sign language, 26
Silver salmon. See Quisutsch
Simpson, David, 84
Siouan (lang.), 63. See also
    Macro-Siouan
Sioux crape myrtle, 141
Sioux Indians, 105, 129,
    133, 136. See also Hun-
    kpapa Sioux; Oglala
    Sioux; Quapaw Sioux
Sipapu, 122
Siscowet, 90
Sitka cypress, 121
Sitka spruce, 108, 121
Sitting Bull, 105, 116, 118
Siwash ("college"), 140–41,
    149
Siwash (Indian), 90, 140
Siwash (jargon), 149
Siwash (rough it), 149
Siwash Indians, 140
Skookum, 90
Skookum-house, 107, 120
Skunk (animal), 37, 90,
    145, 251n.16. See also
    Hog-nosed skunk; Striped
    skunk
Skunk (v.), 141
Skunk bear, 120
Skunk cabbage, 65
Skunk currant, 89
Skunkery, 122
Skunk porpoise, 121
Skunk spruce, 122

Skunkweed, 64
Skunk works, 151
Skunky, 122
Slaves: African, 47; captured
    Indians as, 42, 45, 48, 50
Sleep (time period), 135
Smilax, 10
Smith, John, 16–20, 22, 23,
    32, 69, 249n.9
Smoke signal, 135
Snakeroot. See Canada
    snakeroot
Sockeye salmon, 106, 120
Sofkee, 62, 66
Song of Hiawatha, The
    (Longfellow), 102–103
Sons of Tammany, 113–14
South Dakota, state of, 72
Southwest, American: loan-
    words from, 109–11
Spaghetti squash, 151
Spoon bread, 21
Squanter-squash, 37–38,
    251n.16
Squanto, 33–34
Squantum, 89
Squash, 9, 40, 251n.16. See
    also Acorn squash; But-
    tercup squash; Butternut
    squash; Cushaw; Hubbard
    squash; Marrow squash;
    Pattypan squash; Pump-
    kins; Spaghetti squash;
    Squanter-squash; Summer
    squash; Turban squash;
    Winter squash
Squash beetle, 120
Squashberry, 150
Squash blossom, 141, 149
Squash borer, 122
Squash bug, 90
Squaw, 34–35, 116, 251n.16
Squawberry, 116, 119
Squawbush, 90
Squaw cabbage, 149
Squaw currant, 149
Squaw dance, 116, 120
Squawfish, 116, 121
Squaw hitch, 121
Squaw huckleberry, 116, 119
Squaw man, 116, 120
Squawroot, 89
Squaw vine, 116, 119
Squaw-weed, 89
Squaw winter, 116, 120
Squaw wood, 138, 149

Squeteague, 88
Squirrel, flying. See *Assapan*
Stick-dice, 135
Stikine River, 68
Stogie (cigar), 58–59, 122
Stogie (shoe), 90
Strachey, William, 20–22, 249n.9
Striped skunk, 121
Sturgeon, 61
Succotash, 40, 251n.16
Suffixes, 142
Sugar, Latin American, 47
Suicide, Indians and, 143
Sumac, smokable. See *Kinnikinnick*
Summer squash, 37, 40, 89
Sumner, Charles, 98
Sun (time period), 123, 124
Sunapee Lake, 139
Sunapee trout, 139, 148
Sun Dance, 135
Supawn, 21, 249n.9
Susitna River, 68
Susquehanna River, 68
Susquehanna salmon, 120
Sweat lodge, 135
Swift, Jonathan, 53
Syllabary, Cherokee, 87
Syphilis, guaiacol for, 44

Taconic, 91
Taconite, 122
Tahoe, Lake, 69
Tahoe, trout, 139, 149
Taino (lang.), 47
Talking leaves, 135
Tamale, 48
Tamanend, 114
Tamarack, 80, 88. See also *Hackmatack*
Tammany, 113–14
Tammany Hall, 114
Tammany Societies, 114
Tanager, 49
Tanana River, 68
Tapioca, 49. See also *Cassava*
Tautog, 40 & n, 251n.16
Tawkee, 64
Tea, medicinal, 56
Tecumseh, 81
Tegua, 121
Telescope, Harriot-designed, 10
Tempest, The (Shakespeare), 20, 45

Tennessee, state of, 71
Tennessee River, 68, 71
Tennessee Walking Horse, 150
Tennessee warbler, 82, 89
Tepee, 58, 63, 65, 145
Terrapin, 22, 250n.9(ch. 2).
   See also *Diamondback terrapin; Painted terrapin; Red-bellied terrapin; Salt-marsh terrapin*
Texas (riverboat enclosure), 110, 119
Texas, state of, 72, 110, 140
Texas bluegrass, 110, 121
Texas fever tick, 110, 120
Texas leaguer, 140, 149
Texas longhorn, 140, 149
Texas millet, 119
Texas Ranger, 90
Texas sparrow, 149
Texas star, 149
Texas tower, 140, 151
Texas umbrella tree, 149
Tex-Mex, 140, 150
Thoreau, Henry David, 104, 113, 115, 133, 148
Tillicum, 91
Timber, of Pacific Northwest, 105
Timucua(n) (lang.), 10, 63
Tipi. See *Tepee*
Tippecanoe Creek, battle of, 81
Tiswin, 121
Titi, 89
Tizwin. See *Tiswin*
Tlingit (lang.), 107
Tobacco, 47. See also *Kinnikinnick; Poke; Stogie; Uppówoc*
Toboggan(-er; -ing), 82, 89, 90, 91, 121
Toboggan chute, 149
Toboggan slide, 121
Tomahawk (cruise missile), 140
Tomahawk (hatchet), 16, 43, 141, 249n.9
Tomato, 48
Torture, Indian recourse to, 45, 56
Totem(-ic; -ism; -ist{ic}; -ite), 22, 65, 90, 103, 120, 121, 149, 249n.9
Totem pole, 107, 121
Toucan, 49
"Trail of Tears," 81

Travois, 135
Tribes, Tammany, 114
Tsinaw, 10, 248n.14
Tuckahoe, 19, 20, 249n.9
Tucket, 119
Tullibee, 66
Tump(line), 62, 66
Tuna (plant), 46
Tupelo, 58, 62, 64. See also *Water tupelo*
Tupelo gum, 121
Tupi(an) (lang.), 49
Tupik, 97
Turban squash, 149
Tuscarora Indians, 56
Tuskegee crape myrtle, 141
Tustumena, Lake, 69
Tuxedo, 115, 121
Tuxedo Park, N.Y., 115
Tuxedo sofa, 115
Twain, Mark. See Clemens, Samuel L.
Tweed, William M., 114
Tweeg, 89
Two Moons, 137
Tyee, 63, 66
Tyee salmon, 120

Ugh (interjection), 135
Uintaite, 121
Ulu, 97
Umiak, 96
Unakite, 120
United States: westward expansion of, 79–91, 103, 104, 116, 119 (*see also* Lewis and Clark Expedition). *See also* Carolinas; East; Jefferson, Thomas; Midwest; New England; Pacific Northwest; Southwest; *and individual states by name*
Universities, American Indians in, 147
Upland moccasin, 119
Upper *Klamath* Lake, 69
Uppówoc, 12, 248n.14
Utah, state of, 72
Utah Lake, 69
Ute (lang.), 48
Ute Indians, 72
Utley, Robert M., 105, 119
Uto-Aztecan, 122

Vicuña, 50
Virginia, commonwealth of:

colonization of, 5–7, 14, 16–17, 32, 36, 41, 124; Indians of, 41, 55 (*see also* Powhatan; Virgina, commonwealth of— colonization of); place-names of, 70. *See also* Jamestown; Raleigh, Walter; Roanoke Island; Smith, John; White, John
Virginia Company, 17
Virginia daffodil. See *Atamasco lily*
Virginia poke, 121
Vision quest, 134
Vizenor, Gerald, 147
Vocabulary(-ies): English, 64n; as *Hiawatha* appendix, 103; Indian, 79, 80. *See also* Syllabary
Vulpine opossum, 66

Wabeno, 88, 103
Wahoo, 65, 119
Wakan, 65
Wampanoag Indians, 34, 41–42
Wampee, 88
Wampum, 35, 54, 103. See also *Peace belt; Roanoke*
Wampumpeag, 35
Wampum snake, 64
Wanchese, 5, 10
Wanigan, 91
Wankapin, 90
Wapatoo, 80, 88
Wapiti, 81, 88
Warbonnets, 131
War club, 128
War dance, 128
War eagle, 131
War feast, 131
War hatchet, 128
War of 1812, 81
War paint, 131
Warpath, 128
War pole, 128
War post, 128
War song, 128
War whoop, 128

Washington, George, 59, 126
Washoe process, 120
Watap, 65
Water chinquapin, 90
Water hickory, 89
Water lily. See *Wokas*
Water moccasin, 89
Water opossum, 90
Water tupelo, 63, 64
Wavey, 65
Wawaskeesh, 65
Waw-waw, 107
Waymouth, George, 14–16, 40n, 93
Weatherford, Jack, 142, 145
Wejack, 65
Werowance, 9, 248n.14
West Indies: Harriot to, 6; loanwords from, 44–47, 51
Whales, as Indian prey, 15–16
Wheat, European, 124
Whiskey, Indians and, 107. *See also* Alcoholism; *Firewater; Hooch(inoo); Manhattan* (cocktail); *Monongahela;* Rum
Whisky jack, 65
Whispering spirit, 123, 124
Whitaker, Alexander, 250n.9(ch.2)
White, John, 6–7, 14
White Chief of the Long Hair, 123, 124
White hickory, 65
White Horse, 137
White Mountain Apaches, 76–77
Whitman, Walt, 28, 68
Wickiup, 111, 119
Wicopy, 21, 249n.9
Wigwam, 36, 103, 111, 141, 251n.16; Tammany Society, 114
Wild West shows, 118
Willamette River, 68
Williams, Roger, 39–41, 251n.16

Windigo, 64
Wingina, 7
Winnebago, Lake, 69
Winnibigoshish, Lake, 69
Winninish, 121
Winslow, Edward, 34
Winter squash, 40, 65
Wisconsin (geol.), 122
Wisconsin, state of, 72
Wococon (isl.), 6
Wokas, 108, 121
Wolverine. See *Carcajou*
Wood, William, 37–38, 251n.16
Woodchuck, 42
Woodland caribou, 119
World War II: Alaska during, 100; American Indians in, 28n
Wounded Knee, massacre at, 117
Writers, contemporary Indian, 147
Wyandot(te) (fowl), 121
Wyoming, state of, 72
Wyoming (Pa.) Massacre, 72

Yaghan (lang.), 24
Yamp, 90
Yaupon, 10, 56, 63, 64. See also *Cassina*
Yaws, 47
Year of Reconciliation, 146
Yosemite Falls, 69
Yosemite Indians, 75
Yosemite Valley, Calif., 74–75
Yuca, 46. See also *Cassava*
Yuit (lang.), 24
Yukon River, 68
Yukon Territory, Can., 73, 77
Yukon time, 151
Yuma crape myrtle, 141
Yuma point, 150
Yupik (lang.), 97

Zebra opossum, 119
Zuni crape myrtle, 141
Zunyite, 121